The Shaping of NORTH AMERICA

In series with this book:

The Shaping of

NORTH AMERICA

From Earliest Times to 1763

BY ISAAC ASIMOV

LONDON : DENNIS DOBSON

To Les and Chaucy Bennetts,
for their warm hospitality and friendship

PUBLISHED IN GREAT BRITAIN IN 1974
BY DOBSON BOOKS LTD, 80 KENSINGTON CHURCH STREET, LONDON W8
PRINTED IN THE UNITED STATES OF AMERICA
ISBN 0-234-77175-5

CONTENTS

The Shaping of NORTH AMERICA

1

BEFORE COLUMBUS

THE INDIANS

Mankind, to begin with, was very likely African. The earliest traces of "hominids" (creatures that more nearly approach man in their characteristics than any other form of life) have been found in East Africa. Man's nearest relatives in the animal kingdom, the chimpanzee and the gorilla, are still confined to Africa, except where individuals are taken elsewhere through human agency.

During the couple of million years of hominid existence, individuals spread out to cover a larger and larger range, but were always confined to those regions they could reach without crossing a large body of water. All fossils of those early hominids that are distinctly more primitive than modern man are found only in Africa, Europe, and Asia, the three interconnected land masses that make up what is sometimes called the "World Island." Traces can also be found in the islands off the shores of those continents.

Even as late as 25,000 years ago, when all the early hominids were gone and only one species, "Homo sapiens" or modern man, existed, mankind was still confined to the World Island. The American continents, isolated beyond the Atlantic on one side of the World Island and beyond the Pacific on the other, were still man–free. No trace of any hominid more primitive than Homo sapiens has ever been found anywhere in the Americas.

There is one place, however, where the American continents approach the World Island and that is in the extreme northern Pacific area. There the northwestern tip of North America and the northeastern tip of Asia approach and fall just short of each other. The two continents are separated today by a strait that is 56 miles wide and no more; there are a couple of small islands midway across, too.

There have been times when the strait was narrower still. Through all hominid history there has been a succession of glacial periods during which the polar regions of the Earth were covered with extensive ice caps spreading out for thousands of miles from the pole in every direction. During those periods so much of the planet's water supply was tied up in vast ice sheets covering the land surfaces that the ocean level dropped considerably.

As the ocean level dropped, the strait between Asia and North America narrowed and finally disappeared, leaving a land bridge between the continents.

The last period of glaciation extended from 30,000 years ago to about 10,000 years ago. At its height, the ocean level dropped far enough to leave a land bridge 1300 miles wide between Asia and North America. Once the glaciers began to retreat, the ocean level began to rise; but the continents did not separate completely till perhaps 7000 B.C.

During the last glaciation, Homo sapiens was the dominant

hominid, probably the only one remaining, and he was certainly present in greater numbers than any hominids had been in any previous glaciation. For the first time, perhaps, hominids had penetrated the northeastern reaches of Asia.

As it happened, the glaciations were more extensive on the Atlantic side of the north pole than on the Pacific side. Northeastern Siberia and Alaska were comparatively ice-free. The climate was by no means pleasant, but small bands of men could maintain themselves as hunters of mammoths and other large animals of that era.

Then, perhaps about 25,000 B.C., some hunting group, on the track of the mammoth, found its way across the strait. It is difficult, actually, to tell the exact time this happened or to learn much of the details, because the very early immigrants have left so little behind. There are almost no skeletal remains; only twenty ancient skulls have been found in all the American continents so far. Most of the evidence concerning the early population is in the form of ancient stone arrowheads and other relics of that nature. And perhaps the earliest and best evidence is now under water, buried as the ocean level rose with the melting of the glaciers.

Other hunting groups followed. Those who entered Alaska drifted southward and southeastward, always in search of more and better hunting. Additional groups followed at their heels as long as the land bridge between the continents remained open. For thousands of years, the hunters spread out, and, by 8000 B.C., when the glaciers were beginning their last retreat, man had forced his way into all reasonable corners of the American continents from the polar north to the polar south.

These earliest inhabitants of the Americas show some resemblances to the inhabitants of eastern Asia, if we can judge by their present descendants on both continents. The resemblance is not complete, however. The original Americans (whom we call "Indians" for reasons we will explain later) don't have the shape of eyelids or the rather flat face that the east Asians do.

The Indians have prominent noses and their complexion seems, on the whole, to be ruddier than that of the rather sallow east Asians.*

By the time the Indians had spread out over the Americas, agriculture was beginning in southwestern Asia and the first steps were being taken in that area toward what we call civilization.** The inhabitants of the Americas were insulated from this as far as we know. They did not have the opportunity of trading with civilized areas and learning from them, as did the early inhabitants of western Europe, for instance.

Nevertheless, this did not mean the Indians remained sunk in darkness. They discovered agriculture independently. About 5000 B.C., the first beginnings of agriculture were to be seen in the land we now call Mexico; by 3000 B.C., Mexican Indians had developed a complete farming culture. About 2000 B.C., they made their greatest and most important advance when they learned to cultivate corn (maize), which turned out to be their basic food plant. By 1000 B.C., they were growing beans.

As agriculture developed and the food supply rose and became more certain, enough human energies could be diverted from the bare act of securing the basic essentials of life and turned to those additional activities that make up civilization. By 1500 B.C., there were temples and cities in Mexico.

Nor were the Indian civilizations puny ones. When, in A.D. 1519, Europeans reached Mexico, they found its capital city, Tenochtitlán, (at the site of the present Mexico City) to be larger than Paris or Rome as they then were. They found the Mexican Indians to have a better calendar than the Europeans had, and a better system of public sanitation, too. (The Indians thought the Europeans smelled bad and made it quite clear they thought so — which naturally offended the Europeans.)

---

* Indians are frequently said to be red–skinned and east Asians to be yellow–skinned, but the picture to which such color descriptions give rise is sure to be an exaggerated one.
** See my book, *The Near East* (Houghton Mifflin, 1968).

Agriculture spread outward from Mexico and, by 1000 B.C., it was beginning to penetrate those areas that now make up the United States. The Indians in the Mississippi Valley, from the Great Lakes to the Gulf of Mexico, developed village settlements and were approaching what one might call civilization. The clearest traces we have of this early period is in its burial mounds. These, forming circles, ellipses, squares, octagons, and so on, were sometimes as much as 75 feet high and enclosed up to 25 or even 50 acres. Sometimes the mounds appeared in complex shapes, clearly representing an animal or bird.

Unfortunately, there was a cultural recession in later times, perhaps because of the incessant tribal wars that plagued the Indians, and by the time Europeans appeared in the region, the mound–building culture had disappeared. In the nineteenth century, the mounds were thought to represent a culture of "Mound Builders" who were not related to the Indians. This gave rise to numerous wild speculations about pre–Indian immigration to America from Europe, but all these speculations are abandoned. It seems quite certain now, that the Mound Builders were Indians.

Another type of culture approaching a civilization appeared in what is now the American southwest. The Indians of that region built elaborate buildings out of sun–dried bricks. One such "pueblo" (a Spanish word meaning "city") in what is now New Mexico had four stories, 800 rooms and housed 1200 people. It was built about A.D. 1000 and was abandoned before A.D. 1300, probably because the increasing dryness of the region made it impossible to support such a concentration of people.

Nevertheless, despite their levels of civilization and near–civilization, the Indians were to prove no match for the Europeans, who had a more cohesive unity, a more highly developed art of warfare, and who, above all, had firearms.

It is difficult to tell how many Indians there were in the Americas by the time the Europeans appeared. Some estimates place the total at 25 million. Of these, one million may have been dwelling north of the Rio Grande. (It tells something of the catastrophe that befell the Indians that today, five centuries later, when the total population north of the Rio Grande is something over 220 million, the total Indian population is only 700,000.)

THE GREEKS AND PHOENICIANS

The true discovery of America by mankind came when those first hunting bands crossed over from Siberia 25,000 years ago. This, however, never seems to count. When people speak of the "discovery of America" they invariably mean its discovery by Europeans.

The temptation to do so arises not only out of a natural tendency for people to consider their own history as of prime importance, but also because it was only after the European discovery of the Americas that the continents developed a documented history. We have virtually no details concerning Indian history prior to the coming of the Europeans, and without those details it is easy to be unjust enough to dismiss Indian history altogether, and with it the Indians.

But even if we restrict the discovery of America to the first appearance of Europeans on its soil, there are still some questions to be asked. When *was* this first appearance? The usual answer is that it came about with the voyage of the daring navigator, Christopher Columbus, and certainly from his time on, Europeans have been in the Americas continuously.

Were there, however, voyages before Columbus? Were there discoveries that were forgotten?

If we go far back in the history of civilization, we come across legends that speak of mysterious lands in the far west. It is possible to imagine that these represent misty memories of some American landing. The ancient Greeks, for instance, as far back as Hesiod, who lived in the eighth century B.C., spoke of the "Isles of the Blest." This was pictured as a Utopia–like land in the far western reaches of the ocean where the souls of heroes lived forever.

Yet surely the Greeks of Hesiod's time could not have reached America. They were indeed engaged in colonizing ventures, but to them, the horizon of the known world was the eastern rim of the Black Sea on one side and the western reaches of the Mediterranean Sea on the other.

To be sure, there were men who had penetrated far beyond the Greek horizon and had done so many, many centuries before Hesiod's time. There were men living along the Atlantic shores of Europe and along the Pacific shores of China. These don't count either, somehow, and their discoveries of new lands are ignored. When we speak of a discovery, we usually only count those discoverers who are members of our ancestral Western civilization.

Thus, when we speak of the discovery of the Atlantic Ocean, we don't refer to the early tribes of men who reached the coast of what is now France, Spain and West Africa. We speak instead of ships, from some civilized nation in the eastern Mediterranean, which first passed through the Strait of Gibraltar and into the open ocean.

According to that line of reasoning, the open Atlantic was, in all likelihood, discovered by the Phoenicians,* who were the most daring mariners of the ancient world. As early as 1100 B.C., according to tradition, Phoenician ships passed through the strait and established a trading station at the site of the modern city of Cadiz, fifty miles beyond.

The Phoenicians explored the Atlantic coasts of Europe and Africa and, by 900 B.C., may have reached as far north as the island of Britain. The peninsula of Cornwall, and the Scilly Islands off its tip, may have been the "Tin Islands" of ancient

* See my book, *The Land of Canaan* (Houghton Mifflin, 1971).

times, and the source of the tin so necessary to the manufacture
of bronze.

Working their way down the African coast, the Phoenicians
discovered the Canary Islands, as they are now called, sixty
miles off the coast of what is now Southern Morocco. It may be
the Canary Islands whose existence reached the Greeks of Hesiod's time in a faint and misty way, and these which gave rise to
the legend of the "Isles of the Blest."

The most remarkable voyage of the Phoenicians took place,
however, in 600 B.C. In the pay of an Egyptian monarch, a
Phoenician fleet spent three years circumnavigating the continent of Africa. The only notice we have of that is in the work
of the Greek historian, Herodotus, who wrote about 430 B.C.

Herodotus didn't believe the tale of the Phoenician voyagers
because they claimed that in the southern regions of Africa, the
noonday sun appeared in the northern region of the sky. Since
the noonday sun, when viewed from any Mediterranean land,
was always toward the south Herodotus felt that must be an
invariable law of nature and insisted that the story of the Phoenician voyage must be a fable.

The southern tip of Africa is in the South Temperate Zone,
however, and from there the noonday sun is indeed always to
the north. The mere fact that the Phoenicians should describe
this apparently impossible fact tells us that they really were
that far south and probably *did* circumnavigate Africa.

It may even be that some Phoenicians did something more
startling still. An old inscription, discovered in Brazil in 1872,
was supposed to be in Phoenician and to tell of a vessel that was
driven away by storms from the circumnavigating fleet. Could
that have happened? The distance between the westernmost
part of Africa and the easternmost part of Brazil is only 1600
miles — the narrowest part of the Atlantic. The inscription was
quickly dismissed as a hoax, but in 1968, Cyrus H. Gordon of
Brandeis University suggested it might well be genuine.

If it is, the inscription might represent the first discovery of the Americas by civilized men of the Near East, two thousand years before Columbus. The discovery was accidental, however; news of it never got back to the Mediterranean world, so it was not an effective discovery. It didn't lead to further voyages and to systematic trade or colonization.

The first Greek to venture really far out into the Atlantic Ocean was Pytheas of Massilia. About 300 B.C., he sailed through the Strait of Gibraltar and then turned north. His accounts, which have not survived directly but which reach us through references in later writers, seem to show that he explored the island of Great Britain and then sailed northwestward to a land he called "Thule," which was possibly Iceland or Norway. There, fog stopped the intrepid navigator, and he turned back to explore the northern shores of Europe and to penetrate the Baltic Sea.

If the Greeks remained behind the Phoenicians in the actual practice of venturing out into open ocean, they were ahead in theory. The Greeks were the first to get a notion of the spherical shape of the Earth, and one of them, Eratosthenes of Cyrene, even estimated its size. About 250 B.C., he calculated the circumference of the Earth to be about 25,000 miles, which is quite correct.

The notion of a spherical Earth automatically raises the possibility of sailing west to reach the east (or vice versa), of circumnavigating the world, in other words.

Although circumnavigation may have been seen as theoretically possible, the question still would have remained as to whether it were practically possible. There might well be unexpected dangers far out in the ocean. The tropical regions might be too hot to penetrate, the polar regions too cold. There might be shoals to trap ships that ventured too far, currents that might keep them from returning.

Then, too, there was the fact of sheer distance. If the Earth were 25,000 miles in circumference and if the distance from Spain to the dim eastern regions of Asia were 9000 miles (as it actually is), then to reach eastern Asia by sailing westward would require passage of 16,000 miles of, presumably, unbroken ocean. No ship of ancient times could possibly make that journey.

To be sure, Eratosthenes might be wrong. Another Greek geographer, Poseidonius of Apamea, repeated the work of the earlier man about 100 B.C. and came to the conclusion that the Earth was only 18,000 miles in diameter. He was wrong, but his figure proved the more popular.

The most influential geographer of ancient times was Claudius Ptolemy who, in A.D. 130, wrote a book that proved to be the great and last work on geography and astronomy for some fifteen hundred years. Ptolemy adopted the lower size for the Earth's circumference and that made it "official." What's more, he estimated the stretch of land from Spain to what we would now call the coast of China to be about 12,000 miles (which is 3000 miles too long.)

This meant that the stretch of ocean from the west of Europe to the east of Asia was perhaps only 6000 miles. This was still too long for any ship of the time to cover, but surely it offered more hope than 16,000 miles had.

The hope was not soon to be tested. By Ptolemy's times, the Phoenician and Greek civilizations had been in decay for centuries, and no mariners like the Phoenicians were to arise for a thousand years. Instead, it was the Roman Empire which now ruled all the shores of the Mediterranean.

The Romans spread far and wide over land; and there were Roman cities in western Africa, in Spain, and in Britain. They were not a seafaring people, however, and no Roman ever dreamed of venturing far out into the ocean.

Indeed, after the western provinces of the Roman Empire were taken over by Germanic tribes in the fifth century, geographic knowledge among the people of western Europe actually contracted. The new religion of Islam arose in Arabia in the seventh century and by A.D. 730, all of North Africa, and even Spain, was in the hands of the Moslems, as believers in Islam are called. The west Europeans were cut off from the south and the east, and both Africa and Asia receded into myth and legend.

THE IRISH AND VIKINGS

But if the east and south were cut off, new horizons loomed to the west and north.

Ireland, the island lying to the west of Britain, was never part of the Roman Empire. Even as the Roman Empire receded, however, and the Roman soldiers left Britain forever, Christianity began to reach the smaller island. By the sixth century, Christianity in Ireland, somewhat isolated from a continent in chaos, began to assume distinctive forms of its own and to develop strong communities of monks who preserved learning to a surprising degree.

Craving isolation, perhaps, in order that they might come closer to God, the monks traveled across the ocean in their small boats, locating and colonizing the rocky islands along the northern reaches of the British Isles.

One such mariner was St. Brendan, who, about 550, sailed northward and explored the islands off the Scottish coast, the Hebrides to the west and the Shetland Islands to the north. He may possibly have reached the Faeroe Islands, too, these lying about 250 miles north of the extreme tip of Great Britain. From there, another 300 miles northwestward would have brought him to Iceland and that, too, is not beyond the realm of the possible.

His daring voyages lived on long past his death and in the repetition, his deeds were greatly improved upon. About 800, a narrative was written of his voyages that was undoubtedly fiction, but which was a well–written and exciting account and proved popular. By that time, Irish monks had definitely reached Iceland and its existence lent plausibility to the whole narrative.

Out of the imaginative adventures of the St. Brendan tales arose a belief in the existence of a wonderful island out in the Atlantic, one which came to be called "St. Brendan's Island." It was suggested in later centuries that St. Brendan reached the American continent and that that was St. Brendan's Island. This seems extremely unlikely; it is almost certain that St. Brendan's Island was only one of a series of islands invented and placed in the dim reaches of the Atlantic.

They may all have owed much to the Greek dreams of the Isles of the Blest, for one was "Hy-Brasil" which was invented by the Irish, and the name of which is Gaelic for "Isles of the Blest." Another such island was "Antilia," and there were others as well.

Of course, there *were* islands in the Atlantic off the western shores of Europe and Africa, but they were generally uninhabited until Europeans discovered them, and they were nothing like the fantastic Utopias that Europeans imagined and then convinced themselves really existed.

But the fantasies served a purpose. The tales of wonderful lands out in the western ocean gave explorers a goal and kept interest alive among those at home who might be persuaded to finance voyages.

The golden age of the Irish monks did not last long. There were other mariners on the seas; the most daring and expert since the ancient Phoenicians. These were Scandinavian rovers from Norway and Denmark — the so–called Vikings.

From about 800 onward, their raiding ships fell in full fury on all the coasts of western Europe. Vikings occupied most of Ireland and Scotland, reducing them to savagery. They badly ravaged the Anglo–Saxon kingdoms that had been established in Britain after the withdrawal of the Romans and were to form the nation of England. They terrorized the coasts and rivers of what are now France and Germany. They even penetrated the Mediterranean.

Much more to the point of this book, however, the Vikings sailed out into the open northern oceans. Sometimes they were driven westward by storms; sometimes they went in deliberate search of new lands because warfare at home had driven them into exile, or because they were searching for new places to loot.

One exile, a Norwegian chieftain named Ingolfur Arnarson, set sail in 874 and landed in Iceland, which is 650 miles west of Norway. By that time, the Irish monks who had once dwelt on the island were gone — or perhaps, if any remained, they were killed or driven off by the Vikings. In either case, it was the Norse who founded the first *permanent* colony in Iceland.*

During the early centuries of its existence, Viking Iceland maintained the pagan Norse religion even when the homeland was being rapidly Christianized. To this day, the Icelandic "sagas," tales written before 1300, are a better source of knowledge concerning Norse pagan beliefs than anything that can be found in Scandinavia proper.

The Icelanders found the sea to be their most reliable source of food, and they naturally explored the waters about their islands. Tales arose of an island farther to the west and, as a matter of fact, there was an enormous one only 200 miles to the northwest.

From the mountain tops in northwestern Iceland one could dimly make out land on the horizon to the northwest, and in that part of the island there lived, toward the close of the tenth century, one Eric Thorvaldsson. He was generally called Eric the Red, from the color of his hair.

---

* Ever since, for over a thousand years, Iceland has been closely associated with the Scandinavian nations, both culturally and politically. In modern times, Iceland and the Faeroe Islands were part of the Danish kingdom. The Faeroe Islands still are, though they have considerable self–government. Iceland became an independent republic in 1944.

In 982, Eric was exiled for some offense, and he decided to use the three–year period of outlawry imposed upon him to go exploring westward. He reached the distant island at last but found its coast choked with ice that prevented a landing. He followed the coast southwestward till he reached a cape he could sail round, and then he followed the western coast north- ward. This southwestern coast was less bleak and Eric judged it capable of supporting a colony.

By 985, Eric was back in Iceland drumming up colonists for his new land. In order to do so, he outrageously oversold its good qualities, even to the point of calling it "Greenland." In actuality, Greenland, the largest island in the world, is one huge wasteland, covered as it is almost entirely by an immense miles– deep glacier. It is one of the final relics of the Ice Age, and only Antarctica is bleaker. On the other hand, the northern climate was somewhat milder a thousand years ago than it is now, and the coastal strip along southwestern Greenland may not have been very much worse than Iceland.

In any case, Eric found volunteers to settle the new land, and, in 986, he headed west with twenty–five ships. Fourteen ships made it, and a colony was founded on the western coast of the island near its southern tip.

The latitude of the Greenland colony was actually more southerly than that of Iceland by perhaps 200 miles. Whereas Iceland gets the tag end of the warm Gulf Stream, however, Greenland gets the frigid Labrador current. Nevertheless, the Viking colonists hung on and stubbornly persisted for over four centuries. At its height, about 1200, as many as 3000 Vikings may have dwelt on the island.

While the Greenland colony existed, it served as a base for explorations still farther west. About 1000, a Viking named Bjarne Herjulfson was telling the tale that he had been sailing from Iceland to Greenland, that a storm had caught him and driven him past Greenland's tip and on farther to the west. He managed to turn about and return to Greenland, but not before he had sighted land to Greenland's west.

Listening to this tale was Leif Ericsson, the son of Eric the Red. He had been visiting Norway, where he had been converted to Christianity, and now he was back in Greenland. His imagination was fired by Bjarne's tale, so he bought Bjarne's ship, gathered a crew of thirty-five, and went exploring westward.

He reached land where Bjarne said he would. What he encountered first was the rather barren coast of Labrador, but he sailed southward to more inviting territory and probably reached the northern tip of Newfoundland.*

That Leif reached Labrador and Newfoundland is quite easy to believe. The great mystery concerning this voyage of exploration (at least as described in the later tales) was the discovery of a land where wild grapes grew in profusion. The region where the wild grapes grew, Leif called "Vinland."

It is possible that the tale of the vines was merely an attempt to make the land more inviting to settlers (following the precedent set by Leif's father, Eric the Red). Or it may have been a later embellishment. If the account is literally true, however, it introduces difficulties, for wild grapes do not grow as far north as Newfoundland, nor is it at all likely that they did so a thousand years ago.

Some people speculate that Leif did find wild grapes and that this means he penetrated far south of Newfoundland, perhaps even as far as the present state of New Jersey. This seems unlikely but it is a romantic belief, since it would make Leif the first European ever to sail along the shores and perhaps set foot on the soil of what is now the United States. There has been an

---

* Beginning in 1960, a Norwegian archeologist, Helge Ingstad, has been uncovering traces of houses on that northern tip; houses which may well have been relics of an ancient colony founded by Leif or by those who followed.

assiduous search, therefore, for any signs of Norse relics in New England, for instance. Despite some claims of success, no such relics that are acceptable to historians have been found.*

After his exploring voyage, Leif returned to Greenland and traveled no more. In 1002, however, an Icelandic merchant, Thorfinn Karlsefni, visited Greenland, and heard Leif's tales — just as Leif had once heard Bjarne's.

Thorfinn was fired in his turn. He fitted out a much larger expedition than Leif's, one that included three ships and 160 men, plus some women and cattle. A landing was made in Vinland (wherever it might be) and a settlement established that lasted for some years. About 1007, according to one tale, a Viking child named Snorri was born in Vinland. If this is true, Snorri might be the first child of European ancestry to be born anywhere in the Americas.

Unlike Iceland and Greenland however, Vinland was not empty. It was already populated with people the Vikings called "Skrellings," who were, presumably, Indians. The Indians were hostile and this posed a greater barrier to colonization than all of Greenland's ice. In the end, troubles among themselves and with the Indians finally wore out the Vinland colonists, and those who survived returned to Greenland.

Even though no permanent colony was founded in North America by the Vikings, the western lands remained in their consciousness for a while. The Greenland colonists seem to have continued making trips to the shores of North America to collect wood (for no trees grew in Greenland). Such voyages may have continued until as late as 1350.

---

* The most remarkable find was not in New England, but was far inland. It is the "Kensington Rune Stone" discovered near the village of Kensington, Minnesota, by a Swedish-born farmer in 1898. It was inscribed in runes (that is, in the form of the alphabet used by the Vikings) and was dated 1362. It described a small exploring party of thirty which met disaster, presumably at the hands of Indians. Experts in the field are quite convinced the stone is a hoax.

As for the Greenland colony itself, it continued to exist, but always in a marginal fashion. It barely managed to hang on, and its existence depended on constant communications with Iceland and Norway, and on constant infusions of new settlers.

In 1349, the Black Death, a vast pandemic of the plague, which had been devastating Europe, reached Scandinavia and Iceland, and the economy shrank there as it did everywhere. The link with Greenland grew more tenuous, and the last ship sailed from Norway to Greenland in 1367. In addition, the Earth underwent a slight cooling trend and Greenland's climate, very poor at best, became so bad as to make agriculture virtually impossible.

As if that were not enough, a human enemy appeared as well. . . .

About 2500 B.C., the retreat of the glaciers had left the northern regions of North America in their present condition. New immigrants from Siberia negotiated the narrow strait between Asia and North America which then once more existed and penetrated the hitherto unpopulated areas uncovered by the retreating ice. These new immigrants, whom we call Eskimos, are more clearly related to the people of eastern Asia in appearance than the more southerly Indians are.

By A.D. 1, the Eskimos had developed a remarkable ability to maintain themselves in stark polar regions by hunting seals and walruses and by learning how to protect themselves against the cold. They were able to colonize the coastal shores of the polar regions. They worked their way eastward and by A.D. 1000 had reached Greenland at a point to the north of where the Vikings were establishing their own settlements. They gradually made their way south until they impinged upon the Viking settlements; their hostility may well have added to the troubles of the Greenlanders.

About 1415, the Greenland colony came to an end and the

knowledge of land west of Iceland seemed to fade from European consciousness.* Or did it?

It was announced, in 1965, that a map based on Norse explorations had been found and that it might have been available to European scholars in the years before the great western explorations that finally established permanent European colonies in the Americas.

The map shows an island west of Iceland that has indisputably the shape of Greenland. To Greenland's west is another island representing Vinland (so that it is called the "Vinland Map"). Vinland is shown as an island with two inlets that might well represent the southern portion of Baffin Island, which is to the west of Greenland about where the map shows Vinland to be.

Baffin Island, however, is every bit as bad as Greenland from the standpoint of climate, and it could not possibly have been Vinland. Actually, the genuineness of the map is doubted by a number of historians, and it is perhaps safer to assume that the great voyages of the fifteenth century were carried out without reference to the Viking feats.

THE MONGOLS AND VENETIANS

In western Europe, to the south of Scandinavia, knowledge of the world continued to contract even as the Vikings ventured far into the polar seas. Partly, this decline was due to the ravages that accompanied the Viking expansion, so that as the Vikings were venturing out to Greenland and Vinland, western Europe was at its darkest and most contracted.

---

* Greenland was not left empty, however. The Eskimos remained and even today there are about 25,000 Eskimos living in Greenland. To a great extent, however, they now depend on Western technology to maintain their comfort.

But then came a series of events that began once more to push the horizon outward. The west Europeans ventured eastward and their view of the great eastern mass of Asia very slowly sharpened.

Beginning in 1096, there were the Crusades, a long series of wars in which west Europeans (chiefly Frenchmen) tried to wrest Palestine from the hands of the Moslems who had held it for over four centuries. On the whole, these wars were unsuccessful from the military standpoint, but they familiarized west Europeans with the Mediterranean Sea from end to end, and gave them the vision of a civilization in Syria and in the Near East generally — one that was older and more advanced than their own.

Beginning with the twelfth century, then, there arose a European longing for an east they thought of as a land of wealth and comforts, of spices and sugar, of advanced technology and handicraft. The longing was to continue and to grow more acute for centuries.

In the mid–thirteenth century, the tide of invasion, which had flooded eastward during the Crusades, turned the other way. Under Genghis Khan, the Mongol tribes of Central Asia, who had periodically poured southward and westward against civilized areas in China, the Near East, and Europe, mounted the greatest nomad offensive in all history. By 1260, a vast Mongol Empire was in existence under the rule of Kublai Khan, grandson of Genghis Khan. It included China, Central Asia, Persia, Iraq, and Russia.

For the first time, the vast stretch of land from the Baltic Sea to the Pacific Ocean was under a single, efficient rule. It was possible to travel from end to end of Asia, some six thousand miles, in reasonable security, and some Europeans did.

The most important of these were two brothers, Niccolo and Matteo Polo, who were natives of the great trading city of Venice, and who had commercial connections in the still greater city of Constantinople (which, for some decades, Venice had been dominating economically). In 1261, these brothers set out for the east and made their way as far as Peking, which was Kublai Khan's capital.

They returned, in 1269, with a message for Pope Clement IV from Kublai, asking that a hundred missionaries be sent eastward to instruct the people of China in Christianity. Unfortunately, Clement had died the year before, and it took three years for a new Pope to be elected, by which time Kublai's enthusiasm had waned.

In 1271, the brothers delivered the message to the new Pope, Gregory X, and then went on another journey eastward, this time taking Marco, the seventeen–year–old son of Niccolo, with them. Only two missionaries could be found willing to accompany them, and these did not stay with them long. In 1275, they were in Peking again, with no religious representatives.

The Polos stayed there for nearly twenty years and did very well. Marco, particularly, learned to speak the Mongol language and showed himself so capable a man that Kublai Khan trusted him with missions to various parts of his dominions. Marco had the opportunity to study parts of Asia that no European had ever seen and wherever he went, he took copious notes.

Eventually, the Polos began to dream of returning. Kublai was aging, and after he died, his successor might be less favorably disposed to Europeans. Getting away was difficult, however. Fortunately, a pretext arose when the Polos received permission to escort a Mongol princess to Persia. They traveled to Persia by sea, passing the coasts of China and India and completed their task. While en route, they heard that Kublai had, indeed, died, so they just kept going. In 1296, they were back in Italy.

In those years, Venice was frequently at war with Genoa, another trading city of Italy. In a naval battle between the cities, in 1298, Marco Polo, fighting for his native Venice, was taken prisoner by the Genoese and kept in prison for some months.

During those months he passed the time writing a book about his many years in distant Asia. His book, *The Travels of Marco Polo*, proved very popular, as well-written travel tales always are, but not all his fellow Europeans believed his tales. They wouldn't accept Marco's description of Asia's size, its wealth, its advancement. They called him "Marco Millions" in derision, because all his statistics concerning Asia dealt in millions.

And yet Marco's book differed from all other travel tales written in the Middle Ages in that it was remarkably accurate. It was the real thing, as Europeans found out in later centuries when they learned to know Asia better.*

Whether the stories of Marco Polo were believed or not, they helped to make even stronger the popular European conception of Asia as a land of fabulous wealth. He had succeeded in further intensifying the longing of Europeans for the gorgeous East.

* One mistake that Marco did make turned out to be even more influential than his correctnesses. Perhaps influenced by the ancient Ptolemy, Polo badly overestimated how far eastward China and Japan extended from Europe. As we shall see, this gave rise to a fortunate misunderstanding.

BY SEA TO THE INDIES

THE RISE OF PORTUGAL

There had been a trickle of trade between Europe and the Far East for centuries. Silk, for instance, had found its way westward; so had spices. Always, though, goods had been transported from nation to nation, with each insisting on its own profits.

For a while, during the Mongol era, it looked as though overland trade between the nations of the Atlantic and the Pacific would grow more direct, and would increase and flourish. It might easily be imagined that the Polos would be followed by others.

By 1368, however, less than half a century after Marco Polo's death, the Mongols were driven out of China. In their place, a native dynasty ruled, and they made it quite plain that foreigners would no longer be welcome among them. About that time, too, Tamerlane, a descendant of Genghis Khan, began a career of conquest that placed all western Asia under his control. His realm wedged itself between Europe and the Far East, and he, too, did not welcome foreigners.

The Far East, which had been placed before European eyes for a tantalizing moment, was blocked off again and the overland route to the Indies* was to remain closed and never truly to open again. Never again would the rulers of western Europe and the rulers of eastern Asia come as close together and be so free of middlemen as in the Mongol era.

That was by land though. What about the sea? Marco Polo had made a sea voyage that had taken him along the coasts of China and India. Was there no way in which those coasts could be reached by a sea voyage from Europe?

The sea best known to the Europeans was the Mediterranean. That led eastward, but had no opening on its eastern end. If one went to the southeast corner of the Mediterranean and crossed the Sinai Peninsula, one could pass into the Red Sea and from there reach the Indies quite easily by sea. The trouble though was that the Sinai Peninsula and, in fact, all the southern and eastern coast of the Mediterranean, was controlled by Moslems. Between these Moslems and the Christians of western Europe there was nothing but enmity, and there was little chance of finding a practical route from Europe to the Far East if such a route had to cut across Moslem territory.

In that case, was there any chance of avoiding the Mediterranean Sea entirely? Suppose ships took off into the Atlantic, sailed southward, then turned eastward. They could circumnavigate Africa and bypass the Moslem world altogether in their voyage to the Far East.

That part of Europe which was both farthest west and far-

---

* In ancient times, the easternmost land known to the Greeks and Romans was India. As a result the name was given in a vague sort of way to all the east beyond India as well. To indicate that there were various lands that made up this distant India, the plural was used and "the Indies" became the common term in English.

thest south and therefore had a headstart in any plan for circumnavigating Africa was the Iberian peninsula. In the eighth
century, the peninsula had been captured by the Moslem
"Moors" from north Africa, but Christian principalities remained in the northern mountain range; the long counterattack
had begun almost at once. By the beginning of the fourteenth
century most of the peninsula had been won back, and the Moslem power was confined to the kingdom of Granada in the far
south.

The Christian portion of the peninsula was never united but
consisted of separate kingdoms, each clinging jealously to its independence and often warring with one another.

The easternmost part of the Iberian peninsula was taken up
by the kingdom of Aragon. Its seacoast was entirely on the
Mediterranean, and it looked eastward — not toward the Atlantic — for room to expand. It made itself a Mediterranean
power, and, by 1300, held large sections of Italy and a number
of the islands between itself and Italy.

The central part of the peninsula was the kingdom of Castile.
More than half the entire peninsula lay within its borders and it
had seacoasts on both the Mediterranean and the Atlantic. To
its south, however, lay Granada, and much of Castile's energies
was taken up by the continuing fight against the Moslems.

The kingdom that made up the westernmost part of the Iberian peninsula had its origins in 1095. At that time a region
along the mouth of the Douro River was granted to Henry of
Burgundy, an adventuring knight from France. The region had
been called Cale in Roman times, and the town at the mouth of
the Douro was "Portus Cale." The town's name was slurred to
"Oporto," and the name of the region was altered in another
way to "Portugal." Gradually, the rulers descended from Henry
of Burgundy expanded their dominion southward at Moorish
expense. By 1249, the Portuguese had taken the entire strip of
the Atlantic coast south of their original holdings and Portugal

(the name was applied to the entire country) reached the boundaries it has now.*

After 1249, Portugal, like Aragon, no longer had a Moslem foe at its borders. Like Aragon, too, it looked out upon the sea — but not upon the Mediterranean. Portugal has an Atlantic sea-coast only, and, from its southernmost section, Africa lies dim and misty on the horizon.

Portugal's land boundary was with the considerably larger Castile and that, of course, represented a danger. Castile had absorbed two small northern kingdoms, Leon and Navarre, and Portugal might suffer the same fate.

The danger came close after the death of Ferdinand I of Portugal, in 1383. Ferdinand was the last male descendant of Henry of Burgundy, and he left no sons. His only daughter, Beatrice, was married to John I of Castile. Naturally, John claimed that Portugal was now under the rule of Beatrice, and that their son, Henry, would rule both countries after the death of his parents.

The Portuguese would not hear of this. The dead Ferdinand I had a brother, also named John,** whose only trouble was that he was illegitimate. The Portuguese decided, however, that they would far rather be ruled by the illegitimate son of a Portuguese king than by the legitimate son of a Castilian one. The illegitimate John was acclaimed as John I of Portugal and that, of course, meant war between him and John I of Castile.

In August 1385, John I of Castile led his army into Portugal, and, on August 14, a great battle was fought at Aljubarrota, about sixty miles north of Lisbon. John of Castile was roundly

* The boundaries of Portugal have not changed in nearly 800 years — a record for Europe.
** Actually, the Spanish versions of John and Henry are Juan and Enrique, while the Portuguese versions of John and Ferdinand are João and Fernão. In an English–language book for the general public, however, it doesn't seem worthwhile to use unfamiliar foreign names that would be troublesome to pronounce, when familiar English equivalents would suit the situation just as well.

defeated; his army was smashed and scattered; and he himself barely escaped.

One factor in the victory was the help sent Portugal by England. England was then fighting a war with France and since Castile was allied to France, England was willing to help Castile's enemies.

In fact, in 1386, an English expedition was sent to invade Castile. It was under the leadership of John of Gaunt, Duke of Lancaster. He was the uncle of Richard II, who was then king of England, and a son of the previous English king, Edward III. The expedition proved a complete failure, but, before he returned home, John of Gaunt arranged a marriage between his daughter, Philippa, and John I of Portugal.

By his English wife, John I had four sons and a daughter. The eldest was named Edward (Duarte, in Portuguese) after his English grandfather, and he ruled over Portugal after John I's death. John's third son, born in 1394, was named Henry, and he goes down in history as "Henry the Navigator."

Portugal's victory over Castile had raised its morale sky-high, and it was spoiling for additional victories and triumphs. With Castile taken care of, the nearest place the Portuguese could find another enemy was in Africa, just across the narrow strait that separated that continent from the Iberian peninsula.

A fleet was gathered. The target for Portugal's first overseas venture was Ceuta, a city located on the northernmost tip of what is now Morocco. John and his sons accompanied the fleet and, on August 24, 1415, Ceuta was stormed and taken. Prince Henry particularly distinguished himself, and his standard was the first to be carried over the city wall.

DOWN THE COAST OF AFRICA

In the course of the expedition against Ceuta, Prince Henry

was bitten by Africa; it became his entire and only interest. From then on, for forty–five years, till his death in 1460, he had but one aim, and that was to explore the coasts of Africa, to find a way around the continent, and to master the sea route to the Indies.

In 1420, after he had returned from a second expedition to Ceuta designed to help the Portuguese garrison there survive a siege, he founded a center for navigation at Sagres, at the extreme southwestern tip of Portugal. This became a haven for experienced navigators, a place where ships were built according to new designs; where new aids to navigation were devised and tested; where crews were hired and trained; and where expeditions were carefully outfitted.

Year after year, Prince Henry sent out ships to sail down the Atlantic coast of Africa, each one trying to go farther than the one before had. It was a kind of Cape Kennedy of the 1400s: the African project of the time was as daring and as exciting as the Moon project of our own time.

The first fruit of Henry's effort came even before he had established his center at Sagres, for, in 1418, a small group of islands, 580 miles southwest of Portugal and 400 miles off the coast of Africa, were discovered by a Portuguese navigator, João Gonçalves Zarco. He made his discovery after he had been blown away from the African shore by a storm. (Such storm–driven discoveries took place both before and after Zarco's time.) Zarco named the largest island, "Madeira," a Portuguese word meaning "timber," because it was well wooded.

Madeira may well have been sighted by earlier voyagers, and islands in about the proper place were shown on an Italian map dating back to 1350. It was after the Portuguese discovery, however, that Madeira entered the European consciousness fully and remained there. When Zarco reached the island, it was uninhabited. Henry the Navigator set about establishing a colony there and had the forests cut down so that the land could be turned to agriculture. The island is still Portuguese today.

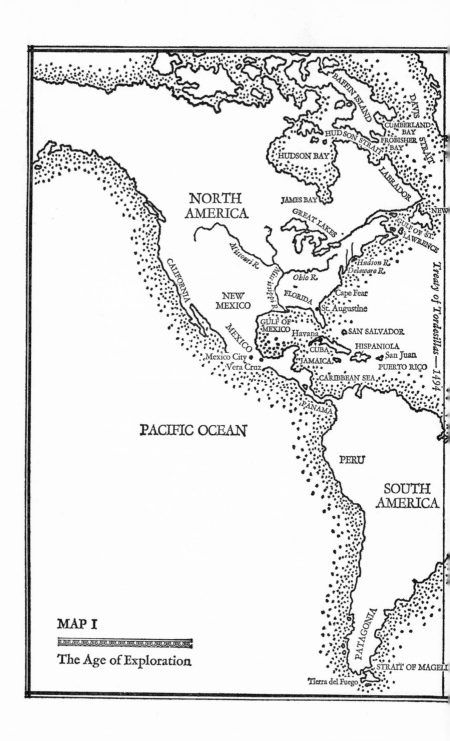

MAP I

The Age of Exploration

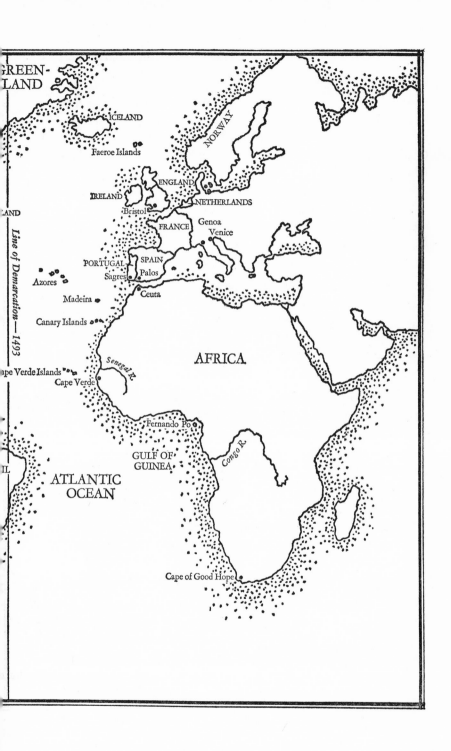

GREEN-
LAND

ICELAND

Faeroe Islands

NORWAY

LAND

ENGLAND

IRELAND
Bristol
NETHERLANDS

FRANCE
Genoa
Venice

Line of Demarcation — 1493

PORTUGAL
SPAIN
Sagres
Palos

Azores

Madeira
Ceuta

Canary Islands

AFRICA

Senegal R.

ape Verde Islands
Cape Verde

Fernando Po

GULF OF
GUINEA

Congo R.

IL

ATLANTIC
OCEAN

Cape of Good Hope

Three hundred miles south of Madeira is a much larger group of islands only fifty miles off the coast of Africa. These islands were apparently known to the Romans, who called them "Canaria" from the Latin word for "dog" because they were reported to have wild dogs upon them. We now call them the Canary Islands.*

Various navigators from various lands had spied these islands before Prince Henry's time. Adventurers who had tried to establish themselves on the islands turned to Castile for help and, by the time Prince Henry began his explorations down the African coast, Castile had a substantial foothold there. In 1425, Henry, fearing Castilian interference with his coastal exploration, sent an expedition to conquer them. It failed, and despite repeated Portuguese efforts, the Canary Islands remained Castilian.

West of Madeira, 800 miles out into the Atlantic Ocean, there is still another group of islands, which seem to have appeared on Italian maps of a century earlier. Prince Henry may have seen such maps, or heard mariners' tales of them, for, in 1431, he sent an expedition westward to locate them. Gonçalvo Velho Cabral, who commanded the expedition, found the islands and, because of the hawks he saw there, named them the Açores, which is the Portuguese word for "hawks." To us, they are the Azores.

The Azores, which were uninhabited at the time of the Portuguese discovery, were colonized by them, and they remain part of Portugal to this day.

By reaching the Azores, Prince Henry, had he only known, had sent men one–third of the way across the Atlantic toward America; but it was not his chief concern to penetrate westward. He wanted to circumnavigate Africa, and the main thrust of his expeditions was southward.

---

* A yellow finch with a cheerful song, native to the islands, became a popular household pet in later centuries, and such birds are now known as canaries.

Year by year, the daring Portuguese navigators thrust farther down the African coast. By 1433, they had sailed nearly a thousand miles along the shores of the continent, and in the next decade, eight hundred miles more were inched out.

Then a milestone of sorts was reached.

All along that 1800 miles of coast, the Portuguese had moved past relatively barren land, for they were skirting the western edge of the great Sahara desert. But the southern limits of the desert were finally reached, and, in 1444, the navigator, Nuño Tristram reached the mouth of a great river, tumbling into the sea. This was the Senegal River.

The next year, Dinis Dias went 120 miles farther still and reached Cape Verde, from the Portuguese word for "green" — because of its color, so different from that of the drab Sahara.

And Cape Verde represented another milestone.

For more than a quarter century, Henry's expeditions had been moving steadily down the African coast, for nearly two thousand miles; but always, through all that length of coastal travel, they had gone south*west*. Every mile brought the ships farther away from the east, farther from the riches of the Indies. By the time Cape Verde was reached, the ships were about five hundred miles farther to the west than Portugal was.

But Cape Verde, as it happened, was the westernmost part of the African continent. Beyond that cape, the shore ran directly southward and then started trending more and more to the south*east*. From here on, the ships began to move toward the final goal instead of away from it.

In addition, the African coast had become useful in its own right. As it grew fertile, the Portuguese found it populated with a native population ready to barter gold and ivory for items that the Portuguese sailors could offer.

The native population could, in fact, offer themselves. The African tribes fought among themselves and prisoners of war were routinely enslaved. The tribal leaders saw nothing wrong with selling these slaves to the Portuguese, and the Portuguese saw nothing wrong with buying them. The natives were dark–skinned, so that they were considered apelike and therefore half–animal and naturally adapted to enslavement. What's more, they were pagan, and the men who bought them could always tell themselves that they would be converted to Christianity and that the salvation of their souls more than made up for the enslavement of their bodies.

Prince Henry tried to stop this traffic in human bodies but failed, and in this way the horrible era of Black enslavement by the Christian nations began. It was to continue for four centuries (with the United States the last to give it up) and was to leave a heritage that has troubled the world, and particularly the United States, down to this day.

In 1455, Alvise da Cadamosto, a Venetian navigator working for Prince Henry, explored the Gambia River, 150 miles south of Cape Verde. He also discovered the Cape Verde Islands, a group of fourteen islands about 280 miles west of Cape Verde — islands which have been Portuguese possessions ever since.

In 1460, Pedro de Sintra explored the coast for about 800 miles south of Cape Verde, and, through that entire stretch, the shore continued to trend southeastward. There was no reason to doubt that the shore would continue to do so and that the ships hastening onward would approach closer and closer to the Indies. When Henry the Navigator died, on November 13, 1460, it must have been with that comforting thought in mind, that the project he had worked on for so long must be nearing completion.

Alas, it wasn't. In terms of miles, the longest stretch covered by Prince Henry's ships, was only one–fifth of the way to the goal, and difficulties lay ahead.

It didn't seem so at first. Henry's driving personality was missed, but commercial success continued to push the Portuguese onward. By 1470, the Portuguese reached a portion of the coast where the trade in gold was particularly lucrative, so that the region came to be known as "Gold Coast," a name it was to keep for nearly five centuries. What's more, by that time, the African coast was no longer trending merely southeast, but had turned so that the navigators were going due east. They were heading straight for the Indies.

With great excitement, the navigators leap–frogged each other's efforts and, by 1472, Fernando Po had discovered the island that bears his name. By now the navigators had followed the African coast to a point 1800 miles farther east than Africa's westernmost point at Cape Verde. They were 1300 miles farther east than Portugal itself was. Surely, it was only a matter of continued eastward sailing and the Indies would be reached.

Then came a heartbreaking discovery. At the island of Fernando Po, the African coast unexpectedly turned southward again, southward . . . southward. . . . It showed no signs of any further eastward trend.

For a while, the Portuguese were disheartened and the attempt to reach the Indies languished. There seemed consolation in the fact that the African coast, as far as it had been explored, was lucrative. Why look farther?

But then, in 1481, John II, a great–grandson of John I and a grandnephew of Henry the Navigator, came to the Portuguese throne. He was an energetic king, considered by many the greatest in Portuguese history, and he took up the work of Prince Henry. Forcefully, he urged the navigators to go on and on; and if the coast trended southward to follow that trend to the point where the continent turned again; for turn (he was sure) it must.

In 1482, Diogo Cão led an expedition that carried him a thousand miles south of Fernando Po, to the mouth of the Congo River, and then 600 miles farther still. By 1486, he had reached that area of Africa now known as Angola, a large section of southwestern Africa that is still a Portuguese colony today.

But still the coast drifted southward, ever southward.

John II did not give up. In 1487, he organized an expedition that was to reach the Indies by way of the Mediterranean and the Red Sea. It might not be a practical trade route, but the information it brought back might be valuable.

Under the leadership of Pedro de Covilhão, the Portuguese passed through Cairo, then traveled to the other end of the Red Sea at Aden. There, Covilhão took a ship that carried him to India. Then he sailed back to the eastern coast of Africa, which he explored as far south as the mouth of the Zambesi River. (The area on the southeastern coast of Africa, centering about the Zambesi, is now known as Mozambique, and is still a possession of Portugal.)

Covilhão settled in Ethiopia but sent back a full report. By calculation, the continent of Africa couldn't be more than 1500 miles wide at the southern points reached by Cão and Covilhão. The continent was nearly 4000 miles across at its northern end, so it seemed to be coming to a point. One more good push, perhaps, was all that was needed.

The push was under way, for in the same year that Covilhão left, another sea voyage was undertaken. With two ships under his command, Bartholomeu Dias sailed from Lisbon, in August 1487. He sailed along the shore of Africa till he passed the uttermost limits reached by any of the navigators who had ventured southward before him.

He sailed 400 miles beyond Cão's farthest reach and came to a spot now called Dias Point. There a severe storm struck, and forced him southward willy–nilly. Nor could he hug the shore. He had to go where the wind drove him and counted himself lucky that he remained afloat at all.

When the storm lifted, Dias found himself in the open sea with no sign of land anywhere. Assuming that the African shore lay somewhere to the east, he sailed eastward — and struck nothing. He then turned northward in order to retrace the route along which the storm had driven him, and, on February 3, 1488, he struck land at what is now known as Mosselbai. To his astonishment, the African coast (assuming that that was what it was) was running east and west. Somewhere, the southerly trend must have ended and the coast must have turned eastward — and he had missed the turning point in the storm.

He began to sail eastward along the coast and after going 250 miles, he reached the Great Fish River (as we now call it), and there the coast was definitely tending *north*eastward. He was convinced he had reached the eastern shores of Africa at last and it seemed to him that it remained only to sail northward and eastward to reach India.

Dias was perfectly right, but his crew was tired and rebellious. They had gone farther than anyone before had done (unless we count the legendary Phoenician voyage of 2000 years before), and they had clearly passed the southern tip of the continent. That was enough. They wanted to go home, and Dias had to give in.

Westward they followed the shore, and eventually Dias reached the end of the east–west line and found the place where the shoreline, rather abruptly, turned north–south. This was the point he had missed in the storm and so he named it "Cape of Storms."

When he returned and made his report, however, John II refused to accept the name. It was the turn at that point that gave him at last good hope of reaching India by the sea route, and he named it "Cape of Good Hope," the name it bears to this day.

John II was right in this but, tragically, he did not live to see the final success of his and, earlier, Henry's great project. In 1497, the Portuguese navigator Vasco da Gama completed the turn around Africa, and reached India.

By that voyage, the Moslem World was bypassed. Portugal proceeded to build a great colonial empire in Africa and the Far East; other nations followed; and Europe grew rich and powerful, spreading out to populate continents hitherto unknown and to dominate ancient nations which could not compete with the new dynamism of Europe. Portugal initiated a European control of all the world that was to last for four and a half centuries and end only in our own times.

CHRISTOPHER COLUMBUS

But the consequences of da Gama's voyage do not immediately concern us in this book. The Portuguese explorations of the coast of Africa interest us only insofar as they led to a westward thrust across the Atlantic Ocean.

After all, by the 1480s, just before Dias's crucial discovery of Africa's southern tip, Portugal had been trying to make its way around Africa for over sixty years, and had not succeeded. Even if it did succeed at last, was not the route an enormously long and difficult one? Was there no simpler and more direct alternative?

It is important to remember that, whatever uneducated people of the time believed, all educated Europeans and certainly all experienced navigators, were quite firmly convinced that the Earth was a sphere. That was understood even as far back as Roman times, and no educated man doubted that if one sailed westward from Europe far enough, one would reach the Indies.

The only quarrel was, how far was "far enough"?

If Eratosthenes was right and the Earth was 25,000 miles around, ships would have to sail westward at least 16,000 miles from Portugal to reach the Indies. An unbroken voyage of that length across open seas could not be made.

To be sure, there might exist islands along the way; even large bodies of land, rich and inhabited — but the cynical Portuguese navigators doubted it. The Earth might be smaller than 25,000 miles in circumference, but who would take a chance on that?

Besides, the Portuguese had sent several quiet expeditions

probing westward just a bit, to see what could be seen, and these invariably encountered contrary winds for, in the temperate zones, the winds tend to blow from west to east.

The Portuguese, therefore, much preferred the African route, long and arduous though it was. There, at least, one could hug the shore every inch of the way; one could find harbors against storms; and, what's more, one could obtain gold, ivory, spices, and slaves.

But there were those who dreamed of the westward route just the same and of these, the most important was Christopher Columbus.

Columbus, the son of a wool weaver, was born in Genoa, Italy, about 1451, but there is some doubt as to whether he might truly be considered an Italian by descent. He seems to have been completely Iberian in culture, he spoke and wrote only in Spanish even before he went to that peninsula. There are speculations that he came of a Spanish–Jewish family that had settled in Genoa some time before his birth and that had been converted to Christianity. Columbus himself was, of course, thoroughly Catholic in religion.

Columbus went to sea as a teen–ager, according to his own account, and, in 1476, he was engaged in a sea battle off the coast of Portugal. He was fighting on the Portuguese side, and when his ship caught on fire, he managed to swim to shore. As it happened, he landed fairly close to where Prince Henry's center for navigation had existed.

He didn't need the coincidence, however, to set him dreaming about the Indies. He had been thinking of it for several years, and, to his way of thinking, it was the westward route that was bound to succeed. He had consulted a famous Italian geographer of the time, Paolo Toscanelli, who had sent him a map representing his own theories. To Toscanelli, the Earth was only about 18,000 miles in circumference, and from the Azores to the islands lying off–shore from the eastern coast of Asia (Toscanelli having accepted Marco Polo's overestimate of the eastward thrust of Asia), there might be little more than a mere 3000 miles of open ocean.

There is a story (not universally accepted) that Columbus, while still young, visited Iceland. If so, he may have heard rumors of the Norse voyages of five centuries before, and vague tales of Vinland to the west. More certainly, he settled for a time in Madeira, about 1479 or 1480, and there he heard tales of large pieces of wood and of other materials drifting eastward across the ocean, indicating the existence of land somewhere to the west — and perhaps not very far to the west.

Then, too, of course, he followed the reports of the Portuguese voyages along the African coast with avidity, and he read and reread the travel tales of Marco Polo.

By 1483, Columbus was appealing to John II of Portugal for ships, men, and money with which to undertake a westward expedition in search of the Indies. John II, a daring and for-ward–looking man, was tempted. But then it would mean the investment of a lot of money, and the voyage would be risky, very risky. John's own navigators assured him the scheme was hare–brained, and John hesitated. He did not entirely close the door, however, until 1488, when the news of Bartholomeu Dias's discovery reached Lisbon. With the Cape of Good Hope passed, John II was exultant, certain that the Indies were in his grasp, and he gave up all thought of westward voyages.

Columbus, however, held to his dream. If Portugal refused to help him, there were other maritime nations that might. Indeed, just across Portugal's boundaries, there was a new nation which might well be fired into trying to outdo Portugal.

The nation that had bordered on Portugal was Castile, but Castile was vanishing from the map. It came about this way. In 1469, Isabella, the half–sister of Henry IV of Castile, married Ferdinand, the son of John II of Aragon. It was a love match and a completely successful marriage.

In 1474, Henry IV of Castile died without sons, but left a daughter, who married Affonso V of Portugal (who was the father of the future John II). Castile had to choose between two princesses each of whom was married to a foreign king. In the end, they chose Isabella; and, as Isabella I, she became Queen of Castile.

Then, in 1479, John II of Aragon died, and his son became Ferdinand II of Aragon. Together, Ferdinand and Isabella, served as joint king and queen over the double nation of Castile and Aragon. At the time, it seemed to be a mere union of monarchs, with the nations themselves remaining separate. As it turned out, however, the two nations have remained under a united government ever since, so that, after the accession of Ferdinand and Isabella, we don't speak of either Castile or Aragon, but only of Spain.

With the founding of Spain, all the Iberian peninsula, except for Portugal and the Moorish kingdom of Granada, was under united rule. Spain, thus enlarged, and with the wealth of two kingdoms at her disposal, simply exploded with ambition and looked for room where she might expand further.

The obvious victim was Granada, and, in 1481, Granada did Spain the favor of initiating war. For eleven years, Ferdinand and Isabella carried on a difficult compaign in the southern mountains. Granada, weakened by internal dissension, gradually lost ground. In April 1491, the capital city of Granada was put under siege, and, on January 2, 1492, it was taken. The last bit of Moorish dominion in Spain was wiped out — nearly eight centuries after the Moors had first entered the peninsula.*

With Granada eliminated, and with an air of victory and triumph permeating all of Spain, it was natural that Ferdinand and Isabella should look about for still further deeds of greatness. After all, while Spain had been occupied with internal affairs and the war with Granada, the neighboring kingdom of

* In the process of winning this war, Spain first tested its military mettle. Under the shrewd leadership of the two monarchs, it became a great power. In fact, the Spanish army came to be the best in Europe and was to maintain that position for nearly a century and a half.

Portugal, much smaller than Spain, had been making the world resound with its African triumphs and had been finding new lands to make its own. Could Spain do nothing to counter this?

Columbus was eager to take advantage of this new mood in Spain, this spirit of emulation. He had gone to Spain as early as 1484, and had there used a new argument. The very fact that the Portuguese had established a stranglehold on the African route made it advisable for Spain to find some alternate. The westward route was not only more practical than the African route (said Columbus) but it offered a way for Spain to get to the Indies without having to compete with Portugal.

Various Spaniards listened to Columbus and were interested in his arguments. They pleaded his case with Ferdinand and Isabella and, in 1486, arranged a royal hearing for Columbus. Columbus was very impressive in his presentation of his case, and Isabella, particularly, was attracted by the idea. And yet the royal couple could not help but realize the project was a risky one; that the money invested might be lost; and that every cent they could raise was needed for the war against Granada.

Ferdinand and Isabella temporized, therefore, in the usual way of rulers; they set up a commission to study Columbus's proposals. The commission's decision was, in the end, unenthusiastic.

Columbus kept following the monarchs about for four years, pressing his case. He managed to gain enough converts to his views to keep up his spirits and to offer powerful help in keeping Ferdinand and Isabella interested.

In the end, what put off the Spanish monarchs was not so much the notion of the trip itself, but Columbus's own demands of titles and of percentages of the proceeds. Columbus (a very stubborn man) would not lower his demands, and Ferdinand (a very tight–fisted man) kept shaking his head. Ferdinand was besieging Granada now, and the distant Indies just didn't mean much to him at the moment.

Finally, as 1492 opened, Columbus gave up. He would just

have to try still another nation, and he left for France.

He had hardly gone, however, when Ferdinand began to have second thoughts. The war was over, Granada was taken, Spain was bathed in glory. Perhaps it *was* time for another great venture. Those who backed Columbus continued to urge, and the monarchs finally capitulated. Messengers were sent after the difficult and demanding dreamer, and Columbus, almost at the border, turned back.

Columbus's demands were accepted, all of them, but the financial backing was not of the greatest. He was given three small ships, rather well worn, with a total tonnage of but 190. His crew consisted largely of men freed from prisons on condition they take the voyage. They might have been glad to be at liberty but that didn't mean they were enthusiastic to sail into the dim west. The total cost of the expedition has been estimated as anywhere from $16,000 to $75,000, not very much even for those times.

And yet perhaps we ought not to look down our noses at the royal pair. The chance was a great one, and few could honestly think they would ever see Columbus, his ships, and his crew again. It was an investment in a long shot; but Isabella is supposed to have been so enthusiastic over it, just the same, that she said she would have pawned her jewels, if necessary, to supply Columbus with money. (But she didn't have to; the money was raised in other ways.)

THE GREATEST VOYAGE

On August 3, 1492, Columbus, with a total crew of 90 on his three ships, left Palos, a port in southern Spain, just 30 miles east of the Portuguese frontier.

Those who watched the ships melt into the southwestern

horizon probably didn't realize that they were witnessing the beginning of the greatest sea voyage of all time. Perhaps Columbus, for all his fervor, did not quite realize it either. The fact is, however, that as a result of the voyage that was now beginning, Europe was to be forced out of its shell forever.

The voyage brought new horizons, a new world, a new Earth to the consciousness of Europe, a new outlook, new hopes, new deeds. After this voyage, European ships would make the whole ocean their home and European men and women would probe every continent, even every island.

The result is that many historians, searching for some date that might conveniently be used to divide the Middle Ages from modern times, have chosen 1492 — and the voyage of Columbus that began on August 3 of that year represented to them one of the great hinges of human history.

Columbus sailed for the Canary Islands, the only Atlantic islands in Spanish hands, and, on September 6, 1492, took off into the unknown. It was a shrewd move on his part, for he had sailed far enough south to take advantage of the trade winds which blew him westward on his way. (Portuguese navigators who had tried to travel westward in the more northerly latitude of the Azores had the prevailing westerlies blowing in their faces.)

For seven weeks, Columbus's ships sailed steadily westward. Amazingly, it was an entirely smooth passage, the smoothest on record. Not once in all those weeks was there a storm — which was fortunate indeed, for Columbus's three hulks would very likely have foundered in a real storm.

Nevertheless, for those seven weeks there was only unbroken sea, without any sign of even the smallest island. The miles they traveled were greater than Columbus had anticipated; and, even though he kept a false log that made the distance less than it really was, the crew grew steadily more nervous and rebellious. It was only Columbus's indomitable will that kept the ships moving westward.

Finally, on October 12, 1492, land was sighted. It was not the Indies, of course. It was not even the American continent. It was just a small island — but it was one that was over two thousand miles west of the Azores. No European (barring forgotten voyages by Phoenicians and Norsemen) had ever ventured so far west before.

It was an inhabited island and Columbus, who was firmly convinced that he had reached the Indies, called the inhabitants "Indians" for that reason. This grotesque misnomer has persisted to this day.*

The Indian name for the island on which Columbus had landed was "Guanahani," or at least that was how the Spaniards pronounced and spelled the Indian name. Columbus, however, started at once with the European notion that no non–Europeans had rights that need be considered at all. He calmly took possession of the island in the name of Spain and called it "San Salvador" ("Holy Savior").

The name eventually dropped out of use, and, astonishingly enough, the identity of the island was forgotten. Nobody is quite certain exactly what piece of land it was that Columbus first stood upon. San Salvador is, however, generally identified these days with Watling's Island, named after an English pirate, John Watling.

This island, part of the Bahamas, lies well to the east of the island group, which is what makes it reasonable to suppose that it represents Columbus's first landfall.

Again, because of Columbus's certainty that the islands he first discovered were part of the Indies, islands off the American coast are called the "West Indies" to this day. Islands off the southeastern shore of Asia, which deserved the name much more, had to be distinguished as the "East Indies," and these make up the modern nation of Indonesia.

---

* To distinguish them from the natives of the Asian country of India, the native inhabitants of the American continents are sometimes called "Red Indians," "American Indians," or even "Amerinds." The common name, however, is simply "Indians."

Columbus hastened on to find better examples of the wealth of the Indies (for San Salvador was only three times the size of Manhattan island and showed no signs of being part of the gorgeous east). Searching for the golden lands, he came upon Cuba, on October 28. Following its northern coast, he could see at once it was a sizable piece of land and thought it might well be the "Zipangu" that Marco Polo spoke of (the land we now call Japan). To its east, on December 6, he came across another island he named "Hispaniola" ("Spanish island"), one that is now occupied by the nations of Haiti and the Dominican Republic.

Off Hispaniola, his largest ship, the *Santa Maria*, was wrecked. He used wood from the ship to build a fort on the island, which he manned with thirty–nine volunteers. This was the first attempt at settling the new lands to the west. Then, on January 3, 1493, Columbus turned his remaining two ships eastward and began the voyage home.

He reached the shores of the home continent, on March 4, near Lisbon. He entered Lisbon harbor with the Indians he had taken with him (who were the living proof that he had indeed reached new lands) and was received by an undoubtedly chagrined, but sportsmanlike John II, who accorded him full honors.

Columbus then went on to Spain and arrived back in Palos, on March 13, 1493, eight months after he left. Suddenly, he was the most famous man in the world and admired by the public much as Lindbergh was to be in our own time and for the same reason — he had undertaken a feat few had thought possible and had carried it through with style. He was wildly acclaimed in Seville and would have been treated to a ticker–tape parade if such a thing had been possible then. Toward the end of April, Ferdinand and Isabella received him in Barcelona, treating him as though he were himself a king.

A second voyage was planned at once, and this time there was no difficulty at all in getting men or money. On September 25,

1493, a fleet of seventeen vessels, carrying some 1500 men, left Spain. This second voyage took Columbus again to the West Indies, where he discovered Puerto Rico ("rich harbor"), in November 1493. This was the first definite occasion in which Europeans set foot on land now flying the flag of the United States.

Columbus then visited Hispaniola, on April 24, 1494, and found the fort he had built a year before destroyed and the men who had held it gone — presumably killed by the Indians. A stronger fort was built, and Hispaniola then became the first portion of the western lands to be permanently settled by men of European descent. What's more, the fate of Columbus's first fort was used thereafter to justify harsh treatment of the Indians. It was a precedent that was to be applied everywhere; for any attempt of the Indians to protect their own lands against invasion was to be considered atrocious conduct which deserved the strongest and most punishing counteraction.

So far, though, on Columbus's two voyages, only islands had been discovered. He had not yet touched a continental shore. He corrected that situation with his third voyage, which left Spain, on May 30, 1498, and which involved a considerably smaller investment than the second. This time he penetrated farther to the south and discovered the island of Trinidad ("Trinity"). He actually sighted the coast of the continent lying immediately to the south of Trinidad, which he took, however to be another island.

On May 9, 1502, he undertook his fourth and last voyage, which took him to the islands again. He then sailed to what we now call Central America, the narrow isthmus connecting the northern and southern continents and sailed along its shores. He returned to Spain, on November 7, 1504, after having been marooned on the island of Jamaica for over a year.

To the day of his death (on May 20, 1506) Columbus was convinced he had sailed westward to the Indies.

As for the Portuguese, they recovered from the chagrin they

must have felt on Columbus's return from his first voyage. After all, by 1497, Vasco da Gama had reached India, the *real* India, and Portugal was well on its way to empire in Africa and Asia. By contrast, the Spaniards merely had a few distant, barbarous islands, and though they called them the Indies, they did not bring back any evidence of Far Eastern wealth.

In fact, Portugal even shared in the western world. On March 9, 1500, a Portuguese navigator, Pedro Álvares Cabral, set sail for India. It occurred to him that, if he skirted Africa in a wider sweep than usual, he would take further advantage of the trade winds. Though he might travel a longer distance, he would make better time.

He wheeled so wide, in fact, that he touched the eastern bulge of South America, on April 22. He did not expect a continent to be that far east and he assumed he had sighted an island, perhaps even the legendary Hy–Brasil. At any rate, the region making up the eastern bulge of the continent is called Brazil to this day; and it remained Portuguese for over three centuries.

As a result of the voyages of Columbus and Cabral, and of others who followed, the entire area of the western world south of the Rio Grande (with inconsiderable exceptions) is either Spanish– or Portuguese–speaking. Since Spanish and Portuguese belong to the group of Romance or Latin languages, the area south of the Rio Grande is still referred to as "Latin America."

But where does the term *America* come from? It stems from an Italian navigator named Amerigo Vespucci. In Latinized form, the name is Americus Vespucius.*

Vespucius was born in the same year as Columbus and was

---

* It was common in medieval and early modern times to Latinize names of people who wrote books, or about whom books were written, since Latin was the language of scholarship and the language in which serious works were written. Christopher Columbus is itself a Latinized name of which the Italian form is Cristoforo Colombo, and the Spanish form, Cristóbal Colón.

present in Spain when Columbus returned from his first voyage. He was involved in the preparations for the second and third voyages. From 1497 onward, he went on voyages to the west himself and seems to have explored the coast of South America, first in the employ of Spain, and then of Portugal.

His voyages were not as important as those of Columbus, but, whereas Columbus insisted on the view that the western lands were part of the Indies, Vespucius said otherwise. In 1504, Vespucius maintained that what existed in the west was a new and hitherto unknown continent, a "new world," as he called it. What's more, accepting 25,000 miles as the length of the circumference of the Earth, he was the first to maintain that there were *two* oceans between Europe and Asia; one, the familiar Atlantic and the other, an unknown sea on the western side of the new world.

Vespucius's views were accepted, in 1507, by a German geographer, Martin Waldseemüller. Waldseemüller published a map showing the new continent as existing by itself and not as part of either Europe, Africa, or Asia. He proposed that it be named "America" for Americus Vespucius, who may not have been the first to discover it (neither was Columbus, after all, we now know), but the first to recognize the discovery for what it was. He included the name on his map.

The name was instantly popular and was soon in universal use. At first it was applied exclusively to the southern portion of the new world for the northern portion might still have been attached to Asia. (Alaska, the first portion of the Americas to be discovered by the Indians, was the last to be discovered by Europeans.) Eventually, though, the northern portion was also recognized as separate. It became North America while the southern portion became, naturally, South America.

3

EXPLORING THE NEW WORLD

ENGLAND DISREGARDS THE LINE

As the 1400s closed, Portugal and Spain stood astride the world. One had rounded Africa, and one had reached the western lands. Each claimed for itself all the pagan–occupied territory it had discovered, and each settled wherever it could. What wealth was to be made out of the non–Christian world, each intended to make. Well, then, was all the world to become an Iberian monopoly, with Spain and Portugal each taking half?

So it seemed just at first, as a matter of fact. No sooner had Columbus returned from his first voyage, than the Spanish monarchs realized that there might be trouble with Portugal. Since both nations were rigidly Catholic, it seemed to Spain that the easiest way out was to have the Pope rule on the matter. Ferdinand and Isabella probably felt they could rely on a favorable ruling since the Pope at the time was Alexander VI, who was a Spaniard by birth.

On May 4, 1493, the Pope drew a line from the North Pole to the South Pole a hundred leagues west of the Cape Verde Islands, or at about the line of 38° West Longitude. All newly discovered lands to the west of that line were to belong to Spain; all newly discovered lands to the east were to belong to Portugal.

From our modern point of view, this "Line of Demarcation" is rather curious. In the first place, it seemed to assume that Europeans could divide the world freely without any consideration for the non–European people who might be living in the various regions, and that the Pope was lord of the Earth and could do the dividing.

And then, too, the line of division was drawn only half way around the world, from the North Pole to the South Pole through the Atlantic Ocean. The Pope seemed to forget the Earth was a sphere. The Spanish could sail west of the line as they were supposed to, but by sailing far enough west they could reach any point in the east, and the Portuguese by sailing eastward could reach any point in the west. The division was no division at all.

Both the Spanish and Portuguese probably realized this and let it go, each planning to use it against the other at some appropriate time. Portugal, however, found herself discontented with the Pope's line, thinking that it didn't give her enough elbow room in making her way around Africa. To take advantage of the winds she might want to swing wide and she didn't want Spain forever telling her she was overstepping the bounds.

On June 7, 1494, therefore, the two nations signed a treaty at Tordesillas (a town in central Spain, 60 miles east of the Portuguese border). The principle of the dividing line was kept, but it was shoved 700 miles farther west to the line of 46° West Longitude.

What neither nation knew was that the new line passed

through the eastern bulge of South America (or did Portugal have an inkling of this from some of her less publicized explorations?). Thus, when Cabral reached that bulge, it was on the Portuguese side of the line. As a result, it was Portugal that colonized Brazil, and this largest of all Latin–American nations speaks Portuguese, whereas the rest speak Spanish.

But if Spain and Portugal really thought they could divide the non–Christian world between them, they were being rather naïve. The other maritime nations of Europe could not possibly let it go at that.

Consider England, for instance. . . .

During the 1400s, England had gone through the trauma of a war with France, one which England first seemed to have won, but then lost after all. This was accompanied and succeeded by the even worse experience of a series of civil wars.

Finally, in 1485, at the Battle of Bosworth, those civil wars ended with the defeat of King Richard III, and the accession of his third cousin, once removed, Henry Tudor, who reigned as Henry VII.

Henry VII was a capable king, if an unlovable one, ruling firmly and parsimoniously. He gave England a period of peace, which it needed, and filled its treasury (though not without some stern taxation). He was interested in turning English energies to ventures outside the nation, if only to make it forget the partisan passions of civil war, but did not wish to wreck his treasury in the process. He did not wish, therefore, to take the obvious course of starting a popular, but expensive, foreign war.

What about turning the national interest toward exploration? That would occupy the English with thoughts away from home, and, if the Indies could be reached, the result might be very profitable. In 1488, while Christopher Columbus was trying to persuade Ferdinand and Isabella to back his westward venture, the navigator's brother, Bartholomew Columbus, was in England trying to sell the notion to Henry VII.

Nor was Columbus the only man in England with this notion. There was another Italian navigator in the land who was born Giovanni Caboto, but who is better known by the Anglicized version of his name — John Cabot.

Cabot was born at about the same time that Columbus was, and possibly, like Columbus, in Genoa. Cabot moved to Venice, however, and became a citizen of that city in 1476. He traveled in the Moslem East and was familiar with the tales of Marco Polo. Again, like Columbus, he speculated on the possibility of a western route to the Indies. To Cabot, however, it seemed that England, rather than Portugal or Spain, was the logical place to seek support.

For one thing, of the nations of Europe, England was at the farthest end of the trade route from the East and, therefore, had to pay the highest prices for spices and other desirable eastern commodities. For another, Cabot had the notion that the eastern shore of Asia trended northeast (as in fact it does) so that the distance from England westward to Asia would be shorter than that from Spain westward. Then, too, northern Europe was particularly rife with tales of western lands. The Irish, Welsh, and, of course, the Scandinavians, all spoke of them.

Cabot came to England some time in the 1480s, therefore, and settled in Bristol, the greatest west–coast port in the nation. There he gained considerable local support for his notion of a venture westward, since Bristol would become the key to trade with the Indies if the idea worked and it would grow wealthy. He, too, like Bartholomew Columbus bombarded the king with petitions for support.

Henry VII hesitated. He was intrigued by the notion, but not by the thought of spending money on it. And while he hesitated, Columbus sailed for Spain and returned in triumph. That convinced Henry VII, of course; but, naturally, Bartholomew Columbus was no longer available. The king turned to Cabot, granted him the right to sail under royal auspices, to govern the lands he found (under the overlordship of the English king), and to make what profits he could in trade, provided he paid one–fifth to the crown.

On May 2, 1497, Cabot set sail from Bristol in one ship with a crew of 18 men. The ship sailed around Ireland and then traveled westward. It reached land on June 24, having crossed the Atlantic in not quite seven weeks, which was fast going for that latitude. The distance it traveled was about 2000 miles, considerably less than the distance Columbus had to travel, so that Cabot was right in his feeling that the western route was shorter in the north (in miles, if not in weeks).

Exactly where Cabot first landed is uncertain, but the best guess was that it was at or near the northern tip of Newfoundland, quite close, in fact, to where the Norse had landed centuries before (though Cabot did not know that, of course). For the next month, he sailed up and down the eastern coast of the island, describing it as a new–found land. Newfoundland has been the name of the island ever since.

Cabot reported the wealth of fish off the Newfoundland shores, and it wasn't long before all the maritime nations of western Europe were sending out ships to fish along its shores. From 1500 onward, fishermen landed all along its shores and along the shores of what are now Nova Scotia and Maine in the course of their fishing. No effort was made to settle any point along those rather inhospitable shores for a century, however.

When, on August 6, 1497, Cabot returned to England with his report, Henry VII gave him ten pounds outright and a pension of twenty pounds a year. This was considerably more in those days than it would be now, but even so it was not exactly an example of overflowing generosity.

Like Columbus, Cabot was convinced he had reached Asia, and, though he had met with no signs of the wealth of the Indies, he persuaded Henry to let him try again. In 1498, he sailed off on a second voyage with five ships. This time, he seems to have sighted Greenland (now empty of its Norse

colonists), passed by it to Labrador, and sailed southward, as far as New England possibly.

If we ignore the Norse discoveries, John Cabot was the first European to sight the North American continent, as opposed to islands off its shores.

Again, though, he returned with nothing and died before the end of the year. There were no signs of the gorgeous east on the forested shores he followed.

Henry VII lost interest. If there were no signs of profitable trade to be gotten out of these ventures, he was only too ready to turn his mind to other matters. Cabot's voyages were, eventually, to give England an excuse to claim as much of North America as she could hold, but for the time being nothing was done about it.

Henry's son, who reigned as Henry VIII on the death of the old king in 1509, grew involved in religious controversies and the New World dropped out of English consciousness for the better part of a century.

SPAIN PUSHES OUTWARD

Spain, meanwhile, was exploring the far more hospitable shores to the south, moving out in all directions from the first base that Columbus had established in Hispaniola. In 1508, Juan Ponce de León, who had been with Columbus on his second voyage, established a permanent Spanish base on Puerto Rico, the island east of Hispaniola, and was made governor in 1510. (The second largest city on Puerto Rico is named Ponce in his honor.) Diego Velásquez, who had also been with Columbus on his second voyage, began the takeover of Cuba, the island west of Hispaniola, in 1511, and founded Havana, in 1515.

In Puerto Rico, Ponce de León heard rumors of a fountain of youth (one which would restore youth when its waters were applied internally or externally) on some small island to the northwest. It is hard to believe that Ponce de León could take such a thing seriously, but it was an age of wonders and a new world might be the very place for wonders. Besides, leaving youth aside, Ponce de León was making his fortune in Puerto Rico as a slave dealer, and he was not averse to finding further lands whose inhabitants might be enslaved. *

On March 3, 1513, Ponce de León sailed northwestward from Puerto Rico, and, on April 11, during the Easter season, reached what he first thought was an island, but which turned out to be the North American mainland. Easter is celebrated in Spain as a feast of flowers so it is called "Pascua Florida" ("flowery Easter"). In honor of the time of the discovery, and because the new land seemed green and flowery, Ponce de León called the region "Florida." In 1521, Ponce de León led a second expedition to Florida, landing on the west coast this time. There he was wounded by Indians he was trying to capture and enslave. He was taken back to Cuba and there died of the wound.

An even more momentous discovery was made shortly after the discovery of Florida, by the Spanish explorer, Vasco Núñez de Balboa. He had settled first in Hispaniola. There he went into debt and had to smuggle himself, with great difficulty, to the South American coast near what is now called the Isthmus of Panama.

In 1510, Balboa founded a settlement on the eastern side of the isthmus (without having the faintest idea he was on an isth-

---

* Nor was it only Indians the Spaniards enslaved. In 1501, Ferdinand and Isabella granted permission to import African Blacks to Hispaniola and the history of Black slavery in the Americas began. The Blacks were thought to adapt to slavery better than the Indians did, but probably no people enjoy being slaves. The first Black revolt in the Americas took place in Hispaniola in 1522. It was beaten down.

mus, of course). Later, he heard rumors of tribes with much gold living to the west. Since he was in financial trouble again, he decided to look for that gold. On September 1, 1513, he headed a party of men westward across the isthmus and, on September 25, climbed a last hill and found himself staring at the limitless expanse of what seemed to be an ocean. He called it the "South Sea" because at that point it lay to the south of the shoreline.

Balboa was the first European to see the ocean lying to the west of the American continents, the one whose existence had been predicted by Americus Vespucius a decade before. The discovery strengthened Vespucius's contention that the land discovered by Columbus was not, after all, the shores of Asia, and that a second ocean must lie between it and the greatly–longed–for wealth of the Far East.

What might have been surmised from Balboa's discovery was shown to be fact by a Portuguese navigator, Ferdinand Magellan. Magellan had served Portugal well as a navigator and had fought for his country against the Moroccans. In the war, he had been wounded, in 1515, and lamed for life. Nevertheless, he was accused of trading with the Moroccans and, in 1516, was denied a pension. Hot with feelings of injustice, he then offered his services to Spain.

There was a new Spanish king on the throne now, who had just succeeded on the death of his father, Ferdinand II. The new king, Charles I,* listened with interest as Magellan pointed out what must have been obvious all along: that by sailing west, one could eventually reach the east, Portugal's east, without crossing the boundary line which had been set only in the Atlantic.

Charles I agreed to support a voyage westward. Magellan

---

* Charles I became Holy Roman Emperor in 1519. He was the fifth Charles to be Emperor and he is better known in history as the Emperor Charles V.

left Spain, on September 20, 1519. He reached the eastern bulge of South America and began to sail southward looking for some end to that continent, as the Portuguese had once searched for a southern end to Africa.

On October 21, 1519, he found a salt–water strait which he began to probe. It might be a strait leading between two bodies of land to the second ocean Balboa had sighted, or it might be a river estuary. He had earlier entered an inlet farther north, which turned out to be nothing more than an estuary (the Rio de la Plata which, on modern maps, lies between Argentina and Uruguay).

For over five weeks, Magellan felt his way through the passage amid storms, and then, on November 28, it opened into an ocean, and the storms ceased. As Magellan sailed on and on through good weather, he called the newly discovered sea the "Pacific Ocean."

However, the Pacific Ocean was far larger than anyone could have expected and sadly free of land. For 99 days the ships sailed through unbroken water, and the men underwent tortures of hunger and thirst. Finally, they reached the island of Guam where they caught their breaths, then sailed westward to what afterwards came to be known as the Philippine islands. There, on April 27, 1521, Magellan died in a skirmish with the natives.

The expedition continued westward, however, and a single ship with eighteen men aboard, under the leadership of Juan Sebastian del Cano, finally arrived back in Spain, on September 7, 1522. This first circumnavigation of the globe had taken three years and, if the loss of life can be set aside, the single returning ship carried enough spices to make the voyage a complete financial success.

The voyage showed beyond doubt, at last, that the Earth was 25,000 miles in circumference, as Eratosthenes had calculated eighteen centuries before and that the estimates of smaller size (which Columbus had accepted) were wrong. It showed, more-

over, that the westward route to the Indies was not really practical, at least if one followed the "southwest passage" through what was ever after called the "Strait of Magellan."*

The voyage also demonstrated, quite vividly, the necessity of extending the Line of Demarcation between Spain and Portugal to the eastern hemisphere. On April 22, 1529, a treaty signed at the Spanish city of Saragossa drew the dividing line from North Pole to South Pole at about 150° East Longitude. Now the Earth was really divided in two, with about 45 percent going to Spain and 55 percent to Portugal, provided other nations respected the division — and of course they didn't.

Even though Spain had the smaller and less civilized part of the world, she had no reason to complain. Though on the whole less civilized than the Old World, the Americas were not entirely without civilization even by European standards. In 1517, the Spanish soldier, Francisco Fernandez Cordoba explored Yucatán and found evidence of past cities and wealth — a civilization that was now in ruins.

Where a dead civilization of great wealth existed, a living civilization might also exist. When Velásquez, governor of Cuba, heard the news of interesting ruins in Yucatán, he commissioned Hernando Cortes to head an expedition to explore the interior of the land that came to be called Mexico.

Cortes set sail from Cuba, in February 1519, with eleven ships manned by 700 soldiers. He found the Aztec civilization centered about its capital Tenochtitlán (Mexico City) which he entered, on November 18, 1519. The Aztecs thought the Europeans to be gods, and Cortes, taking advantage of this, and of his own possession of horses and artillery, which the Aztecs lacked, took over Mexico.

---

* At first it was thought that the Strait of Magellan passed between two continents, South America and a large polar land mass. The polar land mass "Antarctica" exists, but it is fairly far from South America. The land south of the Strait of Magellan turned out to be an island called "Tierra del Fuego" ("Land of Fire") because fires had been seen on it from Magellan's ships.

In succeeding years, he and others explored the land. Cortes himself first sighted the peninsula we now call Baja (Lower) California and the Gulf of California. The Aztec civilization was wiped out; the Mexican Indians enslaved; and Spain finally had what it wanted — gold.

An even more astonishing conquest was made by Francisco Pizarro, who had been with Balboa on the expedition that had resulted in the first sighting of the Pacific Ocean. In his explorations of South America, Pizarro encountered the remarkable Inca civilization, centered in Peru and stretching out along the region of the Andes mountains. This he destroyed with great cruelty, and more gold flooded into the coffers of Spain.

The wanton destruction of two civilizations, the wholesale theft of their possessions, and the enslavement of their peoples did not satisfy the Spaniards. Where two existed, more might, and every Spanish explorer longed to duplicate the feats of Cortes and Pizarro. All the coasts, and much of the interior of tropical America, had now been blocked out and the place to look for more gold was in the largest area of unexplored land that still existed, the region north of Mexico.

The first of the northward searchers for gold was Pánfilo de Narváez. He had served with Velásquez in the conquest of Cuba and had been sent by Velásquez to Mexico when it looked as though Cortes was growing too powerful. Narváez had been defeated in Mexico by Cortes, and he longed to win laurels of his own in another direction.

In 1528, he followed up Ponce de León's discovery of Florida by exploring the Gulf Coast immediately to the west of that peninsula. From what is now Pensacola, he struck inland looking for the kind of civilization and gold that had been found in Mexico not many years before. He was disappointed and had to struggle back to the coast. There he built five ships and tried to sail across the Gulf to Mexico, but was lost in a storm.

Some of the party, however, under Álvar Núñez Cabeza de Vaca, who had been second in command, survived the storm

and were wrecked on the Gulf Coast of what is now Texas. Cabeza de Vaca was imprisoned by Indians for six years, but finally escaped and wandered across northern Mexico, finding his way back to Mexico City, in 1536.

Once returned, Cabeza de Vaca told colorful stories of his adventures, describing vast herds of buffalo and retailing rumors of great wealth somewhere in the north. These reports reached Hernando de Soto who had been second in command under Pizarro in the conquest of Peru and who was now in retirement in Spain. Reading of Cabeza de Vaca's adventures, De Soto now yearned to lead an expedition north of Florida to find there another golden Peru.

Having received permission from Charles I, De Soto landed on Florida's west coast (near what is now Tampa), on May 25, 1539. Heading a party of 500 men and 200 horses, he struck inland, passing through the forests of what are now the southeastern states of the United States.

Somewhere in what is now southwestern Alabama, he fought a battle with Indians in which he and most of his men were wounded. It was the first Indian battle fought with Europeans in what is now the United States. He then continued westward, and, on June 18, 1541, he and his men became the first Europeans to set eyes upon the Mississippi River, which he appropriately named Grande ("great"). The site at which the discovery was made is not certainly known, but it was probably some miles south of the modern city of Memphis, Tennessee.

The expedition crossed the river, still heading westward, then south, skirmishing with Indians and suffering further losses. On May 21, 1542, De Soto died of a fever at a time when the expedition had worked its way back to the Mississippi to a point some 230 miles south of the original sighting. De Soto was buried in the river. The rest of his men made boats, floated down the river and sailed back to Mexico across the Gulf.

Almost simultaneously, another Spanish expedition was exploring what is now the southwestern United States. This one was under the leadership of Francisco Vazquez de Coronado. He, too, had listened to the tales of Cabeza de Vaca concerning the rich cities rumored to exist north of Mexico. (Actually, these were Indian pueblos, housing people who lived quite comfortably, but who were not at all rich by European standards which viewed riches in terms of gold and silver.)

Between 1540 and 1542, Coronado and the men he led wandered widely over Texas and the southwest. Among other things, one of his lieutenants, García López de Cárdenas, discovered the Grand Canyon, along the lower reaches of the Colorado River. (The Colorado was named the Spanish word *red* because of the reddish color of the rocks making up the canyon.) Coronado himself followed the course of the Rio Grande, then went northward, penetrating far enough to see and describe the grass huts of the Wichita Indians in what is now the state of Kansas.

As things stood by the mid–1500s, then, Spain claimed all the Americas (except for the Portuguese holdings in Brazil). It was, moreover, the only European nation that was systematically exploring and occupying North America.

The Spaniards still viewed the Americas primarily as a device for growing rich, a realm to be exploited, rather than a place where new homes might be made and new nations built. Many Spaniards were living in the Americas by 1560, but few Spanish women came with them, and there was much interbreeding, beginning the broad spectrum of racial intermixture that now characterizes the Latin American population.

The centers of Spanish power in North America, up through the mid–1500s, lay in Mexico and the West Indies. As yet there were no actual settlements in Florida or north of the Rio Grande, but the Spanish government had no doubt that the land to the north had been discovered and explored by Spaniards and therefore belonged to Spain. What's more, Spain was then at the peak of her military power and she expected no interference from other European powers.

THE FRENCH INTRUDE

Once Spain had found the gold it had sought in the Americas, it settled down in content to control the continents. Other European nations were not entirely content, however. Even if they did not care to dispute possession of the Americas with Spain's strong armies, what about the Indies which lay beyond the Americas?

To be sure, Magellan had shown the southwestward route to the Indies was impractical. South America was a solid land mass with a sea passage through it only far to the south, and an incredibly large and unbroken ocean lay behind that passage.

What about North America though? There might be a passage through North America somewhere that was nearer to Europe than the Strait of Magellan was and beyond which there might be a narrower and island–filled Pacific Ocean. In short, if Magellan's southwest passage was not practical, a northwest passage might be just the thing. Nations other than Spain might best compete with her by finding such a passage.

There was France, for instance. The French king, Francis I, who had reached the throne in 1515, was engaged in bitter war with Charles I of Spain, and was quite willing to intrude (if it could be done safely) on the Spanish dominions in the west. He therefore sent an expedition westward under the command of Giovanni da Verrazano, an Italian navigator* with instructions to search for a northwest passage.

In January 1524, Verrazano sailed westward and, on March 1, he landed on the eastern coast of the North American conti-

* It is an odd coincidence that the first westward voyages sponsored by Spain, by England, and by France, were all under the leadership of Italian navigators.

nent at Cape Fear (in what is now North Carolina). There was no use following the coast southward for that way lay the Spaniards with whom he didn't want to tangle. Besides the coast southward was known and was solid. If a northwest passage existed it would have to lie to the north.

So he sailed northward, exploring the coast, and, on April 17, entered what is now called New York Bay, passing through the narrow strait between Brooklyn and Staten Island where now the span of the Verrazano Bridge stands.

Verrazano decided the bay was not the opening of the northwest passage and continued to trace the coast northward. Narragansett Bay also struck him as useless. Finally he reached Newfoundland, and, having run out of stores, he returned to France, landing there, on July 8, after an absence of half a year.

The result of Verrazano's voyage was disheartening. The eastern coast of North America looked solid all the way up to what is now known as Nova Scotia. If the northwest passage existed, it would have to be north of that peninsula.

Francis I was not able to follow up Verrazano's voyage at once. In 1525, he was defeated by Spain and taken prisoner. He was released the following year only after making humiliating concessions and then had to fight another war to try to retrieve his losses — but didn't.

Not for ten years could Francis I spare the time to think of the northwest passage again. This time, he sent a French navigator, Jacques Cartier, on the mission, to see what might exist north of Nova Scotia.

Cartier, with two ships and 61 men, left France, on April 20, 1534, and reached Newfoundland, on May 10. Newfoundland was by now well known to all European nations even though it had been settled by none of them. Indeed, the continental shore west of Newfoundland had a Portuguese name, of all things. It seems that a Portuguese navigator, Gaspar Corterreal, had sailed along that section of coast, in 1501, and had picked up a group of the tribesmen he found there and carried them off as slaves. He called the coast "Terra del Laboratore" (Land of Slaves), and it has been Labrador to us ever since.

Cartier did something, however, that no European navigator had done before him (except possibly the Norse). He sailed through the narrow Strait of Belle Isle, only 10 miles wide at its narrowest, which separates Newfoundland from Labrador. Having done that, he sailed south along the hitherto unexplored western coast of Newfoundland. On August 10, 1534, he sailed into the large ocean inlet to the west of Newfoundland. Since this was the day dedicated to St. Lawrence, the inlet was named in his honor and is the "Gulf of St. Lawrence."

Cartier laid claim, in the name of France, to the territories he touched. He tried to find out what the name of the territory was from the local Indians, for in high excitement, he felt that this large inlet might be the opening of the strait that would carry him through to the Pacific Ocean. The Indians, however, thought he was asking them what certain small structures were, since it was to those that he seemed to be pointing. They gave him their word for "huts" which was something like "canada." As a result, Cartier called the region "Canada."

Cartier returned to France with captured Indians and with the news of his discovery of this promising inlet. He then made two further voyages to the area, one, in 1535, and a second, in 1541. In each case, he sailed up the river now known as the St. Lawrence as far as a hill which he called "Mont Réal" (Mount Royal), near where the city of Montreal was eventually founded.

It became clear to him that the St. Lawrence was a river and not a strait and that it could only lead into the interior of the vast continent and not to the Pacific. Clearly, if the northwest passage existed at all, it would have to lie so far north as to pass through polar ice–choked seas. Francis I, disheartened, lost interest.

Some Frenchmen, however, retained an interest in the new world for reasons that had nothing to do with the northwest passage or the wealth of the Indies. There were new reasons to leave Europe for a far–off coast, for Europe had become a religious battleground.

In the time of Columbus, all of western Europe acknowledged the Roman Pope as head of the Church and accepted his authority. In 1517, however, a German monk, Martin Luther, began to question that authority, and in a surprisingly short time, large sections of Germany and the Netherlands, all of Scandinavia, and most of England, had fallen away and their people had become "Protestants" of one kind or another.

This was not done without a great deal of controversy and, eventually, war. About 1546, there began a series of religious conflicts in Europe that was to continue with increasing severity for a century.

In France, the Protestants were called "Huguenots." These were only a minority of the population, although a militant minority, and there was increasing friction between them and the Catholic majority. The most influential of the Huguenot leaders was Admiral Gaspard de Coligny, and it occurred to him that Huguenots might find a new home in which they could worship as they pleased.

Coligny was thus the first to think of the Americas as a refuge, a place where colonists could build a new and better home, a place where they could escape the injustices of Europe, and not just a place where one might seek wealth.

The young French King, Charles IX (a son of Francis I), granted him permission to establish colonies in the Americas. The king was only ten years old at the time, but his mother, Catherine de Médicis, who was the real ruler, had her own reasons for agreeing. If the Huguenots wanted to leave, let them and good riddance; she was giving away nothing, since the Americas were, theoretically, Spanish territory.

Two shiploads of Huguenots, under the leadership of Jean Ribaut, set sail, on February 18, 1562, and, on May 1, they landed in northern Florida. They pushed northward and finally reached the coast of what is now South Carolina. There they established a settlement which they called Port Royal. (The site is now occupied by a town that still keeps that name.) The region round about they called "Carolana" after the Latin version (Carolus) of the name of France's King Charles.

Ribaut left thirty men behind and sailed back to France. The colonists quickly grew homesick, however, stranded as they were at the edge of nowhere. They built ships and tried to make their way back to France. They would surely have died if they had not been found by an English ship and taken to England.

By then the friction between Huguenots and Catholics in France had resulted in actual civil war, the first of eight that were to stretch over a period of thirty–six years. It seemed more than ever desirable to the Huguenots to establish a colony in America.

In 1564, a second and more elaborate attempt was made by 300 colonists who sailed to America under one of Ribaut's lieutenants. This time it was at the St. John's River in northern Florida that the colonists landed. Some miles up the river they established a settlement they called Fort Caroline, again after the king. They were in Spanish territory, of course; but at that time, Spain still had not established any actual settlements on the peninsula, and the colonists felt safe. In 1565, Ribaut himself arrived with additional colonists and things looked rather well for the Huguenots.

The Spaniards, however, were furious. Frenchmen were bad enough, for Spain was fighting a long drawn–out war with France at the time, but French Protestants were far worse. Spain was the most fanatically Catholic country in Europe and to have Protestants living on territory they claimed as their own was intolerable.

Charles I of Spain had abdicated in 1556, and his son now ruled as Philip II. Philip considered himself to be the head of the forces of Catholicism in Europe, and he took action. He ap-

pointed Pedro Menendez de Avila governor of Florida and gave
him specific instructions to wipe out the Huguenot colony.

Menendez sailed for Florida and, in late August 1565, founded
St. Augustine, a settlement on the coast about forty miles south
of the Huguenot colony. The site has remained occupied ever
since so that it is the first town to have been established by
Europeans anywhere in the territory of the continental United
States. (San Juan, Puerto Rico, which flies the American flag, is
older, for it was founded in 1510.)

Menendez took his ships northward against the Huguenots.
While feinting naval action to keep Ribaut's ships at sea, Menendez sent a party of men overland to the Huguenot settlement. The Spaniards took it and then killed every Frenchman
they could find, announcing that this was done, not to Frenchmen, but to Protestants. Later, Ribaut's ships were damaged in
a storm and Ribaut himself was taken by the Spaniards and
killed.

Thus ended the attempts of the Huguenots to found a colony
in the United States; the first test of America as a religious refuge was a failure. It had resulted only in pushing Spain into establishing itself firmly in Florida and in strengthening the Spanish hold on the continent.

THE ENGLISH LOOT

Spain, however, was overextending itself. It placed its men
and its ships over the oceans of the world in a far–flung Empire
that included not only the Americas, but various regions in Europe and the Far East. It continued to fight constant wars
everywhere in an effort to crush Protestantism, and it was driving itself into bankruptcy.

To be sure, a great deal of apparent wealth in the form of

gold and silver reached Spain from the mines in the Americas, but this did little good. The metals flooding into Europe merely raised prices, and Spanish King Philip II found that the more gold he had, the more gold everything cost.

What's more, Spain did not develop agriculture and industry at the rate other nations in Europe were doing. The result was that the gold from America had to be exchanged for the goods that other nations could supply Spain; the nations with shipping and industries grew rich.

Among the nations growing steadily more prosperous in the 1500s was England. About 1530, Henry VIII of England had broken with Rome, and, under him, as well as under his son, Edward VI, who succeeded in 1547, England became officially Protestant.

Edward VI died in 1553, and his Catholic half–sister succeeded as Mary I. She married Philip II, and, for a while, it seemed that England would be Catholic again. In 1558, however, Mary died, childless; her Protestant half–sister succeeded as Elizabeth I. England was Protestant for good.

During Elizabeth's long reign there was rising hostility against Spain, since Philip II yearned to get rid of Elizabeth by any means and place her cousin (another Mary) on the throne instead. Mary was queen of Scotland and a Catholic. She had been driven out of her own country by hostile Protestant noblemen and had taken refuge in England. Elizabeth kept her in close imprisonment, but even so, Mary remained the center of anti–Protestant plotting.

Elizabeth was a cautious queen who, like her grandfather, Henry VII, did not like to spend money or make war, so she refrained from taking actual, warlike measures against Spain, no matter how clear Spanish enmity and intrigue was. On the other hand, she did nothing to stop English navigators from enriching themselves at Spanish expense by actions that were virtual piracy. Elizabeth always insisted to the Spanish that she was not responsible for the actions of her seamen, but she honored them, knighted them, and (most important for herself) shared in their spoils and delighted in the needle pricks with which they bled and weakened the Spanish Empire.

One of these navigators was John Hawkins. His father had engaged in the slave trade, and he himself followed the practice. He picked up Black slaves in West Africa for virtually nothing and carried them to the West Indies, where he sold them for large quantities of useful commodities, such as sugar. It was a most profitable enterprise, and both the Portuguese in Africa and the Spaniards in West Indies were furious — not at the immorality of such trafficking in human beings, but because they wanted the profits for themselves.

Hawkins further angered the Spaniards when, in 1565, he donated supplies to the Huguenot settlers at Fort Caroline.

In 1567, Hawkins prepared six ships for another trading expedition to the West Indies. With him, this time, was a distant relative, Francis Drake, who was in his middle twenties at the time. Hawkins picked up his slaves, sold them very profitably, and young Drake found himself a rich man. Then, as Hawkins was sailing back to England in the summer of 1568, he was struck by a storm.

The six ships managed to make their way to a Spanish port on the coast of Mexico (the modern Vera Cruz). The English ships were permitted to enter and make repairs, largely because the Spaniards on the spot had no ships with which to risk hostile action.

While the English ships were in the harbor, however, thirteen large and well-armed ships happened to arrive from Spain. Aboard was the new governor of Mexico (or "New Spain" as it was called). The English might have prevented the Spaniards from entering the harbor, since they could control the passage inward with their guns. The English were not, however, anxious for a fight. All they wanted was to complete their repairs and get home safely with the cargo of wealth. So Hawkins par-

leyed with the Spanish ships and offered to let them in safely, if
the Spaniards would in turn let him leave safely when his repairs were done.

The Spaniards agreed, but once inside they may have felt
that promises made to Protestants need not be kept. They attacked! The English, surprised and outnumbered, were overwhelmed. Only two English ships, one under Hawkins and one
under Drake, got away. These made their way back to England only after great difficulty and carrying very few survivors.
And the wealth that had been theirs in Vera Cruz was utterly
gone.

The consequences were worse for Spain, though, than for the
English. Till then Hawkins had been interested in peaceful
trade, which the Spaniards might have resented, but which
served them as well as England. Afterward, however, Hawkins
and, even more so, Drake, felt an inveterate hatred of Spain and
a longing for revenge.

Drake began a career of harassment all up and down the
shores of Spanish America. In 1572, he sailed for Panama,
where he destroyed Spanish shipping and pillaged Spanish settlements. He took the town of Nombre de Dios on the northern
shore of Panama and then made his way across the isthmus, as
Balboa had done half a century before, and, on February 3,
1573, gazed upon the Pacific Ocean.

The sight of the ocean gave Drake the idea of pillaging the
western coasts of the Americas. These were less exposed and
therefore even less well defended. He began to lay plans, therefore, for a voyage into the Pacific. Aside from the loot it might
bring him, it would serve as a means of searching for the western end of any northwest passage through North America.

On December 13, 1577, with three armed ships and two aux-
iliaries, Drake set sail from Plymouth, England, intending to
follow the track of Magellan. The two auxiliary ships were
abandoned by the time the southern part of South America was

reached, but the three remaining ships passed through the Strait of Magellan and entered the Pacific Ocean, on September 6, 1578.

This time the ocean was anything but pacific. A month–long storm wrecked one of Drake's ships and drove the remaining two apart. One gave up and returned to England and that left only Drake on his ship, *The Golden Hind*.

The storm drove him southward and into the open sea south of South America. It was Drake, then, who proved that the land to the south of the Strait of Magellan, the Tierra del Fuego, was not a continent but an island of only moderate size. The part of the ocean between that island and the tip of Antarctica is still called "Drake Passage" in his honor.

By November, the ocean was finally clear and Drake sailed *The Golden Hind* north along the South American coast, taking Spanish vessels and confiscating their cargoes. By the time he reached North America, he had captured so much gold and other valuables that he dared not take any more. He simply had no room for it.

Drake continued up the western coast of North America and was the first Englishman ever to see the coast of California.* He entered San Francisco Bay and then sailed as far north as the coast of what is now Oregon before deciding he was not going to find the western end of any Northwest Passage. He claimed the territory for England, calling it "New Albion," and then, in July 1579, turned westward and sailed across the Pacific Ocean. He reached the East Indies, then sailed around Africa and returned to Europe.

He reached Plymouth, on September 26, 1580, nearly three

---

* The name is derived from another one of the mythical islands that filled the western seas. This one appeared in a fictional narrative written in 1510. When the southern tip of a long narrow peninsula off the western coast of Mexico was first sighted by Cortes's men, it was thought to be an island and was called "California." The name was later applied to the entire peninsula and to the regions lying north of it as well.

years after he had left. He was the second man, and the first Englishman, to circumnavigate the world. He also brought back, in his single ship, cargo worth more than half a million pounds, which delighted Queen Elizabeth so greatly that she knighted him on board his own ship, on April 4, 1581.

This made it difficult for her to insist to Spain that she had nothing to do with Drake's voyage and that she deplored his pillaging actions, but she managed to do it with a straight face. Naturally, she never returned any of the material that had been pillaged.

4

THE ENGLISH FOOTHOLD

FIRST ATTEMPTS

While Drake was on his way around the world, partly to search for a western end to the Northwest Passage, other English navigators were taking up the search once again for the eastern end — a search abandoned since the time of Cartier, a generation before. By now, it was quite certain that the passage, if it existed at all, had to lie north of Labrador.

The English navigator, Martin Frobisher, therefore sailed northward. He had sailed with Hawkins against the Spaniards and was an accomplished mariner. In June 1576, he sailed to the Americas, explored the coast of Labrador and, for the first time, ventured beyond it toward the Pole.

He crossed a strait and reached a large island — the fifth largest in the world, in fact. Both the strait (Hudson Strait) and the island (Baffin Island) are now named for English explorers who did their work a generation after Frobisher. However, Frobisher penetrated the southern of two large inlets into the western coast of Baffin Island (in the hope that this was the beginning of the Northwest Passage) and named it Frobisher's Strait. (It isn't a strait, but we still call it Frobisher Bay in his memory.)

He returned to England, on October 9, 1576, but not empty-handed. He brought with him something he called gold ore, which showed yellow glitters but which was only iron pyrites, or "fool's gold." The worthless rocks were enough, however, to enable him to get backing for two more voyages. In the second voyage he brought back no less than 200 tons of fool's gold; and during the third voyage, on June 20, 1578, he sighted the southern tip of Greenland, as Cabot had done a century before.

This time (a century and a half after the last Norse colonists had disappeared), the icy island was never lost sight of again.*

Another English navigator, John Davis, took up the search for the Northwest Passage where Frobisher had left off. In 1585, he sailed to Baffin Island and entered the more northerly of the two inlets, and that, too, proved a blind alley. In another voyage, in 1587, he sailed up the western coast of Greenland, through the narrow ocean passage separating it from Baffin Island. That passage is still called Davis Strait in his honor. He reached a latitude of 73° North, a record for that time.

Yet another Englishman of the time, Humphrey Gilbert, who had also gone sailing against the Spaniards and who was also interested in the Northwest Passage, turned to another aspect of the New World. His enthusiasm for the Americas as a

---

* Nobody seemed to want it, however, and small wonder. Certainly the English never claimed it despite the sightings by Cabot and Frobisher. In 1721, a Danish missionary, Hans Egede, landed to work with the Eskimos on the island. Since then, Greenland has been a Danish colony, and Scandinavian again — which seems appropriate enough.

source of short–term wealth faded with the fiasco of Frobisher's "gold ore" which was eventually used for road repair. Gilbert began to look for better goals, and, like Coligny, a quarter century before, he began to think of colonization, of new homes.

He persuaded Queen Elizabeth to let him launch a colonizing venture. The Queen, to stay out of trouble with Spain, stipulated that only heathen lands might be colonized — no one worried about the heathen — and not such lands as were already occupied by a Christian power.

On June 11, 1583, Gilbert left Southampton and set sail across the Atlantic to regions well north of the farthest Spanish reach. He was aiming for Newfoundland, which had been touched by John Cabot nearly a century before, the harbors and coasts of which had been used freely by fishermen ever since. There were, however, no settlements upon it, and this was scarcely surprising since its climate was by no means attractive.

Gilbert, intent on colonization, landed and proclaimed the entire island to be a possession of England. Though it was to be a full century before any settlement worthy of the name was made on the island, it has remained an English possession ever since and became the first English colony beyond the seas (if we don't count the medieval possession of parts of France, or the English grip on the neighboring island of Ireland).

Gilbert's own fate was a sad one. His exploration of the island did not reveal it to be very suitable for colonization, and on his way home, his vessel was sunk in a storm off the Azores and he died. He was last seen, shrouded in rain, calling out, "We are as near to God by sea as by land."

Though Gilbert died, his dream did not. Gilbert had a half–brother, Walter Raleigh, who had fought with him in Ireland and had sailed with him on some of his voyages against the Spaniards. At the time Gilbert was sailing for Newfoundland, Raleigh was chief favorite of Queen Elizabeth and had become a wealthy man through the privileges she showered on him.

When Gilbert died, Raleigh took over his charter for the colonization of North America. Unlike his brother, Raleigh did not go himself (the Queen would not allow him to risk his life), but he outfitted ships and sent them. What's more, he aimed farther south, where a better climate might be expected. In fact, he aimed as far south as he could go without running into Spaniards.

On April 27, 1584, two ships set sail and reached the coast of what is now North Carolina. They explored it and returned with glowing reports. Pleased, Raleigh named the region "Virginia" in honor of Elizabeth, the "Virgin Queen." (She was flattered enough at this to knight him for it.) The name was applied broadly at that time and took in what would now be the entire east coast of the United States north of Florida.

The explorers are supposed to have brought back samples of potatoes as typical of the native flora. Raleigh, anxious to boost the value of the new lands, encouraged the planting of potatoes in Europe, and the new food item quickly attained a peak of popularity from which it has never receded.

The first group of actual settlers reached Roanoke Island, off the North Carolina shore, about 400 miles northeast of the Port Royal settlement attempted by the Huguenots (and, therefore, 400 miles farther from the Spaniards). They quickly grew homesick, however, and were picked up, in June 1586, by Francis Drake, who had just struck at Spain, again, by sacking St. Augustine in Florida. He carried the colonists back with him and some tobacco plants as well. Raleigh, still intent on proving the worth of the American coast succeeded in popularizing this plant as well and bears a heavy responsibility for fastening on Europeans the harmful practice of inhaling the smoke of burning leaves.

In 1587, under John White, a group of a hundred men, plus

twenty–five women and children, settled on Roanoke Island, for a second and more serious attempt at colonization. There on August 18, 1587, a child was born. She was a grandchild of White and was named Virginia Dare. She was the first child of English parentage to be born on the territory of what is now the United States.

White returned to England for supplies. He was delayed there because England and Spain were at war. When he finally came back to Roanoke Island, on August 15, 1591, the colony had vanished. Not a living person was left. What happened, no one knows, but presumably, all were killed, or carried off, by Indians.

THE COMPETITORS

When we come to the opening of the 1600s, then, it would seem that Spain was still triumphant. An attempt at French colonization on the North American shores north of Florida had been wiped out by direct Spanish action. A later attempt at settlement farther north by England had also been wiped out, though not by the Spanish.

The Spaniards were still the only Europeans who had actual settlements in North America and their grip on Mexico, Florida, and the West Indies seemed stronger than ever.*

The Spaniards no longer had even the competition of the Portuguese to contend with. In 1580, the royal line of Portugal came to an end, and of the various claimants to the throne, Philip II of Spain proved successful (through military action).

---

* In 1581, the Spaniards brought Black slaves into Florida. It was the first appearance of Blacks (a quarter century before the first permanent English settlement) on the territory that now makes up the continental United States.

Spain controlled Portugal and its Empire, and all the American continents were either Spanish or unsettled.

And the Spaniards were continuing to expand into the unsettled part. They assiduously explored the California coast, for instance. Then, in 1598, the Spanish explorer, Juan de Onate (who was married to a granddaughter of Cortes) pushed north of the Rio Grande. As Mexico (a native name) came to be known as "New Spain" to the Spanish settlers, so the northern extension of Spanish territory beyond the Rio Grande became "New Mexico." In 1610, Sante Fe ("Holy Faith") was founded and became the capital of New Mexico.

Spain had never seemed so nearly ruler of the world as when its flag flew over all the New World and over large stretches of the Far East. Even in Europe itself, the German Empire and much of Italy was ruled by other members of the family of Philip II. In western Europe, only France and England were outside the Spanish sphere — but for how long?

And yet Spanish strength was largely an illusion. Its economy was weak, its population impoverished, its military force dispersed, and the deadening hand of conformity sapped its vigor. As the 1600s opened, it might have seemed to some that Spain could not possibly maintain its monopoly in the Americas for much longer. There were eager competitors on the scene.

England was one of these, of course, and it was against England that the limits of Spanish power first became apparent.

In 1587, Queen Elizabeth I, tiring of conspiracies, reluctantly acceded to the demands of her advisers and ordered the execution of Mary of Scotland. To Philip II of Spain, this was the last straw. The English mariners who had been looting his American property and hijacking his ships on the open seas could be borne only because he had been constantly expecting the overthrow of Elizabeth by internal uprising. With Mary of Scotland, the very nucleus of anti–Elizabethan hopes, gone,

Philip II decided the uprising must be supported by military aid from abroad.

He sent a huge fleet to England, one that would carry a Spanish army from the continental possessions of Spain just across the Channel into England itself. This army would support a Catholic rising in the island, set up a government friendly to Spain, and put an end to English piracy.

The Spanish fleet (called the "Invincible Armada") was, however, plagued with misfortune from the start and never made it. Against it were the ships led by England's battle-scarred, salt-caked veterans Hawkins, Drake, Frobisher, and the rest. Storms battered the Armada, too, and in the end it broke up and was almost totally destroyed. Spanish prestige never quite recovered and English self-confidence rose high.

In 1598, Philip II died and though the Spanish Empire seemed as extensive as ever on the map, and as rich as ever in theory, his ill-advised policies had overstrained it. Spain was exhausted, and each year after his death it grew weaker and sank lower.

France, too, the other possible competitor of Spain, was entering a period of increased self-confidence and power. The civil wars of religion had ended. The Huguenot leader, Henry of Navarre, was the legal king, Henry IV, of France. In 1593, he agreed to accept Catholicism. This made him acceptable to the French majority. He arranged to have the Huguenots allowed to worship as they pleased and in his reign France began to grow rapidly in power.

There was still a third region of Europe that had an interest in overseas activity and that was now making itself felt for the first time. This was the Netherlands, so called because the territory referred to is the very low-lying plain about the mouth of the Rhine River directly east, across the North Sea, of southern England.

During the medieval period, the Netherlands (which included not only what we now think of as the Netherlands, but

Belgium and parts of extreme northern France as well) was far advanced in culture and in wealth. It was the most urbanized area of Europe outside of Italy, and its cities, filled with clever artisans and thrifty merchants, steadily resisted foreign domination.

In early modern times, the Netherlands was part of the Holy Roman Empire and was therefore part of the dominion of Emperor Charles V (who also ruled Spain as Charles I). When Charles V abdicated, in 1556, one son, Philip II was awarded Spain, while a younger son, Ferdinand I, ruled as Emperor.

Charles, however, had spent his life fighting France and he didn't want France to benefit by this division. He therefore turned over those parts of Italy and Germany which bordered on France to Philip II of Spain. He hoped in this way to keep France surrounded by forces under the control of a single will. One of the areas turned over to Philip II was the Netherlands.

But this meant trouble, not for France, but for Spain. The northern portions of the Netherlands had turned Protestant and this was anathema to the ultra–Catholic Philip II. Philip attempted to force Catholicism on the population of the Netherlands and managed only to drive them into open revolt. For almost all his reign, Philip fought stubbornly in the Netherlands without ever quite managing to crush the rebels.

Desperately, the rebels developed a fleet that allowed them to control the coasts of the Netherlands. Between that and occasional help from England, the rebels remained in the field. At the time of Philip II's death, Spain was still fighting; but the northern provinces of the Netherlands were virtually independent and remained so.

Today, the name "the Netherlands" is confined to these northern provinces that gained their independence. The chief of these provinces, the most powerful and the richest, with the great trading city of Amsterdam as its capital, is Holland, and this name is sometimes incorrectly applied to the entire nation. The people of the Netherlands are commonly referred to as the

Dutch (a corruption of "Deutsch," the German word meaning "German," for the Dutch were a branch of the Germanic peoples).

The southern provinces, which remained in Spanish hands throughout the 1600s, were called "the Spanish Netherlands."

Under the pressures of the long and harrowing war with Spain, the Netherlands had worked up a merchant fleet that was the best in the world. Dutch ships were on every ocean; Dutch enterprise was everywhere; Dutch industry was flourishing. While Spain was declining into decadence, the Netherlands were becoming a great power.

In 1600, then, each of three powers, England, France, and the Netherlands, were ready to settle the eastern coast of North America in those regions north of Florida where Spain was no longer strong enough to take action. Each succeeded and we will consider each in turn, with England first.

VIRGINIA

Queen Elizabeth I died in 1603. Her successor, James I of the House of Stuart, had been King of Scotland as James VI (he was the son of the executed Mary of Scotland), so now England and Scotland were united under a single monarch.*

James I was a man of peace and retreated from Elizabeth's rather aggressive foreign policy. Since the defeat of the Spanish Armada, Spain was no longer to be greatly feared, but James nevertheless sought her friendship. Since Spain persisted in claiming all of the American continents, true friend-

---

* The two nations remained separate in every other way throughout the 1600s, however, and I will continue to speak of England as a separate country.

ship would have meant that England would abandon efforts
to colonize North America. This, however, did not happen.

Indeed, the drive for colonization grew stronger under James
as life at home grew more difficult. The cost of living was going up and the switch from agriculture to sheep raising, while
more profitable for the large landowners, turned many small
farmers into paupers. There were increasing numbers of Englishmen who would be willing to ignore the ill fate of the
Roanoke colony, to dare the ocean and the wilderness, and to
hope for the chance of building a new and better life in a new
world.

The pressure toward colonization brought about the formation of private companies intended to control and exploit the
movement for (it was to be hoped) profit. Such private companies had succeeded in the past. In 1553, a group of London
merchants had formed the "Muscovy Company," intended to
organize the trade in furs with Russia by way of the Arctic
port of Archangel. In 1600, the East India Company was
formed to exploit the possibilities of trade with the Far East.
Profits had resulted. Why not, then, companies to colonize
North America?

On April 10, 1606, two groups of Englishmen, one group
living in London, and one in the south English port of Plymouth (and therefore distinguished as the "London Company"
and the "Plymouth Company"), obtained official permission to
colonize the eastern coast of North America between the lines
of 34° and 45° North Latitude (that is, from what is now
North Carolina to Maine).

The companies were at first interconnected, though the London Company was expected to concentrate on the southern
half of the region and the Plymouth Company on the northern
half. The shareholders were to supply the settlers and the
capital, and in return they were to decide policy in the pro-
spective colonies, appoint the governor, and were to reserve

for themselves some fair share of any revenue that might be obtained from the colony.

The London Company sent out its first boatload of colonists, on December 19, 1606. On April 26, 1607, they reached the entrance of Chesapeake Bay. The land to the north of the opening they called "Cape Charles," and the land to the south, "Cape Henry," after the sons of King James. Sailing into the Bay due west, they came upon the wide mouth of a river they called the "James River" after the king himself.

They reconnoitered the river and finally, on May 13, they chose the site for a settlement on the northern bank, about 25 miles upstream. This settlement they named "Jamestown," again in honor of the king. It formed the nucleus of the colony of Virginia (the use of Raleigh's name persisted) and proved to be the first permanent English settlement in North America.

During the first year of its existence, however, Jamestown did not give the appearance of being permanent. It seemed fated to be no luckier than the Roanoke colony, and that is not surprising, for the difficulties in the way were many.

After all, the English in North America were trying to make homes for themselves in a wilderness that was like nothing they were used to or could imagine. What's more, there was a waste of water stretching between them and home that, in modern terms, could be compared only to the stretch of space between Moon and Earth. Indeed, astronauts on the Moon, in constant communication with Earth and able to return in three days, were less isolated and closer to home than the first colonists in Virginia were.

In addition, America had been oversold. The first colonists were convinced they were coming to a fruitful land in which food could be plucked from the trees and in which man could relax in a latter–day Eden. The picture of Virginia to the Englishman of 1607 was something like the picture of a South Sea

Island to an American subjected to the kind of movies Hollywood produced before World War II.

It is not surprising, then, that the first colonists contained many men of good birth who had no experience with manual labor and who considered it beneath them. They had not expected that such manual labor would be necessary.

When it turned out that to make Jamestown succeed, there had to be a good deal of sweating of the type necessary to build houses and plant crops, there was considerable disillusionment. Of course, the colonists might have avoided the labor of agriculture if they had been content to hunt and fish, Indian style, but that they could or would not do either.

For months, then, they sat around doing nothing; and, of the hundred settlers, half were dead of hunger and disease within six months. That the rest did not give up and that Jamestown did not become just one more failure was due to one man who bore the undistinguished name of John Smith (perhaps the most important John Smith in history).

He was twenty-eight years old at the time of the Jamestown settlement and had already been knocking about the world for twelve years. He had served in wars against the Turks, according to his own account, and (still according to his own account) had engaged in a variety of daredevil exploits and adventurous feats.

He was an opinionated man, without very much tact, and, being low-born besides, did not get along with the men of good birth among the Jamestown colonists. However, when provisions began to run low and all the gentlemen of Jamestown turned out to be useless at any occupation but that of eating, it fell to John Smith to find food.

For that, Indian help was required, and Smith undertook to persuade Indians to supply the necessary food. This he did by dealing with Powhatan, who ruled a confederation made up of some 9000 Indians in 128 villages spread out over what is now the states of Virginia and Maryland. Powhatan supplied the food that kept the colony alive.*

The most famous story about John Smith is one he himself told later on and which we can't be sure is actually true. In December 1607, he said, Powhatan was going to have him executed for the crime of having killed an Indian in a skirmish. Even as the executioner raised the stone axe with which Smith's head was to be smashed, Powhatan's young daughter, Pocahontas, only twelve years old at the time, intervened. Smith had apparently told her interesting tales of Europe and intrigued her with the strange foreign objects he had on his person. Now she placed her head over his and begged her father to forbid the execution. The Indian "savage" showed a mercy an Englishman in his place might not have, and Smith's life was saved. (Pocahontas was eventually converted to Christianity and took the name of Rebecca though, mercifully, it is only by the name of Pocahontas that she is known.)

Smith kept the colony going till new supplies and colonists arrived, in January of 1608. By that time only 38 of the original colonists remained; two-thirds of them had died.

Once the winter was over, Smith made a thorough exploration of Chesapeake Bay and of the lower courses of the rivers that ran into it. That spring he also bullied the colonists into planting corn, using techniques learned from the Indians.

He remained head of the colony till the fall of 1609, even though under fire from the distant merchants of the London Company, which now called itself the Virginia Company, and which was discontented over the fact that the settlement had

---

* It is part of the folklore of the United States that the Indians were cruel and bloodthirsty barbarians. Actually, they were invariably friendly and even helpful to the white settlers who invaded their shores; much more so than Europeans would have been to Indian invaders. They were content to allow the Europeans to share their hunting grounds. It was only when the Europeans began to treat Indians as inferiors and exclude them from areas which had belonged to the Indians in the first place, that relations deteriorated into enmity and warfare.

not yet proved hugely profitable. Finally, after he was hurt in a gunpowder explosion, on October 5, 1609, Smith was forced to give up his post and return to England.

Although Jamestown seemed well off now, with the harvest gathered, the disappearance of Smith's strong hand led to a complete breakdown. The winter of 1609–1610 was called the "starving time." An expedition under Sir Thomas Gates that ought to have arrived with supplies and men encountered a hurricane. Some ships rode out the storm, but others were wrecked off the Bermudas. The survivors were stranded there for nearly a year before they managed to construct a couple of ships that took them to Jamestown. (The tale of this ship-wreck and the reappearance of many of the expedition who had been given up for dead is supposed to have inspired Shakespeare with some of the details of his last play, *The Tempest*.)

When Gates arrived, those of the colonists who remained (only sixty) were in such a bad way that there seemed to be nothing to do but bundle them on board ships and make for England again, admitting the whole notion of settlement to have been once more a failure.

But, on June 8, 1610, just as the returning men were ready to pass through the mouth of the Chesapeake into the open ocean, they encountered three ships coming in from England with three hundred new colonists and ample stores of all kinds of provisions. The old colonists turned back, and Jamestown was a going concern once more, having escaped abandonment by a hair.

The man in command of this new flotilla was Thomas West, Lord De La Warr, who had been appointed by the company to be governor of the colony. The ship's captain was Samuel Argall. He made voyages to various points off the coast that year in search of supplies and spied a bay to the north of the Chesapeake. He called the point of land to the south of the bay "Cape De La Warr" in honor of the governor. That name did not survive, but "De La Warr," usually spelled "Delaware" was eventually applied to the bay itself, to the river that flowed into it, and finally to the land along the western shore of the bay.

On May 28, 1611, De La Warr returned to England to obtain additional settlers and supplies and remained there for years, dying before he could return. During his absence, the task of running the colony fell upon Sir Thomas Dale, who arrived, on May 10, 1611, and served as deputy governor.

For the first time since the departure of Smith, the colony felt a strong hand at the controls. Indeed, Dale drove the colonists pitilessly, forcing each to pull his weight. No food was supplied for those who did not do their fair share of the work.

One important development was carried through by a settler named John Rolfe. He learned Indian methods of growing tobacco, blended a strain of native tobacco with varieties imported from the West Indies, and, in 1612, produced a product that was superior to anything that had yet been tried. Tobacco was in great demand in England despite the fact that King James was dead–set against smoking; and, in 1614, when the first supplies of Rolfe's blend arrived, they were snapped up at high prices at once. Virginia had found its source of wealth at last.

Rolfe, who was a widower, served Virginia in another way, too. On April 5, 1614, he married Pocahontas and thus insured the continuing friendship of Powhatan.*

Between Dale's drive and Rolfe's tobacco, the colony began to spread up along the banks of the James. Though over ten thousand settlers had come and died, the survivors numbered at least a thousand, by 1617. To be sure, the winters always

* In 1616, Pocahontas went with Rolfe to England and was presented to the king. The next year, however, she died, still only 22 years old, before she could return to America. Her infant son survived, settled in Virginia, and was the ancestor of a notable Virginia family.

took their toll, but the population was high enough now to insure survival, barring extraordinary catastrophes.

In 1619, Sir George Yeardley was governor of the colony, and under him a notable bit of progress was made. The population was large enough and sufficiently spread out to make one–man rule difficult. Great Britain had a tradition of the collaboration of elected representatives of the population with the king, and Yeardley had his instructions from the company to establish a similar collaboration in Virginia.

Each of eleven districts in the colony was to elect two representatives (they were called "burgesses," an old English word meaning "freemen") to act as a kind of local parliament. On July 30, 1619, the twenty–two burgesses so elected met in a log church as a "House of Burgesses" and this was the first elected representive assembly in an English colony overseas. In the two weeks it sat, it passed laws and made recommendations for changes in old laws, and the precedent was set.

Until 1636, the House of Burgesses was elected by the vote of all male adults; but, as the colony developed, a kind of social stratification developed. There were those who owned land and those who did not, and the vote came to be restricted to those who owned a certain amount of land. Since the landowners were usually conservative and saw eye to eye with the governor and those who were in power in England, the House of Burgesses was often a puppet body of no importance. Nevertheless, its existence, however far it might fall short of democratic perfection, symbolized the transfer of representative government from England to the colonies, and this was, in some ways, the greatest gift the mother country could have given the future United States.

Also in 1619, young women began to arrive in Virginia, women sent for the precise purpose of serving as wives to settlers. Also in that year, an iron works was set up in Virginia, a small token of the industrialization that was to come.

Finally in that same fateful year came a significant event

indeed. The growing of tobacco increased the need for hands to labor in the fields. The Englishmen coming to Virginia did not suffice for the purpose; nor were many of them eager to do the hard drudgery needed for the cultivation of tobacco. Why not get Black slaves, then, who could be driven to do the work by force?

In August 1619, a Dutch ship brought some twenty Blacks to Virginia. Others trickled in later. It was cheap Black labor that made the tobacco fields (and later on, the cotton fields) more profitable than ever, and it was Black slavery that fastened to the United States an institution that was to do it infinite harm and whose evils have persisted, even after the end of slavery itself, right down to the present day.

Meanwhile, there was trouble brewing with the Indians. As the settlements spread along the James River, it became clear to the Indians that there were no reasonable limits to European expansion (and certainly it never occurred to the English settlers that the presence of "heathens" was any bar to the exploitation of the land). While Powhatan lived, he kept the peace; but he had died in 1618, and his brother, Opechancano succeeded.

Opechancano was nearly eighty years old at this time, but he harbored a grudge against the settlers that dated back to a time when he had been captured by John Smith and had been treated with the kind of indignity reserved for those who were considered ignorant and heathen savages. Opechancano did not forget.

Now he carefully planned an offensive to drive the settlers out of Virginia. In a surprise attack, on March 22, 1622, 347 Europeans were killed — one-third the total population. The rest managed to fight off the attack. More arms arrived and the settlers moved in for revenge, mounting three raids a year in which they killed Indians and destroyed their crops. In 1625, they succeeded in surprising an Indian settlement and slaughtered a thousand Indians.

After the first Indian attack, the settlers were not again in danger. Only the Indians suffered, and, in 1636, Opechancano was forced to agree to peace on terms very unfavorable to the Indians.

This set the pattern for two and a half centuries of Indian history that was to follow. First, there would be steady White encroachment. The hounded Indians would then strike back in the only way they could — given their inferiority in weapons — a surprise attack. Such an attack, invariably called a "massacre" in our history books, would be beaten off after high casualties. Then would come the counterattack which would be pressed remorselessly and cause much higher casualties among the Indians. The Indians killed women and children, this being carefully noted in detail in the histories. The Whites killed women and children, too, this being rarely mentioned.

The result of all this is that the Indians were weakened and thrown back — and farther back — with every conflict. In the end the whole land belonged to the European settlers and their descendants.

The Indian attack of 1622 gave James I an opportunity. He disapproved of having Virginia run by a private company because his theories of the kingship were exalted ones, and he was restless under the gathering and growing pretensions of the English people as expressed through Parliament. Besides, Spain was constantly protesting the very existence of Virginia, and James, eager for peace, felt he might have to withdraw the settlers and wanted them under his control.

He therefore managed to pry Virginia out of the control of the company. On June 16, 1624, it ceased to be a "proprietary colony," that is, one under the control of private proprietors. It became a "royal colony" instead, one under the direct control of the king, to whom the governor would henceforward be responsible. James did not, however, try to put an end to the institution of the House of Burgesses, so the effect on the internal development of Virginia as a result of this change of rule was little. In fact, the Burgesses were even more powerful under the king than they had been under the company.

The colony continued to spread. The loss in population as a result of Opechancano's attack of 1622 was quickly made up for by the steady inflow of settlers, and, by 1630, there were 3000 settlers living in Virginia. Plantations and towns continued to spread up the banks of the James and then along the York River, too, which lay ten miles to the north of the James and followed a parallel course into the Chesapeake.

The whole peninsula between the lower courses of the James and York Rivers were fenced off for protection from the Indians, and the settled region was divided into colonies.

Opechancano, who still ruled the Indians and who had not really given up, tried once more to stop the expansion. On April 18, 1644, this remarkable Indian (who was now nearly a hundred years old) launched another surprise attack which is supposed to have killed some 500 settlers. More were killed than in the first attack a quarter–century before, but the population was higher, too, so that more were left alive to launch the counterattack that was bloodier than before.

Opechancano was captured and killed, and the Indian power in eastern Virginia was permanently broken; the English settlers spread northward to the Potomac River, some sixty miles north of Jamestown.

North of the Potomac, however, it was no longer Virginia, and to explain how that came to be, we must refer back to England.

MARYLAND

The official religion of England, as set up by Henry VIII, and reinforced by his daughter, Elizabeth I, was the Church of England (or "Anglicanism"), a mild form of Protestantism that was not startlingly different from Catholicism. The greatest single difference was that the supremacy of the Pope was not recognized and that it was the English monarch who was accepted as head of the Church. Against this, many Englishmen felt it necessary to make their stand, and they remained Catholics.

There was no attempt in England to root out Catholicism by force. Nevertheless, there was considerable harsh feeling against Catholics on the part of the government, since, by championing the Pope against the king (or queen), they seemed to be forever on the edge of treason. They were placed, therefore, under many legal disabilities.

In general, though, the intensity of Protestantism among the English population grew stronger as the 1600s progressed, and increasing numbers found Anglicanism too mild for their liking, too much like Catholicism.

James I found himself more concerned over the extreme Protestants who increasingly dominated a Parliament to which Catholics could not be elected. It was the extreme Protestants, it seemed to James, who questioned the royal prerogatives to which he clung so tightly. Between his dislike for the Protestant radicals and his desire to maintain friendship with Spain, James I found himself tending to be rather friendly toward Catholics.

Some of his advisers were even friendlier than he was. George Calvert, for instance, was an important member of the government and was high in the favor of James. In 1625, he announced that he had been converted to Catholicism. This meant he had to give up all his government offices.

This did not, however, cost him James's friendship. Calvert had large estates in Ireland, one of which was named Baltimore. James therefore raised him to the peerage as Baron Baltimore.

James died that same year, but Baltimore's position was not shaken thereby. James was succeeded by his son who reigned as Charles I, and Charles was even more favorable to Catholicism than James had been. Charles had married Henrietta Maria, the daughter of French King Henry IV (whose son now reigned in France as Louis XIII), and she was herself a Catholic and influenced her husband in favor of Catholicism at every opportunity.

Lord Baltimore had been a member of the Virginia Company and now it occurred to him that a colony might be established in America where Catholics might settle and find freedom. (This was the reverse of Coligny's notion of more than half a century before.)

His first notion was that such a colony might be placed in Newfoundland, which was still an unsettled territory. He even placed settlers there in 1621, but the attempt quickly failed since the island's climate was most inhospitable. Baltimore visited Newfoundland, in 1627, and wintering there, could see that for himself. He went on to Virginia, in 1628, found that climate much more favorable, of course, and returned to England, in 1629, filled with determination to build a Catholic colony in the south.

He asked Charles I to allot him territory in the Virginia region. He did not hide the fact that he intended to settle Catholics there, but, since he was trying to obtain permission from a Protestant government, he made it clear that Protestants, too, would be welcome and would suffer no political disabilities. Thus, from the very start, such a colony was envisioned as a place of a certain degree of religious tolerance.

Charles I was quite willing, but, on June 20, 1632, just before the formalities could be completed, Lord Baltimore died. His son, Cecil Calvert, the second Baron Baltimore, took over the task. That portion of Virginia which lay north of the Potomac River and which was still unsettled, was granted to him for colonization.

In November 1633, under the leadership of Leonard Calvert, a younger brother of Cecil, some 220 settlers (Protestants as well as Catholics) in two ships left England. They arrived three months later at the point of land just north of the mouth of the Potomac.

The new colony, which they intended to administer independently of Virginia, they named "Maryland" in honor of the Virgin Mary and of the Catholic queen, Henrietta Maria. The settlement they founded, on March 27, 1634, at their place of landing, they named St. Mary's City. It was to be the capital of the colony for the remainder of the century.*

Maryland had both the advantages and disadvantages of the existence of Virginia to the south. The original settlement at Jamestown was now over a quarter of a century old and Maryland could profit from the lesson of Virginia's troubles. The Maryland settlers did not pass through the disasters of starvation and disease. Moreover, they benefited from Virginia's victory over the Indians.

On the other hand, the Virginia settlers were by no means pleased at the foundation of a new colony to the north, one which considered itself independent and was founded under Catholic auspices to boot. One Virginian, William Claiborne, had established a trading post on Kent Island in the northern Chesapeake, in 1631, and was dealing profitably with the Indians. Now his island was suddenly in Maryland territory, and he refused to accept that. He carried refusal into force and his ships actually fought with those under the control of Marylanders. He also made the trip to England to get the grant of land to the Marylanders reversed and almost succeeded.

The Marylanders clung to their colony, but their Catholicism made them vulnerable especially as the Protestant radicals were growing steadily stronger in England. The Catholic proprietors of the colony could not exclude Protestant immigration into Maryland, and, within a decade of the colony's founding, the Catholics within it were in a minority.

* The time was to come when the greatest city of Maryland was to be named Baltimore, in honor of the men who had made it a reality.

The Protestants felt their strength. They plundered St. Mary's in 1646, and Leonard Calvert had to flee for Virginia for a while. There he received the help of Virginia's governor (as a fellow governor rather than a fellow religionist, for though Virginia's governor was a Protestant, he did not want to see governmental authority weakened) and was soon back in Maryland.

It was clear that, to survive, Maryland must avoid religious conflict. The colony must specifically tolerate Protestants in the hope that this would set an example of toleration on a larger scale from which they themselves could benefit.

On April 21, 1649, therefore, Maryland passed a law popularly known as the "Toleration Act," under which all people who accepted the Trinity were given free exercise of their religion. It did not represent total toleration, for it extended the freedom only to Christians and excluded Jews, for instance.

Whether there were selfish motives behind the act scarcely matters. The fact is that the Catholics of Maryland set up the first official example of broad religious toleration among the English settlements in America, and this served as precedent for religious freedom in the United States.

In admiring Maryland's policy of tolerance, however, we mustn't forget that the very existence of the colony was a testimonial to a prior example of religious toleration — that of England itself. The Catholic settlement of a portion of the Americas was not only permitted but was even encouraged by Protestant England. This was in strong contrast to the policy of Catholic Spain which at no time permitted any religion but that of Catholicism in any part of the American continents that it controlled.

5

NORTH OF VIRGINIA

NEW ENGLAND

Even as Virginia and Maryland strove to survive, events farther north put vigorous new English colonies on the map of North America. These arose, like Maryland, but for opposite reasons, out of the religious conflict in England.

There were Protestants in England who were dissatisfied with the Church of England and found it far too Catholic in ritual for their liking. They spoke over and over of the need to purify the Church of Catholic ritual, and, in the time of Elizabeth I, those who opposed them called them "Puritans" in derision. The term (as frequently happens in such cases) was adopted proudly by those it was supposed to mock.

In general, the English monarchs were opposed to Puritanism, since the Puritans were always ready to use their consciences as excuse to oppose the king. The kings preferred a church that would be wholly subservient to themselves, and James I made no secret of the fact that he intended to crush the Puritans. They must either abandon those beliefs he found undesirable or he would drive them out of the land.

Some Puritans despaired of ever imposing their views on the Church of England. They felt the only solution was to separate themselves from the Church altogether and set up their own form of worship. These were called "Separatists." One group of such Separatists lived in Scrooby in Nottinghamshire.

Harried by local officials and churchmen, the Scrooby Separatists finally adopted the desperate procedure of leaving England; their destination was the Netherlands.

At that time, the Netherlands had virtually won their independence from Spain. Finding that commerce and industry were the key to prosperity and strength and that religious enthusiasm seemed to count for little in these respects, they established religious tolerance out of indifference rather than conviction. Even Jews were allowed to live and worship freely, something that had been unheard of in Christian Europe for many centuries.

The Separatists would undoubtedly be able to go their way, too, so, in 1607 and 1608, the Scrooby Separatists made their way to the Netherlands. They settled in Leiden and did well for a time.

Still, with the passing of the years, they grew unhappy. For one thing, they were immigrants in a strange land, and felt themselves to be outsiders. Even their children disturbed them, for they learned Dutch and were visibly becoming Dutchmen rather than Englishmen. Then, too, what if the war with Spain (suspended by what was only a truce) began again? It had been marked by many atrocities and the Separatists did not feel secure.

As these doubts and worries grew, it became obvious that the Jamestown settlement in Virginia was a going concern. The Separatists began to consider seriously whether it might not be better to go to America and be in a land of their own (nobody counted the Indians, of course) where they might live as both Englishmen and Puritans. Most of the Separatists flinched at the thought of the long journey and of the uncertainties of the wilderness, but some began to petition King James for permission to go to Virginia.

He finally granted it, and the Separatists who wished to go began the long and hard task of raising funds and of getting ships and supplies. They got two ships, one of which proved unfit for the trip, so that they finally sailed from Plymouth, on September 16, 1620, in one ship, the *Mayflower*.*

On board were thirty–five Separatists from Leiden. Sixty–six others (mostly non–Separatists) from London and neighboring areas joined them. In theory, these were all to sail to some part of Virginia, but the leaders were not eager to travel to a land already occupied by settlers who were not Puritans. Deliberately (and illegally) they headed farther north.

The coast north of Virginia had been explored by such early explorers as Cabot and Verrazano, but the men on the *Mayflower* did not have to depend on that. In the previous two decades, explorer after explorer had followed the northern shore.

In 1602, for instance, the English navigator, Bartholomew Gosnold (who was later to be second in command in the fleet that brought the first colonists to Jamestown) had explored that coast. On May 15, 1602, he came upon a narrow, curved peninsula with neighboring waters rich in codfish. He called it Cape Cod, and went on to explore the shores of an island to the south which he called Martha's Vineyard.

Two years later, another navigator, George Weymouth, ex-

---

* The *Mayflower*, 100 feet long and 180 tons, is known for this one voyage alone, but that is enough to make it one of the most famous ships in history. It has become the symbol of the "Pilgrim fathers" — as the Separatists came to be called because of their journeys — who are themselves, for some reason, the most nearly deified, in the American tradition, of all the early settlers.

plored that section of the coast and brought back glowing reports.

Then, in 1614, John Smith, of Jamestown fame, had conducted an exploring expedition of that section of the American coast. He carefully studied and mapped the shoreline and was sufficiently struck by the resemblance of the climate and appearance of the land to that of the home country as to name the area "New England," a name it has kept ever since.

Perhaps the report that most swayed the Separatists, however, was that of a Dutch explorer, Adriaen Block, who, in 1614, returned to Amsterdam with glowing reports of the southern section of the New England coast. An island 40 miles west of Martha's Vineyard is still called "Block Island" in his honor.

On November 9, 1620, when the *Mayflower* finally reached America, the men on board found themselves at the tip of Cape Cod, rather farther north than they had actually wanted to go. It was the wrong time of year, too, and Cape Cod presented a bleak aspect; but the trip had been long and uncomfortable, and they were in no mood to go much farther.

They sailed past the hook of the cape and began to explore the shoreline beyond for anything that didn't look too bad. They finally located a harbor and, on December 16, the *Mayflower* anchored there. John Smith had already given that portion of the shoreline the name of "Plymouth," and the *Mayflower* passengers accepted that in honor of the English port from which they had sailed.

The passengers were in a peculiar position, however, since they were outside the limits of the land under the control of the Virginia Company under whose auspices they had, in theory, sailed. The Virginia Company could not legally appoint a governor over them in this section of the coast, and they had to govern themselves.

The Separatists among the settlers, to take care of this and also to avoid trouble from the non–Separatist contingent, prepared an agreement whereby they would promise obedience to those laws worked out by the inhabitants of the new settlement. This "Mayflower Compact," signed on November 21, was a kind of prelude to the famous "town meetings" of New England and was a first step toward self–government in the English colonies.

As soon as the Separatists landed, they elected John Carver, one of themselves, to be their governor.

It was still the wrong time of the year, however, and the settlers had to face a winter entirely unprepared. Half of the passengers of the *Mayflower* were dead of starvation and disease before the spring. Governor Carver was one of those who died. The survivors clung on grimly, electing William Bradford their new governor. (He was to remain governor, on and off, for thirty–five years.)

The small group of settlers would certainly not have survived Indian enmity; but, in Plymouth as elsewhere, the Indians were friendly to begin with. Indeed, in this particular case, they had no choice. An epidemic of the plague, in 1617, had carried off most of the Indians of the area, and the few survivors were not disposed to seek trouble.

Came the spring of 1621, and the settlers were able to plant their first crops in deserted Indian fields. One Indian, named Squanto, who had learned English during his stay in London (where he had been carried by English seamen who had casually kidnapped him) helped the settlers by instructing them in Indian methods of agriculture. Another friendly Indian, Samoset, arranged a meeting with Massasoit, the leader of the local tribes and peaceful relations were formally established between Indians and settlers.

By the time the winter of 1621 began to close in, the settlers had a good fall harvest to keep them going, and they declared a three–day celebration, to give thanks to God.* Massasoit and ninety Indians joined in the feast.

* It is this celebration which is now commemorated by our own holiday of Thanksgiving on the fourth Thursday of every November.

It was clear that Plymouth was going to survive. It remained a small colony, the number of settlers rising only to 180, by 1624, but it was vigorous. In 1626, it had raised the 1800 pounds necessary to pay off those merchants who had invested in the venture at the start, and Plymouth residents were founding other little settlements up and down the shore.

Other settlers were beginning to reach portions of the shore in voyages directly from England. The second important town to appear on the map was Salem, founded in 1626, about 40 miles north of Plymouth.

What really put New England on the map, however, was the activity of John Winthrop, an influential Puritan of education and of means. He gathered together a party of Puritans, in 1629, and began to plan for a highly organized expedition to New England, one which would be backed by a royal grant.

Charles I, who now ruled England, was not averse to getting rid of as many Puritans as possible, so he granted permission to establish a "Massachusetts Bay Company." * Charles neglected to specify that the company hold its annual meetings in London, where it could be easily controlled. The settlers, therefore, carried the company, and the government, with them to New England. It was another step, if an inadvertent one, toward self–government in the colonies.

In 1630, seventeen ships, carrying nearly a thousand men, sailed to New England, with Winthrop aboard as governor of the colony to be founded. They landed in Massachusetts Bay, so that the colony was first called by that name and eventually simply "Massachusetts."

A town, established in that year of 1630, on a tongue of land jutting into the bay was named "Boston" after the English town from which a group of the settlers had come. The river at

---

* Massachusetts Bay, immediately north of Plymouth was named by John Smith in his 1614 mapping expedition. The name comes from Indian words meaning "near the great hill" in reference to hills in the area where Indian tribes gathered for discussions.

whose mouth Boston was founded was named the "Charles River" after the king.

Other towns were established round and about Boston and from the very start Massachusetts Bay flourished, with Winthrop continuing to serve as governor, on and off, for twenty years.

Over the next dozen years, Puritans (and some non–Puritans) poured into Massachusetts in wholesale fashion as the government of Charles I continued to be hostile to their beliefs. Some 20,000 settlers in 200 ships landed, and, for a while, New England was far more populous than the older settlement in Virginia. By 1640, New England had a population of 22,500 as compared with about 5000 in Virginia and Maryland.

The new colony of Massachusetts overwhelmed, particularly, the earlier settlement of Plymouth which, at the time of the founding of Boston, still had a population of only 300. Nevertheless, Plymouth staunchly maintained its independence and was to continue to do so for sixty more years.

The new settlers were not the simple artisans who had crossed on the *Mayflower*. Many were university graduates who were concerned lest their children grow up without their own educational benefits.

On October 28, 1636, therefore, a school was founded just north of the Charles River, in what is now the town of Cambridge. Four hundred pounds were voted for the purpose by the settlers. At the time a thirty–year–old minister was dying of tuberculosis. He bequeathed about 700 pounds and his library of 400 books to the new school — an enormous gift by the standards of the time and place. The minister's name was John Harvard, and, on March 13, 1639, half a year after his death, the school showed its gratitude by taking the name of Harvard College. It was the first institution of higher learning to be established in the English colonies.

Another intellectual step forward was taken, in 1639, when a printing press was set up in Cambridge. It was the first device of the sort anywhere in the English colonies. This printing press produced an edition of a book of psalms, in 1640, and this was the first book to be published in the English colonies.

Other sections of New England were also colonized. An Englishman named Ferdinando Gorges (who had fought against the Spanish Armada) had long been trying to colonize the northern portion of New England. As early as 1607, he had tried to found a settlement under the auspices of the Plymouth Company, at a point about 135 miles north of what was later to be the settlement of Boston. It failed to survive the winter and those few of the 120 settlers who survived were returned to England in 1608. It was an expensive blow to the Plymouth Company, all the harder to take because the London Company was having better luck at Jamestown. Nor did the Plymouth Company ever succeed, for New England was settled without them.

On August 10, 1622, Gorges and John Mason (who had served as governor of still–unsettled Newfoundland and who was the first to map all its shores thoroughly) received royal approval to try again to settle the northern stretch of the New England shore. The northern section was called "Maine" at first, because it was customary to speak of the shore as the "main" (mainland) from the viewpoint of the many islands off-shore. Gorges and Mason divided their holdings, in 1629, and Mason called his southern portion of the shore "New Hampshire" after the English county of Hampshire, where he had spent most of his life (though he was not born there).

By the mid–1630s, settlements were springing up along the New Hampshire and Maine shores and these were viewed with the deepest suspicion by the Puritans of Massachusetts. Gorges and Mason were not Puritans, after all, and they believed in the control of the colonies by the crown. Such an example so near at hand would endanger the self–government which Massachusetts was exercising and which it valued.

Massachusetts, therefore, did its best to insist that the entire

New England shore to its north fall under its own jurisdiction. Some of the Maine towns acknowledged Massachusetts sovereignty, and, by 1677, Massachusetts bought out all the claims of the Gorges family. Maine remained part of Massachusetts for a century and a half thereafter.

Massachusetts also managed to dominate New Hampshire on and off, but it retained its independence in the long run and maintained itself as a separate colony.

It was not long before the settlers in Massachusetts were themselves spreading out in search of newer lands. By 1632, they were exploring the valley of the Connecticut River (from Indian words meaning "beside the long, tidal river"). In October 1635, emigrants from Massachusetts towns trekked eighty miles westward and settled Windsor, Hartford, and Wethersfield along that river. This was the nucleus of what was to become the colony of Connecticut* and represented the first large scale overland migration westward — a process that was to continue (it is, in a way, still continuing today).

In 1638, a new party of Puritans arrived from England, lingered only briefly in Boston, then went on to found a settlement on the coast west of the Connecticut River, on April 15 of that year. They called the settlement New Haven.

New settlements were formed out of a desire for religious freedom, too; for, although the Puritans had arrived in Massachusetts to be free to worship as they pleased, they were not the least interested in according others the same privilege.

This meant trouble for Roger Williams, a Puritan who arrived in Boston, in 1631. There he found himself at odds with the leaders of the community because he was more radical than they were and had become a Separatist, wishing no connection whatever with the Church of England. Indeed, logic compelled Roger Williams to the view that it was so difficult to determine the true religion and to persuade others to practice it,

---

* Massachusetts and Connecticut were the only English colonies on the American coast to receive Indian names.

there was no use in trying to make but one form of religion lawful. He, therefore, began more and more to believe in total freedom of religion as the only practical way of dealing with human beings.

This was bad enough as far as the leaders of Massachusetts were concerned, but Williams's views with respect to land ownership were even worse. Williams maintained that the king of England did not own America and could not make grants of its lands to settlers. The only possible way in which a European settler could own land in America, he felt, was to buy it from its Indian owners.

That was too much for the Massachusetts authorities. On October 9, 1635, Williams was banished from Massachusetts. He was allowed to remain the winter but then went off southward and finally came to Narragansett Bay. There, forty miles south of Boston, he bought land from the Indians, and, in June, 1636, founded the settlement of Providence.

The settlement spread to include the shores of Narragansett Bay and the islands within it. The largest of these islands was thought to be the one referred to by Verrazano in his explorations a century and a quarter before as one which had reminded him of the Mediterranean island of Rhodes. It was therefore called "Rhode Island." Eventually, Williams's settlement came to be known as "Rhode Island and Providence Plantations," * although it is usually known simply as "Rhode Island."

Following Williams's lead, Rhode Island practiced full religious toleration (even toward Jews), though unlike the later Toleration Act in Maryland, this tolerance did not represent legal governmental action, since Williams had no charter to govern the land. Even so, this toleration was enough to make Rhode Island anathema to the other New England colonies,

* This is still the official title of the American state that grew out of the colony so that the smallest of the fifty states has the longest name.

who would have nothing to do with this hotbed of radicalism.

Another religious rebel was Anne Hutchinson, who arrived in Boston in 1634, and was the first woman of note in American history. She had something of the "women's liberationist" about her, for she insisted on practicing religion as she saw it, denying the authority of the church leaders. She organized other women behind her and maintained with vigor a belief in a kind of religious democracy, with each man or woman deciding his or her own course. In the end, she was tried, and, on November 8, 1637, also exiled. She found her haven in Rhode Island for a while, then moved on to what is now Westchester County in New York. In 1643, she was killed in an Indian attack.

Of course, there were bound to be troubles with the Indians, for the swarming influx of settlers occupied the land with ruthless disregard for the Indians. Roger Williams was one of a number of idealists who dealt with the Indians fairly, treating them as though they had all the worth and rights of Europeans; in return, the Indians always dealt fairly with him.

Not all men were Roger Williamses, however. In 1637, an arrogant White trader made himself hated by the Pequot tribe, who occupied Connecticut, and eventually he was killed by one of them. That meant war; a war that followed the usual course.

A raiding party of Indians burned the infant town of Wethersfield, killing some settlers, and that was the initial massacre. Then came the deadly counterattack. On May 26, 1637, a group of armed settlers penned 600 Pequot men, women, and children in their village stronghold near the Mystic River in southeastern Connecticut, set fire to it and let them all burn. The Indian power, in Connecticut at least, was broken.

The "Pequot War," though it ended in victory for the settlers, served to make the Whites insecure. In 1643, Massachusetts, Plymouth, Connecticut, and New Haven joined in a "New England Confederation" to present a united front to the Indians and to settle boundary disputes among themselves. (Radical

Rhode Island was ignored.) This union, which lasted a full generation, was the first attempt of separate colonies to unite in order to deal with common problems.

As the 1640s progressed, however, the drive for British colonization of America began to recede. Largely, this was because of troubles back home.

The Puritans, growing steadily stronger in the industrial and populous southeast of England, increasingly dominated Parliament, and grew increasingly hostile to Charles I. Charles returned the hostility, and, from 1629 to 1640, he refused to call Parliament into session at all.

Without Parliament, Charles found it difficult to raise money. He was forced into all sorts of dubious expedients which simply increased his unpopularity. Then, in 1639, the Scots rebelled. Charles needed money so badly that he was forced, much against his will, to call Parliament into session. Parliament tried to use its control of finances to force Charles I to make concessions, and the conflict flared out of control.

By 1642, there was actual civil war, with both the King and Parliament raising armies with which to fight battles. A Puritan squire, Oliver Cromwell, fought on the Parliamentary side and proved to be an unusually capable general. By 1645, it was clear that the King was beaten; and, on January 30, 1649, he was actually beheaded. England remained without a king for eleven years, to the utter horror of the rest of Europe.

The English Civil War was of great importance to the evolution of the colonies. While England was occupied with its internal troubles, the colonies were left to manage their own internal affairs. Even Virginia, a royal colony, was allowed, for a time, to elect its own governor. This habit of self–government could not be entirely undone afterward, so another step toward liberty was taken.

The Puritans of New England were, of course, heart and soul with Puritan Parliament. Virginia, on the other hand, was on

the side of the King, and, after 1649, many of Charles's support-
ers emigrated to that colony.

Hostility between the two sections of Anglo–American coast
seemed almost to mirror the English Civil War. The New England Confederation broke off trade relations with Virginia for
a time, and had the two sections been closer together there
might even have been war between them.

The events of the 1640s are early evidence of the differences
between the North and the South, which were to develop eventually into a deadly crisis and which have not yet vanished. It
was North against South; Parliament against the King; Puritan
against Anglican; commons against aristocracy.

But in the 1640s, at least, the two sections could only glower
at each other across a part of the coast that was not English at
all, but Dutch.

NEW NETHERLAND

In the course of the great civil war against Spain, the Netherlands had built a mighty fleet and established a worldwide system of trade and commerce. The Netherlands was, for its size,
the wealthiest nation of the world and could even be considered
a great power.

As its strength increased, the Netherlands carried their war
against Spain overseas. The Portuguese holdings in the Far
East were particularly vulnerable, for, since Portugal had fallen
under Spanish control, its empire had decayed.

In 1602, a group of merchants founded the Dutch East India
Company to develop trade with the Far East and to snap up
what pieces of Portuguese territory they could. Steadily, they
established themselves in the large islands southeast of Asia.

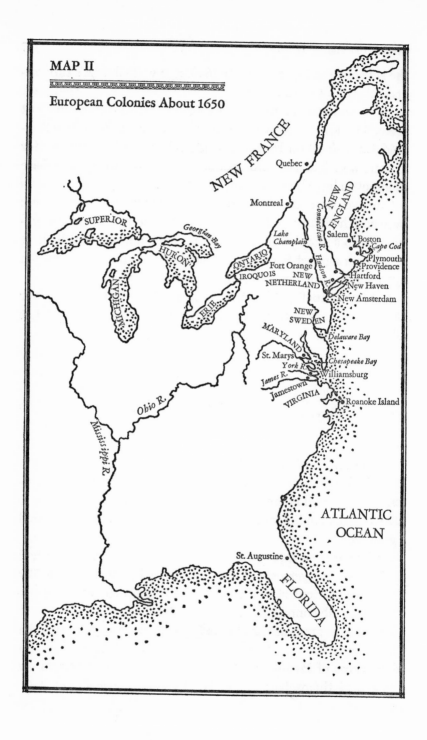

MAP II

European Colonies About 1650

NEW FRANCE

Quebec

Montreal

SUPERIOR

Georgian Bay

HURON

Lake
Champlain

Connecticut R.

NEW
ENGLAND

Salem

Boston
Cape Cod

MICHIGAN

ONTARIO

IROQUOIS

Fort Orange

NEW
NETHERLAND

Hudson R.

Plymouth
Providence
Hartford
New Haven

New Amsterdam

ERIE

NEW
SWEDEN

MARYLAND

Delaware Bay

St. Marys

York R.

James R.

Chesapeake Bay

Williamsburg

Ohio R.

Jamestown

VIRGINIA

Roanoke Island

Mississippi R.

ATLANTIC
OCEAN

St. Augustine

FLORIDA

These eventually came to be called the "Dutch East Indies" (and, after World War II, this area gained its independence and is now the nation of Indonesia). As early as 1619, the Dutch founded, on Java, a city they named "Batavia," after the old Latin name for that region of Europe in which the Netherlands were located. (Batavia has now been renamed Jakarta and is the capital of Indonesia.) The Dutch also took the island of Ceylon from the Portuguese and established themselves in South Africa, where the Portuguese had been established since the time of Dias, a century and a half before. In all this, the Dutch merchants were making fortunes.

In 1609, an exhausted Spain had finally consented to a temporary truce with the Netherlands (she was not to accept the independence of the region for almost forty years more), and Dutch energies mounted still higher. Even while their efforts in the Far East were doing so well, they began to dream of similar attempts in the Far West.

What about the Northwest Passage which had been sought so long and so vainly? Frobisher and Davis had failed a quarter century before, but there was an English navigator who, in the first decade of the 1600s, was still exploring Arctic waters in search of navigable routes. This was Henry Hudson, who, in 1607, had been tracing the Arctic waters north of Europe in the employ of England's Muscovy Company. Hudson had ventured out to Spitzbergen and beyond, and had discovered what is now called "Jan Mayen Island," just about halfway between Spitzbergen and Iceland.

In 1608, he was commissioned by the Dutch to undertake explorations for them. On April 6, 1609, he set off in the ship *The Half Moon*. He began by moving northeastward again, past Spitzbergen, but the discontent of his crew forced him to turn westward.

Hudson headed across the Atlantic to North America, at a time when English settlement of the coast was at its barest beginnings and when Jamestown was hanging on by an eyelash.

Hudson sailed up and down the American coast, exploring Delaware Bay a year before any Englishman saw it. Then, on September 3, 1609, his ship sailed into New York Harbor. Others had preceded him there, notably Verrazano; but Hudson, hoping against hope that it was the entrance of the Northwest Passage, was the first to enter the broad river that emptied into the bay. On September 12, he began to move upstream.

He made his way for a hundred fifty miles up the river until the gradual shallowing of the water convinced him that it was indeed a river and not a strait, and sailed downstream again in disappointment.

In after time the Dutch called this the "North River" and the one that emptied into the Delaware Bay, farther south, the "South River." The latter eventually came to be called the Delaware River, but the former has very justly come to be known as the Hudson River.

Sailing back to the Netherlands with his report, Hudson was stopped in England and prevented from working for the Dutch further.

In 1610, Hudson tried again, farther north this time and in the pay of the English once more. In June of that year, he sailed south of Baffin Island, through the narrow sea passage between it and the mainland, a passage now known as "Hudson Strait." On August 3, he entered a large bay jutting south into the North American continent, one that is now called "Hudson Bay."

It seemed as though it were just possible he had finally rounded the North American continent and that there might be clear sailing west to the Indies. He spent three months in the bay, exploring the eastern shore, and reaching the southern portion (an inlet known as "James Bay" after James I of England) in November.

There he was frozen in for six dreary months. When the ice broke, in June 1611, he wanted to continue exploring the western shore of the bay, but his crew had had enough. Hudson was set adrift, with his son and with seven loyal crew members, and presumably all died of cold and hunger. Those of the mutineers who survived an attack by Eskimos managed to find their way back to England.

The Dutch continued their westward drive even without Hudson. In some ways their most astonishing successes were in South America where, after the expiration of the truce with Spain, they continued to seize portions of the Portuguese empire. In 1623, the Dutch took the city of Pernambuco on the easternmost bulge of Brazil. They extended their conquests, and, for a while, it seemed that there would be a great Dutch empire in South America. However, in 1640, after sixty years of subjection to Spain, Portugal regained its independence and that made a great difference. Beginning in 1645, a popular uprising by the Portuguese colonists ended with the eviction of the Dutch from Brazil.

More permanent conquests were made in the small islands rimming the Caribbean Sea. Such islands as St. Martin and Saba, east of Puerto Rico, and Curacao, just north of the South American mainland, became Dutch and remain Dutch to this day.*

But the Dutch did not forget the coast of North America, the stretch from the North River to the South River. In 1614, Adriaen Block began with the Hudson River and explored eastward. He sailed around Manhattan and Long Island (proving both to be islands) and explored the Connecticut shore, discovering the Connecticut River and entering it. In the same year, Cornelis May explored the shore south of the Hudson and Cape May, at the southern tip of what is now New Jersey, is named for him.

---

* France and England were also seizing islands in this area. France obtained a foothold in the western portion of Hispaniola, Spain's oldest colony; while England took Bermuda, the Bahamas, Barbados, and Jamaica. For a while, these English islands were far more valuable to England than the mainland colonies were. There were more settlers in the islands in 1630 than in all Virginia.

Also in 1614, the Dutch established a fort far up the Hudson, at the point where Hudson's exploration had reached its farthest extent, and used it to trade for furs with the Indians. They called it first Fort Nassau, after their ruler Maurice of Nassau, and later Fort Orange after the family name of the Netherlands's ruling house. In 1624, a small settlement was also placed on an island at the mouth of the Hudson River, one called "Manhattan" from the name of the Indian tribe that lived there.

By that time though, Dutch merchants had established the Dutch West India Company (on June 3, 1621) to organize the western settlements more efficiently and to make of what was coming to be called "New Netherland" a working concern. For the purpose, a strong base at the mouth of the Hudson River was needed.

Peter Minuit was appointed as director–general of New Netherland by the company and was sent to America to establish this base. On May 4, 1626, he landed on Manhattan and made what is, in retrospect, the most astonishing real estate deal in history. He bought Manhattan Island from the Indians for cheap finery worth sixty guilders, a sum usually translated into American money as $24.

At the southern tip of the island, the settlement, then containing 300 people, was named "New Amsterdam," in honor of Amsterdam, then as now the largest city in the Netherlands.

By that time, England's Virginia settlement was clearly successful, and Englishmen were beginning to land on the New England shores. The Netherlands, feeling their own colony being hemmed in both north and south, were anxious to strengthen it by filling it with settlers. Not enough Dutchmen seemed ready to go spontaneously, and the Netherlands, therefore, eagerly accepted settlers from anywhere else in Europe. By 1643, a visiting Jesuit priest reported that he had counted eighteen languages being spoken on the streets of New Amsterdam — which thus gained a polyglot character that it has never since lost.

The Dutch took measures to encourage immigration. On June 7, 1629, they founded the "patroon system." Men who would make themselves responsible for bringing over fifty settlers were given large tracts along the Hudson River, sixteen miles along one bank, or eight miles along both. These men, called "patroons" were given almost sovereign rights over their land. The semifeudal system thus initiated succeeded in opening the Hudson River to European settlement with great rapidity — but it also kept New Netherland a tightly run oligarchy.

The founder of the patroon system was Kiliaen Van Rensselaer, a diamond merchant of Amsterdam who had been one of the original stockholders of the Dutch West India Company. Though he did not come to New Netherlands, his sons did, in 1630. They had a lordly section of the upper Hudson under their control, and even today a county on the east bank of the river, opposite Albany, is called Rensselaer.

The colony expanded. A Danish immigrant, Jonas Bronck, settled on the mainland north of Manhattan, and we still call the area the "Bronx." A Dutch settler with the title of "jonker" (the equivalent of the better-known "Junker" of the Prussians) settled farther north in the area we call Yonkers.

Staten Island was settled (and was named for the States–General, the legislature of the Netherlands). So was Long Island, and places like Brooklyn and Harlem were named after Dutch towns. The Dutch also spread along the coast of Connecticut and New Jersey. In 1633, they built "Fort Good Hope" at the present site of Hartford, before the New England settlers had arrived. Later, when the English settled along the Connecticut River and at New Haven, the Dutch protested vigorously, called it an invasion of their land.

Through it all, the Dutch had to deal with the Indians. Peter Minuit and the Rensselaers dealt fairly with the Indians, and so did Wouter Van Twiller, a nephew of Van Rensselaer, who be-

came governor of New Netherland in 1633. They had no problems.

But then, in 1637, Willem Kieft became governor, and Kieft
was one of those who had the firm opinion that one had to take
no nonsense from the Indians and that killing a few would have
a good effect on the rest. So he killed a few and promptly had
an Indian war on his hands.

Kieft had to build a wall of palisades across the southern tip
of Manhattan (the origin of "Wall Street") to protect New
Amsterdam. In 1644, there were battles in Westchester, in one
of which Anne Hutchinson was killed, and only narrowly did
the Dutch maintain themselves.

Naturally, the colonists strove to get rid of the incompetent
Kieft, and, in 1647, New Netherland received a new governor,
Peter Stuyvesant. He was, by all odds, the most capable man
in the history of Dutch America. He had been wounded, in
1644, during a battle in the Caribbean, and as a result one leg
had to be amputated. He walked around on a wooden stump
thereafter, one that he decorated with silver bands.

He was not a lovable man, and he ruled harshly; but he also
ruled efficiently. He had no easy time of it. To the north and
east were the ever–encroaching English settlers of New England, and to the south there was an unexpected challenge —
from a small group of Swedes, the least–remembered of all the
national groups that established early settlements on the American coast.

NEW SWEDEN

Sweden did not really enter the stage of European history
till after the discovery of America. Through much of the Middle Ages it had been under the domination of Denmark, but, in

1523, it achieved its independence under Gustavus Vesa, who reigned as Gustavus I. It then expanded over the Baltic region and reached a peak of power under a remarkable soldier–monarch, Gustavus II Adolphus.

In 1630, Gustavus Adolphus intervened in the ruinous Thirty Years' War that was then convulsing Germany and, in the course of the next two years, won brilliant victories that raised Sweden to the status of a great power, a role it was to keep for a century. It is not surprising that Gustavus Adolphus, eager to place Sweden on a par with the older powers of Europe, gave ear to projects involving the settlement of the eastern coast of America. In this he was encouraged by Dutchmen who had been ousted (they thought unjustly) from the Dutch West India Company.

Gustavus Adolphus died in battle, in 1632; but Swedish plans continued. The "New Sweden Company" was organized, in 1637, to do for Sweden what the Dutch West India Company had done for the Netherlands. It was Peter Minuit, in fact, the purchaser of Manhattan, who was a leading spirit of the new venture. And, in 1638, when the first group of Swedish settlers left for America, Minuit was at their head.

The expedition stopped at Jamestown for ten days, then sailed north into Delaware Bay and, on March 29, 1638, founded a settlement near the site where the city of Wilmington now stands. They called it Fort Christina, after Gustavus Adolphus's daughter, Christina, who had succeeded to the throne on her father's death.

The Swedish settlers spread farther up the Delaware to the vicinity of what is now Philadelphia, where they established their capital. Still further upstream, however, were the hostile Dutch, who considered the Delaware their own territory. "New Sweden," as it was called, kept the peace with the Indians; and under Johan Bjornsson Printz, a hugely fat man, who had fought under Gustavus Adolphus, the colony flourished — but it always remained small. A couple of hundred Swedes and Finns served as its core and its population never grew larger than that.

The Swedes brought one thing to America that in time came to be inseparable from the legends of American pioneers. This was the log cabin, invented in the Scandinavian north, which, for ease of construction and for warmth through a hard winter, was far superior to anything else in the settlements. It was certainly superior to the English frame houses built by the settlers in New England.

The log cabin was gradually adopted over all the North American frontier.

NEW FRANCE

Nor was France behindhand in the race for the colonization of America. Once Henry IV had made himself king and the religious civil wars were over, France took up once again the matter of America, carrying on where Cartier had left off in his explorations of the St. Lawrence River.

The French had kept up contacts with the region in connection with the fur trade. Beaver fur, in which Canada was rich, had come into great popularity for the manufacture of hats (for which "beaver" became a slang term); and the fur trade, which needed a land base, had become more profitable than the offshore fisheries. Henry IV was, therefore, persuaded to try to make the French hold firmer. For the purpose, he appointed Samuel de Champlain as geographer royal, with instructions to explore the area.

Champlain was no beginner. He had fought under Henry IV while the latter was still struggling to be king and, later on, in the service of Spain, had had great and varied experience at sea and in New Spain.

He had already made two trips to America. In 1603, he had

entered the St. Lawrence River. Then, in 1604, he explored the
New England coast before it had been named New England.
On a peninsula farther north, which the French called "Acadie"
(Acadia in English), from an Indian word meaning "rich," he
helped found a settlement called "Port Royal."

In 1608, under royal sponsorship, he sailed from France on
his third voyage to Canada. Again he sailed up the St. Lawrence River, and, on July 3, 1608, he founded a settlement 400
miles upstream at a point where the river narrowed and where
the precipitous river bank made the settlement easy to defend.
This was the town of Quebec, founded one year after Jamestown.

Quebec had a difficult time of it at first. The harsh northern
winter closed in upon the settlement, and of the twenty–eight
settlers, only eight were alive when spring came. Nevertheless,
Quebec remained in existence and served as a nucleus for what
was to be called "New France."

The French, in their fur trade, depended upon the local Indians who belonged to tribes called "Hurons" and "Algonquins."
These were at war with the Iroquois, a confederation of Indian
tribes who held land in what is now New York State. The Iroquois had formed their confederation about 1570, under the
leadership (among others) of the semilegendary Mohawk, Hia-
watha. This brought a measure of peace and unity among five
hitherto–warring tribes. As a result they became the strongest
group of Indians anywhere in the coastal territory now being
colonized by European nations.

In fact, the Iroquois were perhaps the most remarkable Indian warriors in the Americas. The tribe never boasted of more
than 2300 fighting men, but these, faultlessly brave and incredibly sado–masochistic in their ability to torture and endure torture, had developed the technique of commando–type raids to
a fine art. They conquered the neighboring Indian tribes and
dominated much of what is now the northeastern United States.

Champlain knew nothing of this. He was merely anxious to

explore southward and was willing to help the Indians on whom he relied for furs. Moving south from the St. Lawrence, in July 1609, he discovered a long lake which is still called "Lake Champlain" in his honor. At the southern end of that lake, on July 30, the Algonquin Indians whom Champlain was accompanying, encountered a group of Iroquois.

Battle was joined at once with tomahawks and arrows. The Iroquois were winning, so Champlain and his men interfered. Using their muskets they fired volleys into the Iroquois party. Astounded at the new weapon which thundered and killed mysteriously, the Iroquois turned and fled.

Champlain's interference was probably the most important single act of his life. The Iroquois, humiliated at having been sent into panicky retreat, never forgot nor forgave. From that moment on, the tribes in general remained consistently hostile to the French and served as allies first of the Dutch and then of the English.

From the Dutch, they obtained firearms of their own, and, by 1640, had become the first of all the Indians to be using guns in their warfare. More than once, the vengeful Iroquois brought New France to the edge of extinction. Without Iroquois support, it may be that, in the long run, neither the Dutch nor the English could have held out against the French in this crucial area. If the French had managed to drive a wedge between New England and Virginia, the two areas of English settlement, the future history of the North American continent might have been enormously different.

After returning to France for more settlers, Champlain came to America a fourth time, in 1610; and, in 1611, he founded a settlement 150 miles upstream from Quebec. He called it "Place Royale" and it served as the nucleus for the later Montreal. In 1613, he trekked westward and, by 1615, had reached Georgian Bay, the northern extension of Lake Huron. He was the first European to reach the Great Lakes.

Back in France, Henry IV had been assassinated, in 1610; and there followed fourteen years of relative weakness under his young son, Louis XIII. Though Champlain fortified Quebec, in 1620, it remained a tiny settlement and could not resist a naval attack by the English in 1629. Champlain, who was now governor of New France, was forced to surrender and was held prisoner for three years. The English also took the French settlements in Acadia. Both Quebec and Acadia were, however, returned in 1632.

In 1624, meanwhile, the able Cardinal Richelieu had taken over as Louis XIII's chief minister. Under his firm hand, France quickly revived. In 1627, he organized a company designed to encourage the colonization of Canada. He obtained the return of French holdings from England, and from year to year thereafter New France grew stronger. The river that drains Lake Champlain northward into the St. Lawrence River is named Richelieu River in his honor.

The actual number of French settlers remained small, however, considering the size of the territory France controlled. There were many reasons. The climate was harsh, and the French were more interested in the fur trade and in profits than in building a new home for Frenchmen overseas. To insure a profitable trade, the French government, which was autocratic at home, maintained a despotic control over the settlers and did not make Canada an attractive place for those looking for escape from harshness at home.

Finally, those French who were most apt to seek asylum overseas were the Huguenots, the French Protestants, who suffered the woes of a distrusted minority at home. The French government, however, intent on keeping New France thoroughly Catholic, would not allow Huguenots to enter French territory in America. Huguenots therefore emigrated to the English colonies, where they were welcome and where they served to strengthen France's enemy.

Meanwhile, in Europe itself, France put the final touch on the decline of Spain.

The Spanish had been protesting the colonization of the eastern coast of North America by other nations, for it stubbornly maintained that all the North American continent was its own by right of discovery and exploration. (Discovery and exploration by Indians did not count.)

It could, however, do no more than protest, for its decline continued steadily through the first half of the 1600s. Still considering itself the champion of Catholicism, it embroiled itself in the Thirty Years' War, fighting against Germans, Danes, Swedes, and Frenchmen.

In 1642, at Rocroi, on the borders of the Spanish Netherlands, a Spanish army was thoroughly defeated by French forces. This marked the end of the Spanish military supremacy on the continent after a century and a half, during which Spanish armies had virtually never been defeated.

In 1648, the Thirty Years' War ended with a peace settlement that was clearly a defeat for Spain. Spain was even forced, after eighty stubborn years of failure, to accept the independence of the Netherlands. War between Spain and France continued, however, till 1659, when peace was finally made, again to Spain's disadvantage. Spain sank from the ranks of great powers, then, and has remained a minor power ever since.

Nevertheless, although Spanish dominion in the Americas ceased to expand, and although minor outposts in the islands were lost to other nations, Spain showed, on the whole, a remarkable tenacity. It kept its hold on Mexico, New Mexico, Texas, and Florida all the more strongly since it needed them as a buffer between the vigorous new colonizing powers in the north and its own rich core of empire in Mexico.

6

THE ENGLISH EXPAND

THE END OF NEW NETHERLAND

By 1650, then, the colonies of five nations were strung along the eastern coast of North America, the identity of the nations reflected in the names. There was New France along the St. Lawrence River; New England centered about the Massachusetts Bay area; New Netherland along the Hudson River; New Sweden along the Delaware River; Maryland and Virginia (English) along the Potomac and James Rivers; and New Spain in Florida and southward.

It was not an amicable arrangement, of course. Spain claimed it all, and there were occasional scuffles — between the Dutch and English in Connecticut, between the French and English in Canada, and so on. Until then, however, there had been sufficient elbow room to keep the settlers from serious warfare.

The room, however, was disappearing. By 1650, with each group of settlers spreading out, collisions began to occur, and for a century thereafter there was intensifying competition to see which European nation was to inherit the North American continent.*

New Netherland felt the crowding keenly. Under the dour Peter Stuyvesant, it was continuing to flourish and was growing even more cosmopolitan. In 1654, the first party of Jews arrive; 23 men, women, and children from Brazil, fleeing the decline of Dutch power there and the reestablishment of control by the uncompromisingly Catholic Portuguese. Then, in 1655, Black slaves arrived and the institution of slavery received its first hold in the northern portion of what was to become the United States.

However, New England was expanding, too, and even more vigorously. Connecticut was becoming more English each year, and, though the Dutch had been there first, they had to accept reality. On September 29, 1650, Stuyvesant signed a treaty at Hartford, granting Connecticut its present western boundary and the eastern half of Long Island as well. The Treaty of Hartford was a humiliating defeat for Stuyvesant and he searched for revenge elsewhere.

For the purpose he kept a constant harsh eye on the Swedish settlements on the Delaware River. The more the Swedes prospered under Printz, the worse Stuyvesant's temper grew. In 1651, Stuyvesant sent two hundred men to Delaware Bay and established Fort Casimir, about six miles south of Fort Christina. From that moment on, the Swedes knew they were living under the axe and that whenever Stuyvesant wished, the axe would descend.

Printz tried desperately to encourage new settlers to arrive,

* Perhaps one portent of what the end would be was this: In 1650, the total population of the English colonies is estimated to have been 52,000, at least five times that of the French, Dutch and Swedish settlements combined. Nor would this disproportion be changed if the Spaniards in Florida were added to the latter.

but finally gave up the clearly impossible struggle and left the colony in 1653. The next year, the Swedes, in despair, attacked Ford Casimir and took it. At that, Stuyvesant exploded, sent seven ships with 600 men (twice the total population of New Sweden) up the Delaware River, and let the axe descend. New Sweden was forced to surrender and its existence came to an end, on September 26, 1655. New Netherland now stretched from the Hudson to the Delaware and was at the peak of its power.

Its doom, however, was approaching — through the events that were taking place in Europe.

After the execution of Charles I, Great Britain fell more and more under the harsh but efficient rule of Oliver Cromwell. It was Cromwell's intention to restore the nation to the level of a great power at sea that it had reached under Elizabeth I.

Standing in the way of that were the Dutch who now controlled most of the sea trade of the world. On October 9, 1651, therefore, Cromwell forced the "Navigation Act" through Parliament. By this new law, all goods entering England by sea, must be carried in English ships (with an English owner, an English captain, and an English crew) or in ships of the nations producing the goods. This was designed to cut out the middlemen Dutch, who picked up goods in one nation and delivered them to a second, charging a healthy fee for the service.

Naturally, what applied to England applied to the English colonies and this meant the settlers in America had to use English ships, even when the more numerous and more skilled Dutch ships and captains would have been cheaper. What was conceived to be good for England was economically harmful for the colonies, but this did not bother the English government. At that time, it was taken for granted that colonies were founded and maintained primarily for the profit of the homeland.

The colonists could do little about the Navigation Act but disregard it, and they proceeded to trade as they pleased and use what ships they chose. This began the long tradition of smuggling (illegal trade) on the part of the English colonists in their effort to avoid the disabilities placed upon them by the homeland.

The English found that there was little they could do about the smuggling, too. They were too far away. In those days, three thousand miles of ocean water was an excellent insulator. It took three months to make the round trip.

The failure of the Navigation Act to work well with respect to the colonies was, however, interpreted by the English as caused by too many loopholes. For that reason, the act was continually strengthened even after the time of Cromwell. In 1660, it was decreed that the ships trading with England be built in England or the colonies. In 1663, it was ordered that any ships from some other nation carrying the produce of that nation to the colonies must stop in England first (thus allowing England certain middlemen profits at the expense of higher prices to the colonists). Furthermore, the number of products specifically subjected to the Navigation Act was continually increased, and the colonies had to sell such commodities as sugar, tobacco, rice, molasses, fur, and so on, only to England (and therefore at whatever price English merchants cared to pay).

And with each tightening of the screw, the colonists simply smuggled the more. England never learned that the attempt to milk the colonists at a distance of 3000 miles couldn't possibly work and that the greater profit would have rested with allowing the colonies to develop freely. The failure to learn the lesson would eventually cost England dear.

But if the colonists could do little but disobey, the Dutch, who were the other sufferers of the Navigation Act, could take direct action. A naval war broke out between the Netherlands and England, in 1652. For two years the war raged, with twelve naval engagements fought all told. The war was not decisive, but it ended, in 1654, with the Dutch having rather the worse of it.

The important aspect of the war was that it ended the friendship between the two nations, a friendship that had lasted all through the long Dutch revolt when both nations stood together in their fear of the great Catholic power of Spain. The new enmity extended to America, of course, and further increased the hostility between New Netherland and the English colonies to the north and south.

In 1658, Cromwell died, and with his death, the prospects for a revival of the monarchy brightened. In 1660, the exiled son of Charles I was called back to Great Britain and began to rule as Charles II.

With Charles II came many exiled royalists whose properties had been confiscated by Cromwell's regime. Naturally, they wanted their property back and with added bonuses as rewards for their loyalty.

This, Charles II could not do. He was quite a sensible man, and he knew that if he tried to wrest land from people who had owned it for a decade and more, he would simply create a new civil war and be forced into exile once more. So he assigned his followers land in America, something he could do without trouble.

As it happened, Charles II had no love for the Dutch, who had treated him unkindly during the years of his exile, and a new war was gathering with them anyway. Consequently, one of his first moves was to grant the territory of New Netherland (which was not his, of course) to someone he considered worthy. That someone was his younger brother James, Duke of York and of Albany.

It seemed a good stroke of policy. If the English could take New Netherland, the entire coast from Massachusetts to Virginia would become unbrokenly English. What's more, the English could take over the profits the Dutch were making from the fur trade, and, perhaps, if the Dutch were gone from the American scene, the Navigation Act could be more easily enforced.

So the Duke of York fitted out a fleet of four ships. Under one of his staff, Richard Nicolls, these sailed across the Atlantic and, on August 29, 1664, sailed into the harbor of New Amsterdam and demanded its surrender.

Old Peter Stuyvesant was caught by surprise. He had been led to believe that the ships were heading for New England, where the Puritan colonists were showing a stubborn reluctance to accept the rule of Charles II.

Facing the English without preparations for defense, Stuyvesant, now over 70, energetically called for some sort of resistance. He called in vain. There were altogether 1600 people living in New Amsterdam, and perhaps 8000 in all of New Netherland. In a fight they were sure to be overwhelmed by the far more numerous population of New England. Besides many, if not most, of the inhabitants of New Amsterdam were not Dutch and felt no great patriotic fervor. They simply refused to resist.

New Amsterdam surrendered without a shot, on September 7, 1664. On September 20, Fort Orange on the upper Hudson also surrendered, and, on October 10, the Dutch along the Delaware River, after a token resistance, surrendered as well.

All of New Netherland became an English colony and the name of that portion of it which straddled the Hudson River was changed to New York, in honor of James. New Amsterdam became New York City, and Fort Orange became Albany, in honor of James's other title.

Actual war with the Netherlands came the next year. By the terms of the peace, signed at Breda in the Netherlands, on July 21, 1667, the Netherlands formally relinquished its claim to what was now New York. In return, England recognized Dutch claims to what is now Dutch Guiana on the Caribbean coast of South America. It was a remarkably poor exchange for the Netherlands, as we can now see, but at the time it didn't seem too bad.

The English, with their usual reasonableness, made no effort to dispossess the Dutch or change their way of life. They left the Dutch to the free practice of their religion and the use of their language. They even kept the patroon system. They merely introduced English ways as well and encouraged an influx of English settlers.

Peter Stuyvesant, on returning to the Netherlands, was roundly blamed for the loss of the colony. In anger, he returned to New York and spent his last years in peace under the English flag. He lived on his farm "Bouwerie" in New York City, which gives its name to the section now known as the "Bowery."

Stuyvesant died in 1672 and did not live to see the Dutch return to New York when a new war broke out with England. On July 30, 1673, a Dutch fleet took New York City by surprise; but a little over a year later, the war came to an end, and the Dutch handed the city back to England, on November 10, 1674.

Not all of New Netherland became New York, however. The southern portion of the Dutch holdings, between the Delaware River and the sea, were granted by James of York to two of his friends, on June 24, 1664, even before New Netherland was taken.

One was George Cartaret. He had been born on the channel island of Jersey, and, after Charles I was beheaded, he had held Jersey for two years against Cromwell, before being forced into exile in France. While he was still holding Jersey, he had been visited by Charles's son, later to be Charles II, who had promised him lands in America as a reward, these lands to be called New Jersey. Now, fifteen years later, the promise was made good. Associated with Cartaret was John, Lord Berkeley, who had also fought for Charles I.

THE GIFTS OF CHARLES II

Thus, as Charles II began his reign, the eastern coast of

North America became solidly English from Maine to Virginia.

South of Virginia there was still an unsettled gap of about 500 miles. It had been avoided while Spain was still strong, but Spain was growing weaker. On March 24, 1663, even while New Netherland remained to be conquered, Charles II had granted this stretch to eight of his loyal courtiers (including Cartaret and Berkeley, who were to have New Jersey the next year).

The whole area was named Carolina in the king's honor, from the Latin version of Charles ("Carolus"). As it happened, it was in this area that the first Huguenot settlement had been made a century before and the French had called it "Caro-lana," almost the same, in honor of their Charles IX.

In 1670, a party of settlers, sponsored by the eight propri-etors, came to Carolina and established their farms along a deep inlet which was named Albemarle Sound after General Monk, one of the proprietors. He had been the chief agent in bringing about the restoration of Charles II and had been named Duke of Albemarle as a reward.

The area was only about 80 miles south of Jamestown, and Virginians had been settling in the area for fifteen years. There was considerable friction between Virginia and Carolina for some decades, therefore, as there had been between Virginia and Maryland earlier. (In both cases, Virginia lost in the end, and its boundaries were fixed at the Potomac River in the north and at 31° North Latitude in the south.)

At about the same time, another group of settlers landed in the southern portion of the Carolina colony. They landed, in fact, as closely as they dared to the Spanish dominion, about 330 miles southwest of Albemarle Sound and only 250 miles north of St. Augustine. There, in April 1670, they founded Charles Town (later Charleston), also named in honor of Charles II.

It was not until 1683 that the colonists dared to settle Port Royal, forty miles farther south (where once the Huguenots had tried vainly to establish themselves), and, even at that late date, Spain managed to find the force to drive them out, on August 17, 1686.

For a quarter century, the Carolina settlements grew stronger, some in the north, some in the south, with little settlement between. So disparate were the groups — tobacco–growing, small farmers in the north and rice–growing, plantation owners in the south — and so large the gap between that it was quickly seen to be useless to attempt to govern the entire area as a unit. While the governor remained in Charleston, a deputy governor was established in the Albemarle area.

Another colony founded under the auspices of Charles II, had, like Maryland and New England, a basis in escape from religious persecution. It involved a sect that dated back to Cromwell's time.

In those days, a Puritan preacher named George Fox had gathered disciples about him who believed so completely in the nearness between God and man as to see no need for churches or ministers.

Fox and his disciples were pacifists and would not accept any authority but God's. They would not remove their hats as a gesture of respect to any Earthly authority, and they used only second person singular ("thee" and "thou") because the use of the plural "you" had originated as a sign of respect. They called all men by no other title than "Friend." For that reason they call themselves "Society of Friends." Because, however, Fox used to warn people to "quake at the power of God," his disciples were called "Quakers" in derision. The name was accepted and is now commonly used for them.

To us today, Quakers seem a particularly harmless group, but in the seventeenth century they seemed dangerous radicals and, because of their rejection of ritual and church organization, even atheists. They were widely and harshly persecuted and three thousand of them were thrown in prison soon after Charles II regained his throne.

It was not long after Quakerism came into existence that Quakers began to leave England for the American colonies, partly in the hope of relief from persecution and partly to convert others to their doctrines. There, too, they were met with harsh anger, and, between 1659 and 1661, four Quakers were hanged in Boston by those who felt that they alone had the ear of God.

Nevertheless, Quakerism did spread in the colonies and even found a haven of sorts in New Jersey. Berkeley and Cartaret had divided the colony, the former taking the western half, the latter the eastern. On March 18, 1674, Berkeley sold his share of the colony to two Quakers for a thousand pounds, and, in 1675, the first Quaker colony was established there. On July 1, 1676, the colony was officially made into two; the Quaker half was named West Jersey and the eastern half, still Cartaret's was East Jersey. The two halves were administered separately.

Meanwhile Quakerism had gained a notable convert, in 1666, when William Penn became a Quaker. He was a son of Sir William Penn, a British admiral and man of wealth, who had fought against Charles I and who, under Cromwell, had fought against the Dutch.

The elder Penn became sympathetic to the Royalist cause in the 1650s, however, and was one of the moving spirits in the drive to restore Charles II to the throne. More important still, he advanced a total of 16,000 pounds to Charles. Charles II did not forget and he was grateful not only to the father, but to the son as well, even when the son did something so socially gauche as to become a Quaker.

The younger Penn was deeply involved with the attempts made by the Quakers to turn New Jersey into a haven. After Cartaret died, in 1680, Penn negotiated the purchase of the rights to East Jersey from his heirs, on February 1, 1681. The trouble with New Jersey, however, was that it was too close to New York, which strove to dominate it as New Netherland had done in Dutch times. This introduced complications, and it seemed to Penn that if he found a virgin territory, which only the Quakers would settle and control, things might be better.

He had already petitioned Charles, in 1680, for the right to colonize the unsettled land west of the Delaware River. Charles was willing to make the grant in return for which his debt to the Penn family was to be cancelled, and, on March 14, 1681, the matter was arranged.

Penn proposed to call the new colony "Sylvania" from the Latin word for a wooded area. Charles II, who had a sly sense of humor* changed the name to "Pennsylvania." Penn, as a Quaker, was horrified at being made to seem so arrogant as to name the colony after himself and refused. Charles, smiling, merely insisted that the name was meant to honor his friend, Sir William Penn, who was no Quaker. Penn could no longer refuse.

Penn went about establishing the new colony in a most unusual way. He published a prospectus of the new colony that made no attempt to deceive. He described the area and its prospects with mild accuracy. He himself went to the colony, in 1682, and, like Roger Williams before him, bought land from the Indians and treated them with scrupulous fairness. And, like Roger Williams, he never had trouble with the Indians, who responded to fair dealing with fair dealing.

He made a treaty with the Indians, in fact, which, being a Quaker, he did not solemnize with oaths — but merely with his word. Later, the French writer, Voltaire, pointed out that of all the treaties signed between the English and the Indians, Penn's was the only one not to be sworn to with religious so-

---

* There is a story that Penn, having gained an audience with the King, approached with his hat firmly on his head, Quaker fashion. At once, Charles II removed his own. "Why removest thou thy hat, Friend Charles?" asked Penn. To which Charles replied, "Because it is a custom in this land that when the King is in the room, only one man remains covered."

lemnity, and also the only one not quickly broken by the English.

To the grant Penn had received from Charles II, were added the lower reaches of the Delaware River, which had once been New Sweden and had briefly been part of New Netherland. This Penn bought from James of York (who had held it since the fall of New Netherland), on August 24, 1682.

On the lower Delaware, near where the capital of New Sweden had been, Penn had ordered a new town laid out, in 1681, even before he himself had arrived. He had it laid out in sensible rectangular fashion, with the streets all straight and meeting at right angles. He called the town "Philadelphia," both because the name means "brotherly love" in Greek and because in the book of Revelation (3:8) the church in Philadelphia (a city in Asia Minor) was praised: "thou hast a little strength and hast kept my word, and hast not denied my name." Penn was also the first to give the river on the eastern boundary of the colony its name of Delaware River.

Penn did not attempt to establish an authoritative rule as other proprietors did, but allowed, from the beginning, for an elective assembly to participate in the making of laws. He also established humane criminal legislation and adopted a policy of religious toleration.

As a result, immigrants from everywhere flooded into the new colony. In particular, there were German members of sects with Quakerish tendencies who came in large numbers and who founded the settlement of "Germantown" to the north of Philadelphia. This was the first entry into the colonies of quantities of non–English–speaking peoples. (We can't count Dutchmen and Swedes who were in sections of the country before the English came.)

Philadelphia itself flourished, its population growing and its intellectual life expanding. The first printing press in the English colonies, outside of the New England, was established in Philadelphia, about 1690.

TROUBLE IN NEW ENGLAND

The fall of the Puritan government in England and the restoration of an Anglican monarchy promised trouble for Puritan New England.

Charles II was not of the bigoted temperament that would have found it praiseworthy to attempt to wipe out the religion of New England, even if he had been foolish enough to think it possible. Nevertheless, he felt it would be wise to do what he could to keep the Puritans from going too strong. For one thing he could divide the area into separate colonies. Mutual hostility might then keep them all weak, and they might play into royalist hands.

For that reason, Charles granted Connecticut a separate charter, on April 23, 1662, and Rhode Island one, on July 8, 1663. Then, when New Netherland became the New York, the settlement at New Haven, which, till then, had insisted on ruling itself, began to fear absorption by a New York still strongly Dutch in character. On January 5, 1665, New Haven therefore consented to union with Connecticut.

In this way, Connecticut and Rhode Island received the boundaries they were to keep ever after in their history.

If Massachusetts considered the loss of southernmost New England (to which till then they had maintained a kind of tenuous claim) to be a disaster, there was far worse to come at the hands of the Indians.

Naturally, as the colonists increased in numbers, they spread out, occupying more and more land. If they dealt with the Indians at all in this process, it was by purchasing the land for trivial sums. The Indians assumed they were selling rights to use the land, a kind of rental, with their own rights in no way diminished. They were horrified, and deeply resentful, when they found themselves driven off the land as interlopers after the sale.

Some colonists also engaged themselves in converting the Indians. The chief of these was John Eliot, who arrived in Massachusetts in 1631 and spent many years as a missionary, beginning his drive in this respect among the Indians living in what is now the town of Newton. He even produced a Bible translated into an Indian language, in 1663 — the first Bible printed in North America.

Eliot and other missionaries had considerable success. As many as 4000 of the Indians in southern New England were converted. That, however, made the majority of the Indians, still unconverted, all the more restless at the inroad of the strange ways. This was especially so since the Puritans (with the usual callousness of those too sure of their own righteousness) applied their own religious laws even to unconverted Indians, fining them for violations of a Sabbath which they did not understand.

While Massasoit still lived, there was peace. He had greeted the Pilgrims at Plymouth when they had first arrived, and he lived on for forty years more. He brought his two sons proudly to Plymouth, in order that they might receive English names. The men of Plymouth, thinking of the great warriors of ancient Macedon — and partly in derision — named the elder son Alexander and the younger Philip.

When Massasoit died in 1661, Alexander succeeded and was promptly forced to come to Plymouth and swear loyalty under what were to him humiliating conditions. He did not rule long and was succeeded by his brother, Philip ("King Philip" to the sneering settlers). Philip, flinching under the insults that he and his Indians had to endure, planned retaliation. It had to come soon, he knew, for already there were 40,000 White settlers in New England as compared to only 20,000 Indians, and the settlers were increasing in numbers each year.

Philip gradually built up a league of Indian tribes all through New England and, on June 24, 1675, launched an attack on Swansea, Rhode Island, which marked the beginning of the bloodiest and fiercest Indian war in colonial history.

It began, as Indian wars always did, with surprise attacks by the Indians and with the settlers suffering bloody losses. But, as always, the Indians had fatal weaknesses, and these showed up more clearly in "King Philip's War," as it was called, than ever before.

For one thing the Indians did not fight in the winter and did not post guards at night. Among themselves this was a general rule and did not hamper fighting. When the settlers began to make surprise attacks in the winter dawn, however, an Indian defeat was a sure thing.

Then, too, Indians never learned to build strongly fortified positions, to establish supply lines and to provide food stores. They could never maintain sieges for long, nor withstand sieges, since there was always the necessity of hunting to maintain themselves from day to day.

Though they learned to use firearms (and the New England Indians used them effectively, for the first time, in King Philip's War), they never established an industrial base, so that they could never manufacture them, but had always to depend on their enemies for guns and ammunition.

Futhermore, the Indians never combined to present the White settlers with a united front, except temporarily and then only partly. There were always individuals and tribes of Indians who would fight on the White side, though there were virtually never any Whites willing to fight on the Indian side.

In the case of King Philip's War, the Christian converts among the Indians, the so–called "Praying Indians," could be counted on by the settlers to serve them as spies and as guides.

The first attacks of the Indians in King Philip's War fell heavily on the settlers, and, by the end of 1675, most of the westernmost settlements had been destroyed. Nor could New England find help. England was far away and indifferent. The only nearby colony, New York (just restored to the English by the Dutch, after the latter's temporary takeover), was in no position to do much either. In fact, its governor, Edmund Andros, seemed more interested in using New England's troubles as an opportunity for detaching part of Connecticut and adding it to his own colony. (This failed.)

The New Englanders had to fight without help. The New England Confederation showed its usefulness now as the different colonists combined in alliance. In December 1675, they had managed to organize a counteroffensive and struck toward an Indian stronghold in a Rhode Island swamp.

A thousand settlers, led by a Praying Indian, penetrated the swamps to the base, and there, after a savage fight, on December 19 (the Battle of Great Swamp), the Indians were totally defeated. About two–thirds of them were killed. Eighty settlers were also killed and those who survived suffered severe losses during the winter that followed.

The victory in Rhode Island marked the turning point, and from then on the settlers had the upper hand and moved inexorably toward final victory. Old Roger Williams, still alive, tried for a peace that would be just to both sides, but passions had gone too far. It was war to the death.

Finally, in August 1676, the Indians had been driven back to their last stronghold. King Philip was surrounded and was killed, on August 12, by another Indian. The war was over and the Indian power in New England was broken forever.

It had cost New England much, however. One man out of sixteen, among those settlers capable of bearing arms, had been killed. Of the ninety settlements in New England, twelve had been utterly destroyed and forty others had sustained damage in varying degrees. It was nearly half a century before the colonists spread out to where they had been before the war.

And after the war, efforts to convert the Indians ceased. They were looked upon as inveterate enemies with no fate possible other than their removal and eventual extermination. (King Philip's head was displayed on a pole in Plymouth for twenty years as a reminder to Indians of the price of opposing the White man.)

Far from attempting to aid battered New England, England saw the weakened condition of the area as a good opportunity to further fragment it. On July 24, 1679, New Hampshire was given a charter and formally recognized as a separate colony. Massachusetts, which had just succeeded in buying the rights to Maine from Gorges's heirs, managed to hold on to that part of New England.

As each newly separate part of New England became anxious to hold on to its self–rule, and as the Indian menace had virtually vanished with the death of King Philip, the New England Confederation which had served the region so well in King Philip's War, was allowed to fall into abeyance. On September 5, 1684, in Hartford, the Confederation held its last meeting.

Even this was not enough for England. As long as Massachusetts continued under the charter it had received in 1630, which gave her virtually complete self–government, she was bound to be a Puritanical plague to the mother country. For one thing, Massachusetts avoided the Navigation Act and smuggled extensively, and, since the colonial government refused to take action, there was nothing to be done about it.

On October 23, 1684, therefore, England simply annulled the Massachusetts charter. The colony was made a royal domain, in which all officials were responsible to the king.

Then, on February 6, 1685, Charles II died, and his brother, James of York, became king as James II (which immediately made New York a royal colony, too).

James II was a Catholic, the first Catholic monarch to have ruled in London since the time of Mary I, a century and a quarter before. What's more, he was a narrow and tactless person who could not be made to see that by insisting on his own views too blindly, he was actually defeating them.

Naturally, James II's attitude toward Puritan Massachusetts

was even harsher than his brother's had been. Now that he ruled the area himself under the new system, there was no reason to fragment the area into separate colonies. More strength could be gained against the Indians and greater ease of administration was possible, if there could be one colony in place of many. James therefore established the Dominion of New England, which included six colonies: New Hampshire, Massachusetts, Connecticut, Rhode Island, New York, and New Jersey.

To rule the Dominion in his name, James II chose Andros, who had governed New York during King Philip's War and had made no effort to aid New England then. If the various colonies resented the loss of self–government, they resented this choice of governor even more.

The notion of a unified, large colony was a good one in many ways, and some of Andros's actions were worthwhile by present–day standards. For instance, he tried to put an end to the stiff religious intolerance in Massachusetts, insisted on allowing other forms of Protestant worship, and established an Anglican Church in Boston, on March 15, 1687.

However, Andros, like his royal master, was utterly tactless. Whatever he did was met with a sullen and stubborn resistance.

Andros set about forcing the colonies to accept his rule in a formal manner and to get them to agree to the abandonment of their earlier charters. On January 12, 1687, he forced Rhode Island into line.

Then, on October 31, 1687, he went to Hartford to demand the surrender of Connecticut's old charter which had, in any case, already been annulled. The Connecticut colonists, not recognizing the annulment, would not abandon the written record of their rights.

There was a loud and angry argument in the night, and then, suddenly, the candles were blown out. When they were lighted again, the charter, which Andros had ordered brought to the scene, had disappeared. According to tradition, the charter was hidden in the hollow of a large oak tree (afterwards known as the "Charter Oak") by a Captain William Wadsworth, there to be preserved until such time as it could be retrieved to continue to serve as the basis of the Connecticut government.

Despite this, Andros dissolved the Connecticut government, on November 1, 1687.

In 1688, however, James II was driven from the throne and, in his place, there succeeded his daughter, Mary II and her husband William III (who was also king of the Netherlands).

The news of James's downfall reached New England on April 4, 1689, and there was a joyous uprising at once. Andros was arrested, on April 18, and sent back to England (he later served as governor of Virginia and Maryland). The colonies that made up the short-lived Dominion of New England returned to their separate existences within a month of Andros's removal.

Massachusetts was granted a new charter, on October 7, 1691, and under it she absorbed the seventy–year–old colony of Plymouth. However, not everything could be as before. By the new charter, Massachusetts granted freedom of religion to all Protestant sects.

TROUBLES IN VIRGINIA

Cromwell and the Restoration did not make a quiet time for Virginia, either.

In 1642, Sir William Berkeley (the brother of the Berkeley who, twenty years later, was to be granted New Jersey by Charles II) was appointed royal governor of Virginia. He proved to be a popular governor. For one thing, he encouraged colonial manufacturing and the planting of crops other than tobacco; and, on the whole, Virginia prospered. Then, too, he took a firm stand against the Indians, crushing the 1644 uprising of Opechancano.

The English Civil War was just beginning when he became

governor, and his own strong royalist stand matched the feelings of the colony generally and helped make him popular. He was hard–fisted against Puritanism and, when Charles I was beheaded, promptly recognized his son as Charles II. Proroyalist refugees flooded into sympathetic Virginia, and that colony began to climb steeply in population for the first time since its founding a half–century before.

As Cromwell's regime continued in power, however, his weight made itself felt. Berkeley was forced into retirement, in 1652, and Puritan sympathizers managed to hold Virginia. They took over Maryland, too, in 1654, drove out the Baltimores, repealed the Toleration Act, and outlawed Catholics.

It couldn't last though, and, with Cromwell's death, things quickly began to return to normal. In 1659, Virginia anticipated the Restoration by a full year, declared Charles II king, and welcomed back Berkeley as governor. In 1662, his rule was extended over Maryland as well.

The royalist rebound included the election of a House of Burgesses, in 1661, so subservient to Berkeley that he could rule almost without consulting it. In fact, so satisfied was he with the election that for fifteen years he allowed no other.

But he was growing old, and the Cromwell era had so soured him against the interference of popular feeling in government that he actually began to value ignorance. At a time when Virginia's population had reached 45,000 (including 2000 Black slaves), Berkeley openly rejoiced, in 1671, that there were neither schools nor printing presses in the colony, since he considered both agencies for subversion.

His increasing autocracy and his growing irascibility in dealing with the people began to erode his popularity. In addition, there were economic troubles. Despite Berkeley's efforts, Virginia remained too dependent on tobacco. When enthusiastic growing produced an oversupply, and when the Navigation Act and the wars between England and the Netherland hampered trade, there came a serious depression.

Then, too, there were troubles with the Indians. Berkeley tried to protect the Indians against outright brigandage and murder and favored the establishment of a defensive system of forts against Indian attacks. The western settlers would not hear of that for it would have been expensive. They favored outright extermination of the Indians in every direction and accused Berkeley of favoring the Indians because of his own investments in the fur trade.

And now a young man named Nathaniel Bacon comes on the scene (a distant relative of Francis Bacon, the famous English statesman and philosopher).

In 1674, after a variety of family troubles in England, including involvement in some ill–chosen financial ventures, Bacon was sent off to Virginia by his father. In Virginia, Bacon had a cousin who possessed influence in the government, and Bacon's wife was a relative of the governor's wife. With such connections, the young man did well. He was appointed to the governor's council, even though he was only 28; and he was able to purchase two sizable plantations.

When one of Bacon's overseers was killed by Indians, in 1676, Bacon reacted hotly and suddenly found himself at the head of those frontiersmen who wanted to make war on the Indians. (King Philip's War was raging at this time in New England and anti–Indian feeling was higher than usual.) Unable to resist the flattery of being hailed as a leader, Bacon illegally led his armed farmers against the nearest Indians (who were friendly, peaceable, unarmed, and helpless) and, on April 20, 1676, killed a few against no resistance.

This made him a hero, and he at once called for a thorough–going reform of the government and for the election of a House of Burgesses that would take a stiffer stand against the Indians. Berkeley, furious, was forced to allow the election; and Bacon was one of those elected. When Bacon tried to take his seat, Berkeley had him arrested, but was then forced to release him.

Bacon returned upstream, gathered an armed following, and

marched on Jamestown. Berkeley departed hastily for the east coast of the colony, leaving Bacon to take Jamestown, on September 18, and to burn it the day after. For a while, Bacon controlled almost all of Virginia and prepared to institute the reforms he favored.

Unfortunately for him, he was rather too successful. To many of the Virginians and Marylanders, he began to seem a kind of Cromwell, and a movement back to Berkeley began. Then, with the tide beginning to turn against him, Bacon died of dysentery, on October 26, 1676.

By January 1677, Berkeley was in full control again, and he overreacted. He hanged twenty–three men who had been active in what is called "Bacon's Rebellion." He would have hanged more if he could have caught them. This angered Charles II, who pointed out that Berkeley had taken a sterner revenge for a passing uprising of little importance than he himself had taken for the execution of his father. Berkeley was recalled and died soon after reaching England.

Bacon's Rebellion, even though defeated, succeeded in introducing changes. Most of the reforms it had championed, designed to make the government's power less autocratic, were soon adopted.

One more thing. The burning of Jamestown was, in a way, the end for that city — the first permanent English settlement in North America. It never recovered, and, in 1692, the capital of Virginia was transferred six miles north to Williamsburg, which received its name then, in honor of William III, the king who had succeeded the deposed James II.

The next year, on February 8, 1693, the College of William and Mary, named for the king and queen, was established there. It was the second institution of higher learning to be established in the English colonies, only twenty–one years after Berkeley's expressed gratitude at the absence of schools in Virginia.

7

THE FRENCH EXPAND

BEYOND THE GREAT LAKES

During the reigns of Charles II and James II, while the English colonies were expanding along the eastern coastline, New France was likewise expanding. Led by missionaries and fur traders, however, it expanded far into the interior.

The 1650s and 1660s saw the French increasing their knowledge of, and strengthening their hold on, the Great Lakes country. Four of these lakes eventually received Indian names — Huron, Michigan, Erie, and Ontario. Lake Superior was so called because it was northernmost and therefore on maps, as usually oriented, topmost. The name is also appropriate, in the English meaning of the word, since it is the largest of the Great Lakes as well.

As early as 1634, a Frenchman had even passed beyond the

HUDSON'S BAY
COMPANY

NEW FRANCE

Quebec

Port Royal

ACADIA

Montreal

SUPERIOR

Fort
Michilimackinac

Fort Frontenac

Lake
Champlain

N.H.

Portsmouth

Green Bay

HURON

Albany

Fort
Oswego

MASS.

Boston

R.I.

ONTARIO

Fort Niagara

CONN.

Providence

Hartford

MICHIGAN

Detroit

ERIE

New York

PENN.

Philadelphia

NEW JERSEY

Cahokia

Kaskaskia

VIRGINIA

MARYLAND

Williamsburg

Albemarle Sound

New Bern

LOUISIANA
(FRENCH)

CAROLINA

Charleston

SPANISH

Natchez

Mobile

Pensacola

St. Augustine

Biloxi

New Orleans

SPANISH

English

MAP III

English, French and Spanish Possessions in 1689

Great Lakes. Jean Nicolet, a follower of Champlain, had in that year crossed Lake Huron and Lake Michigan and discovered Green Bay, the thumblike western extension of the latter lake. He then explored what is now the state of Wisconsin (where he yet felt the lingering hope he might find Chinese) and nearly reached the Mississippi River, but gave up too soon in his anxiety to rush back with his reports.

His work was followed in much greater detail by the French Jesuit missionary, Claude Jean Allouez, who, interested in converting the Indians rather than in exploration for its own sake, traveled all over the lands bordering the Great Lakes. He established a mission, in 1666, at a spot between Lakes Superior and Michigan. Another Jesuit missionary, Jacques Marquette, founded other missions on the lakes' shores, in 1668 and 1671.

In 1672, Louis de Buade, Count Frontenac, became governor of New France. He was a capable, if quarrelsome and egotistic person, and he had both imagination and drive. He was anxious to keep New France from becoming totally dominated by the Jesuits and so he wanted more than missions on the Great Lakes. In 1673, for instance, he founded Fort Frontenac at the point where Lake Ontario issues into the St. Lawrence. (For a while, Lake Ontario was known as Lake Frontenac to the French.)

Then, too, it was clear to him that, in going from the Atlantic Ocean to Lake Superior, one traveled deep into the North American interior. If the rivers reported by Nicolet to have existed a short distance beyond Lake Michigan flowed into the Pacific (and they certainly flowed westward), then there would be a water passage through the continent that necessitated only a short overland trip west of Lake Michigan. It was something worth investigating.

For the purpose, he turned to a fur trapper, Louis Joliet, who had already explored the Great Lakes thoroughly. Joliet, feeling the need of someone who knew the western Indians, asked Father Marquette to come along. In May 1673, they began their exploring journey. They followed the footsteps of Nicolet, nearly forty years before, to Green Bay, up the Fox River, then westward over land to the Wisconsin River.

Here they did not turn back but moved on down the Wisconsin River past the farthest point Nicolet had reached and, on June 17, 1673, entered the great river into which it flowed. Joliet and Marquette were the first Europeans to reach the upper portion of that great river and they gave it the Indian name of "Mississippi" (which means "great river").

They then traveled about 700 miles downstream to the point where the Arkansas River entered. They turned back, then, because they were approaching the area of Spanish influence, and they feared capture and the loss of the records of their exploration. Besides they had accomplished their task. It was plain that the waterways beyond the Great Lakes led into the Gulf of Mexico and not into the Pacific. They did not represent the passage through the continent.

One man who was still not convinced was Rene Robert Cavelier, Sieur de la Salle, a favorite of Frontenac. La Salle was an ebullient and eccentric man who was an incurable explorer. It was his dream to find a route to China, and he talked about it so much that his estate on the St. Lawrence River, eight miles upstream from Montreal, was mockingly called "La Chine" (China) by others. The city that has grown up on that site is still called Lachine today.

La Salle restlessly explored the lands south of the Great Lakes which now make up the state of Ohio. In 1677, he obtained permission to explore westward, with the right of exploiting the fur trade in any areas he opened up. La Salle followed in the footsteps of Joliet and explored the Mississippi both upstream and down.

In 1682, La Salle made his way down to the mouth of the Mississippi River, passing unharmed through the southern territory claimed by Spain. On April 9, standing on the shore of the Gulf of Mexico, he formally claimed for France all the land watered by the Mississippi and its tributaries. He named all this vast area (making up virtually all the United States between the Appalachian and Rocky Mountains) "Louisiana" in honor of Louis XIV of France.

By that time Frontenac had been relieved of his post; and La Salle found himself at odds with the new governor. He went to France where Louis XIV confirmed him as governor of Louisiana and gave permission for the founding of a settlement at the mouth of the Mississippi.

In 1684, La Salle left France on this mission. His new expedition was plagued by misfortune from the start, and La Salle, more volatile than ever, quarreled with everybody. When he finally reached the northern shores of the Gulf of Mexico, he completely missed the mouth of the Mississippi River and landed on the shores of Texas to the west. He tried to make his way eastward and was assassinated by his own men, on May 19, 1687.

Nevertheless, Louisiana remained French.

And so, as the 1600s approached their final decade, anyone looking at the map of North America might have felt the English hold on the coast was still precarious, for the vast stretches of the continent were still held by other powers.

Spain was still entrenched in Mexico and in Florida and laid claim to much of what is now the southwestern United States. In the west, in fact, where there was little competition from other European powers, it was even still acting with vigor. Thus, when the Pueblo Indians revolted, in 1680, and forced the Spaniards to evacuate Sante Fe, the latter fought on grimly till the Pueblos were defeated and Santa Fe retaken, in 1692.

Meanwhile, the Spanish survivors of the Pueblo revolt had built El Paso on the Rio Grande, and, after La Salle's futile attempt to colonize the Gulf Coast, the Spaniards spread further into Texas to preempt repetitions. And as the 1600s closed, the Spaniards were probing northward up the California coast and were beginning to establish settlements there.

Spain's ventures in the far west were of no concern to the English colonies, however. It was France, with holdings much nearer and with a program much more vigorous, that concerned them.

France controlled all of what is now southeastern Canada from the Great Lakes to the sea and now was claiming all the vast interior of the continent beyond the Appalachians. This enormous French area was under a unified administration and was under the close control of the home country. It hemmed in the English colonies and confined them to the occupation of what seemed a precarious coastline. What's more, these English colonies were many in number, each separate in its government and out of sympathy one with another; all brawling, internally, among themselves, and with the home government.

It might have seemed to anyone looking at the map that France must eventually extend its enormous holding over the inconsiderable shoreline and wipe out English America as English America had wiped out Dutch America and as Dutch America had wiped out Swedish America.

Against this possibility was the fact that New France, for all its vast extent, had a population of only about 12,000, while the English colonies, as the 1600s closed, were home for nearly a quarter of a million men who were growing in numbers and in prosperity and in the determination to continue growing each year.

Both sides knew that the French and English could not continue to expand for long without coming to blows. Indeed, there had been fighting already.

One site of such conflict was the large peninsula, lying between Newfoundland and New England. Both Newfoundland and New England had been considered by the English to lie in their sphere of influence, and they naturally assumed that the peninsula between was also theirs and wiped out early French settlements there in 1613.

Then, in 1621, James I granted the right to colonize the peninsula to Sir William Alexander, a Scottish poet who was serving as tutor to the royal children. Alexander called the peninsula "Nova Scotia" (Latin for "New Scotland") which was rather appropriate since it lies north of New England as Scotland lies north of England.

There were further French settlements in Nova Scotia (which was "Acadia" to the French), and the peninsula was dragged this way and that between the two powers. In 1667, the Treaty of Breda, which allotted New Netherland to England and made it New York by international agreement, allotted Nova Scotia to France, and it was officially Acadia.

Fighting also took place in the far north. England was aware of the danger represented by the outflanking of its holdings on the north and west by the French. With the thought of outflanking the French in their turn, the English established the Hudson's Bay Company, on May 2, 1670. The English lay claim to Hudson Bay through its discovery by Hudson, in 1610, and the company was intended to establish posts on the shores of that frigid body of water. Not only would these serve as a check on the French, it was hoped, but there would be profits through the fur trade and, who knows, even the chance of a route to Asia.

The French reacted strongly to the founding of English posts along the shores of Hudson Bay and took several of them, in 1686. For several decades, the English claim to the area was more theoretical than real.

The conflicts prior to 1689, however, had been desultory and localized and never very much the concern of the home governments. In 1689, however, events took a crucial turn. England and France began a series of wars that were to stretch out over a century and a quarter, and each war was fought out, in part, on the American continent.

The English colonies found each successive war to be less a local matter and more a part of a distant continental war. To see how this came about, we must return to Europe.

KING WILLIAM'S WAR

In France, Louis XIV had succeeded to the throne at the age of five, in 1643, when his father, Louis XIII, died. For nearly twenty years, France was governed by the shrewd Cardinal Mazarin, who saw to it that France gained by the end of the Thirty Years' War and by the treaty of peace with Spain, in 1659.

By the time of Mazarin's death in 1661, France was the strongest nation in Europe. Louis XIV, now twenty–three years old, took over personal direction of the government and at once initiated a program of territorial expansion, particularly in the direction of the Netherlands. The Netherlands, deeply disturbed, recognized that France had replaced Spain as the great expansionist power of Europe and became the focal point of anti–French resistance.

Between 1672 and 1678, there was war between France and the Netherlands — an unequal one, since France was much the stronger power. Netherlands preserved its independence, but was badly shaken by French victories. This, combined with its naval losses in the wars against England, removed the Netherlands from the rank of the Great Powers, a position it had held through much of the seventeenth century.

During this early period of Louis XIV's expansionist career, England remained generally neutral. Charles II was anxious to keep the peace and was out of sympathy with any but the mildest Protestantism so that he did not hasten to the relief of the Protestant Dutch. In fact, he depended on Louis XIV for a personal (and secret) subsidy which supplied him with funds and made it unnecessary for him to appeal to Parliament. He was therefore actually willing to side with France against the Netherlands, especially since England had been fighting the Nether-lands, too.

English public opinion, however, was slowly drawn into an anti–French position. The turning point came when Louis XIV, driven by religious bigotry, committed a crucial error. On October 18, 1685, he put an end to all toleration of Protestants in France; the French Huguenots were forced, by quite inhuman treatment, either to convert or flee the country. Nor would Louis allow them to enter New France or Louisiana.

The result was that Frenchmen by the hundreds of thousands left France, depriving their native country of their talents and industry, and bestowing those same talents and industry upon the enemies of France (England, Prussia, and other Protestant nations) to which Louis's action had forced them to flee.

Many came to the English colonies. Some went to the south-ern portion of Carolina, a traditional haven for them since Coligny's time a century and a quarter before. There, they added to the aristocratic tone of the colony, with their cultured French ways. In 1688, a party of Huguenots settled in West-chester County, New York, and founded the town of New Rochelle, which was named for the one–time Huguenot strong-hold of La Rochelle, from which many of the refugees had come.

Wherever the Huguenots came, they added elements of strength to the colonies — and brought in their own anti–French sentiment, too.

The effect of Louis XIV's repressive act on public opinion in Protestant England was enormous. When, that same year, Catholic James II became King of England, many English Prot-estants regarded him with horror, since they expected him (once he was strong enough) to follow in the steps of Louis.

These fears helped lead to the uprising in 1688, in which James II was driven from the throne. Parliament placed the crown on the head of his Protestant daughter, Mary II, and her husband, William III. William had been ruling the Nether-

lands (and was William III by Dutch numbering as well) and
had been the very heart and soul of the struggle against Louis
XIV.

William intended to continue fighting Louis from his new
position, and the French king knew that now England could be
counted on to maintain a firm anti–French stand. He felt he
had no choice but to support James II (who had fled to France)
and to attempt to place him on the throne. In 1689, then,
France and England went to war.

Several years before, in 1686, William had completed the
gathering of a league of allies pledged to resist Louis XIV
when he next went to war. The final terms of the alliance were
settled at the city of Augsburg in Bavaria, so the grouping was
called the "League of Augsburg."

When William became King of England, that nation became
part of the League. The war that followed, between all the
League on one side and France on the other, is usually known
as the "War of the League of Augsburg," or, sometimes, the
"War of the Grand Alliance."

William, intent as he was on fighting the hated Louis, with
every weapon at his command, had no intention of allowing the
North American colonies to remain neutral. He knew well that
the English colonies outnumbered New France in population
by 15 to 1; that England and the Netherlands held naval superiority which could be crucial in a war fought across the ocean;
and that the allies had the superiority in industrial and financial
strength which could support distant warfare.

Unfortunately for the English, though, there were disadvantages on their side as well. For one thing, the English colonies
were disunited, and the southern colonies, who were far from
any Frenchmen, saw no reason to take part. Only the northernmost colonies were involved.

Then, too, the French, though few in number, had strategi-
cally placed forts and few large centers of population at which
the English could strike. The French colonists were familiar

with trackless forests, and were on good terms with the Indians. What's more, the French government directly supported its colonists, while the English government, under the pressure of fighting Louis's army (the best in the world at the time) in Europe, left their colonies to themselves, so that the Anglo–Dutch superiority in naval and economic strength went for nothing.

Characteristic of this war (which was known as "King William's War" in the colonies, since it came hard upon the news of William's accession to the throne) and of those that followed was the role of the Indians. The French did most of their fighting with the help of their Indian allies so that the series of wars that began in 1689 are sometimes lumped together as the "French and Indian Wars."

As the story is told from the side of the English colonists, the French are blamed for the conflicts and are described as allowing their Indian allies to commit atrocities against fellow Whites.

The French might argue that given their inferiority in numbers they could do nothing else. They might also point out that the first to use Indians to attack white enemies were not the French, but the Dutch.

In the 1640s, the Dutch had taken advantage of Iroquois hostility toward the French, by arming them with guns and sending them northward. For ten years, the Iroquois made life hell from the French colonials, raiding as far as Montreal and killing Indians whom French missionaries had converted. The raids ended in 1652 by a treaty which left the Iroquois clear victors.

When the English took over New Netherland, they, too, encouraged the Iroquois to fight against the French, though under the vigorous rule of Frontenac, New France, through a mixture of force and diplomacy, managed to hold them off.

Were it not for the Iroquois, there is no telling how strong New France might have grown or how poorly the English colonies might have managed against French–led Indians. Hence the importance of those musket volleys fired by Champlain and his men on that fateful day in 1609.

Then, once King William's War started, the onus of supporting Indians attacks on the opposition fell first on the English colonists. With the support of New York's governor, Thomas Dongan, the Iroquois had been raiding the Great Lakes country and playing havoc with the French fur trade. On August 4, 1689, about ten weeks after King William's War began, the Iroquois struck northward directly at New France, wiping out the settlement of Lachine, slaughtering 200, taking 90 prisoners, and devastating the countryside about.

It is not suprising that the French felt justified in replying in kind.

To handle the crisis, Louis XIV restored Frontenac to his post as governor. Frontenac was now nearly seventy, but he made his energy felt at once. He organized an invasion of New York in reprisal. The expedition set out, in mid–January 1690, and moved silently over the snow on snowshoes. They were planning an attack on Albany as the first step in the conquest of New York, but the weather turned very bad and when they came in sight of Schenectady, on the night of February 8, 1690 (in the middle of a blizzard), they knew they could go no farther.

The Dutch settlers in Schenectady were sleeping quietly. They had refused to believe Indians would attack in mid–winter. So amused were they at talk of the possibility that they left the settlement gate open and placed two snowmen there as sentries. It was a terrible mistake.

The Indians entered the sleeping town and burst into the houses with triumphant cries, slaughtering indiscriminately. Schenectady was completely wiped out and the invaders then retreated rapidly, pursued by Iroquois.

Other frontier towns were similarly victimized by Frontenac's forces. A settlement on the site of what is now Portland, Maine, surrendered to a French attack on July 31, 1690, on the promise

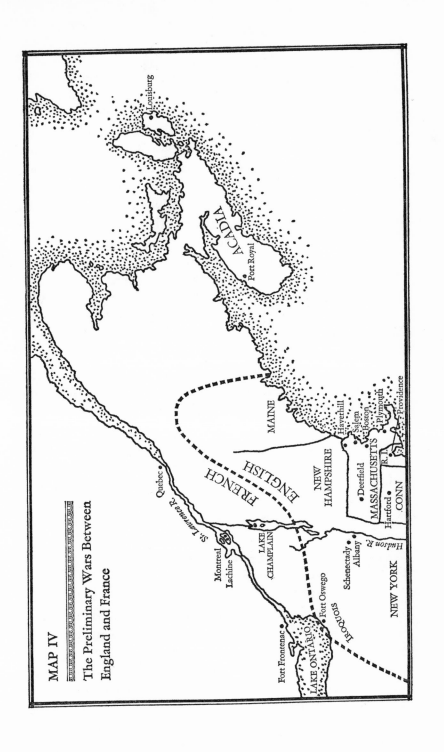

MAP IV

The Preliminary Wars Between
England and France

Louisburg

ACADIA

Port Royal

St. Lawrence R.

Quebec

Montreal
Lachine

LAKE
CHAMPLAIN

FRENCH

ENGLISH

MAINE

NEW
HAMPSHIRE

Haverhill
Salem
Boston
Plymouth
Providence

Deerfield

MASSACHUSETTS
Hartford
CONN
R.

Fort Frontenac

LAKE ONTARIO

Fort Oswego

IROQUOIS

Schenectady
Albany

Hudson R.

NEW YORK

that their lives would be spared. After they had been taken, the
Indians killed them all anyway. (The French were blamed for
such incidents, but they argued that their Indian allies were
sometimes too numerous to be resisted; and too full of hate for
the English to be held back. Had the prisoners been refused
them, they would taken taken them by force, killed them, and
killed the French as well.)

The English colonies found themselves face to face with a
terrible crisis, and New York, the one that was most nearly on
the firing line, was least prepared to meet that crisis.

In 1688, it had come under the rule of Francis Nicholson,
who served as lieutenant–governor under Andros — for New
York was then part of the Dominion of New England. When
news of the ouster of James II and the fall of Andros reached
New York, Nicholson demanded Andros's restoration and refused to proclaim William and Mary.

There was a popular uprising against him, therefore, beginning on June 1, 1689, led by a German–born merchant, Jacob
Leisler, who was a devout Protestant and who strongly opposed
the Catholic James II and his allies. Leisler eventually seized
the strong points of the city and, on December 1, 1689, proclaimed himself governor, while Nicholson fled to England.

Once in power, Leisler instituted some reforms, but then
came the Schenectady massacre and, with the colony in dis-
array, Leisler found himself facing the French and Indian menace. On May 1, 1690, he called for a meeting of representatives
of the various English colonies to concert united action against
the enemy and to provide for a common defense.

The call was not answered by most colonies. Only Massachusetts, Plymouth, Connecticut, and (for a wonder) distant Maryland responded, and in the end nothing much could be done.
It was, however, a notable event, for it was the first call, from
within the colonies, for colonial unity against a common enemy.

Leisler did not last long. He was unpopular with the colonial
leaders in New York, and he did not know how to ingratiate

himself with the people. King William was properly grateful for Leisler's efforts on his behalf against Nicholson, but he appointed someone else as governor. Leisler tried to resist the landing of the new governor, was taken, and, on May 16, 1691, was executed.

"Leisler's Rebellion," like Bacon's Rebellion in Virginia fifteen years before, had failed; but again it pointed up the dangers of too much heavy–handed autocracy on the part of those who ruled.

It was left to Massachusetts to strike back against the French. It was the most populous and strongest colony in the north, and it was fresh from its successful overthrow of Andros. To its northeast, 270 miles away, was Acadia, the most exposed portion of the French dominions and the logical target for attack by sea.

In May 1690, a flotilla of fourteen vessels were placed under the command of Sir William Phips. He had been born, in 1651, in Maine and was said to have been one of 26 children by the same mother. He had kept sheep till he was eighteen; but, when he was grown, he came to Boston, married a rich widow, and became a substantial citizen.

In 1687, he had commanded an expedition to the waters off Hispaniola and there had supervised the recovery of a sunken ship carrying 300,000 pounds of Spanish treasure. For this he was knighted — the first colonial to be so honored.

Between this and the fact that he had been an active opponent of Andros, he seemed a natural for the post of commander of the fleet. Off it sailed for Port Royal, the capital of Acadia. It arrived at that town, on May 11, 1690; and the French governor was bluffed into surrendering. The Massachusetts seamen were able to do a little looting and returned home as conquering heroes.

The success naturally lured Massachusetts into attempting something greater still. A fleet of 34 ships and 2000 men were placed under Phips and sent off to capture Quebec itself. The expedition left in August, but contrary winds delayed it and it did not reach Quebec until October 7, 1690. By that time, Frontenac had received news of what was happening and had had time to fortify and reinforce the city.

Phips felt he had to do something so he tried a frontal assault which was, of course, smashed. He had to return empty-handed; worse than empty-handed, in fact, for the men and supplies involved in the expedition had to be paid for and the Massachusetts treasury was empty. The colony was forced to print paper money with which to pay its debts. It was the first issuance of paper money in the English colonies.

Still Massachusetts passed through a glorious period. The new charter, of 1691, not only added Plymouth to the colony and confirmed its possession of Maine, but conquered Nova Scotia was made part of the colony as well, a direct tribute to its great battle feat at Port Royal. This produced the first case of the political promotion of a war hero, too, for Phips became governor of Massachusetts, in 1692.

The war continued for seven years more, mostly in the form of sporadic raiding on one side or the other. The English made progress in the Hudson Bay area, but the attack on Port Royal, trivial though it was, was the big event of the war, as far as North America was concerned.

On September 10, 1697, the war came to an end with the Treaty of Ryswick (so called from the Dutch town where it was signed). Louis XIV and William III, rather indifferent to events in North America, simply agreed to restore the situation in that continent to exactly what it had been when the whole thing had started.

In particular, Nova Scotia became Acadia again, and indignant New Englanders had an object lesson in how little England cared for them. Not only had they received no help in the war, but what they had won by themselves was given back without even the courtesy of consultation. On the whole, though, any anti–English feeling generated was far outweighed by the anti–French feeling produced by the Indian raids and massacres.

WITCHES!

During the course of King William's War, something had taken place in New England which had nothing to do with the war and which has loomed larger in the minds of Americans since than virtually anything else in colonial history. It involved the matter of witchcraft.

Witches were thought to be individuals in league with the devil and the forces of darkness. With the help of evil spirits and by means of magical arts, they could wreak harm on their enemies and do mischief to humanity in general.

The ancient Hebrews believed in the power of such "black magic" and passed laws against it and against those who practiced it. The Bible has, as one of its verses, a line which is translated into English as follows: "Thou shalt not suffer a witch to live" (Exodus 22:18).

This made it seem necessary to believe in the existence of witches and in the necessity for extreme punishment for witchcraft.

Protestants, who paid more attention to the literal words of the Bible than did the Catholics, were rather more apt to fear witches and find them everywhere. After the Protestant Reformation, a kind of witchcraft mania swept over Europe. Some estimates place the number of people killed in Europe between the years 1500 and 1800, on the pretext of their being witches, as high as two million. In the 1600s, perhaps 40,000 people were executed for witchcraft in England alone.

The English colonies were not exempt. Every colony recognized witchcraft as a crime and provided harsh punishments therefor, and it is not surprising that New England was most harsh. Religious intolerance was extreme in New England in the first century of its existence. In 1644, Massachusetts had ordered all Baptists banished from the colony. In 1656, it had begun to banish or imprison Quakers (who were the next year banished even from the ordinarily tolerant New Netherland) and eventually hung a few of them. Should the self–righteous Puritans not be even sterner with such wicked monsters as witches?

In 1647, a woman was convicted of witchcraft in Hartford, Connecticut, and hanged — the first such execution in the colonies. The next year a witch was hanged in Massachusetts, and, by 1662, fourteen of them had been hanged in those two colonies.

The fear of witchcraft intensified in the 1680s. First there had been King Philip's War and then the rule of Andros. Why should God be punishing the godly men of Massachusetts? Could they be suffering through the evil machinations of witches? Were they being punished for their own sins of omission in not combating witches hard enough?

Tales of witches spread. The most celebrated of all colonial Puritans, the Congregationalist minister, Cotton Mather, considered himself an expert on the subject and his book, *Memorable Providence Relating to Witchcraft and Possessions*, published in 1689, filled all its readers with foreboding on the matter of witches and their dangers and gave them plenty of material for morbid speculation.

In 1692, a group of silly teen–age girls in the town of Salem, fearing punishment for some prank or other, pretended to be possessed and under the influence of witchcraft. They were believed, of course, since everyone knew that the power of witchcraft was everywhere. They accused a family slave as the witch, and in that they were believed, too. After all, the slave was half–Indian and half–Black, each half being powerful evidence against her in itself. She was from the West Indies and had amused the children with tales of voodoo — more dark evidence.

The slave, being a slave, was questioned with a whip. To stop the flogging, she admitted witchcraft and named two other women as her confederates. In a trial involving a two–penny theft, she would not have been believed though she had sworn on a Bible; in a case of witchcraft, however, she was believed at once. The two supposed confederates were drawn into the net, and they, of course, named others.

Governor Phips of Massachusetts set up special courts to look into the matter; and, within half a year, thirteen women and six men were hanged for witchcraft (they were *not* burned), and one eighty–year–old man was crushed to death for refusing to plead at all. (By refusing to plead he kept his property from confiscation and saved it for his children.)

What could possibly stop the mania? The circle of guilt had to spread and grow ever wider since each accused person was considered guilty by virtue of the accusation, and since, under torture, each accused others, who were promptly considered guilty — with the trials merely confirming the prejudice with a show of legality. Moreover, those who tried to point out the illegality, cruelty, and downright madness of the procedure were sure to be assumed to be in league with the devil himself.

But there were no automatic safeguards to protect the leaders of the community. When some of the accused began to name prominent members of the church and the government, the mania had to break. The machinery of the witch hunt worked best when it was brought against only the poor, the old, and the helpless.

Governor Phips's wife was mentioned, and then those few voices which had been raised in opposition to the madness were suddenly multiplied. When the turnabout came, one hundred fifty people were in prison awaiting trial. They were released, and all who were involved in the matter stood there ashamed, well aware they had been judicial murderers.

This horrible affair brought a virtual end to official concern about witchcraft in the colonies. Considering what had gone on in Europe in such matters, one might be tempted to say that the colonies had learned their lesson cheaply.

Furthermore, the witchcraft fiasco badly damaged the reputation of Cotton Mather and other clergymen of his stern and rockbound persuasion. Never again was New England to be quite so hag–ridden by its ministers.

A much more dangerous problem than that of witchcraft was beginning to make itself felt, however. The developing colonies, particularly in the south, became more and more dependent on slave labor. In 1661, Virginia recognized slavery as a legal institution.

Black slavery was particularly pernicious since the slaves were so different in appearance from their White masters that it was easy to suppose slavery was a natural condition for them. And once slavery was associated firmly with Blackness, it became difficult to free them and then treat them as freemen. After all, they were still Black. The excuse that Blacks were enslaved because they were heathens and that in slavery they would learn to be Christian and save their souls (so that slavery was for their infinite good) came to seem a poor one, when Virginia passed a law, on September 23, 1667, that a Black slave remained a slave even if he became a Christian.

In the north, however, where slavery had a weaker economic base, voices were being raised against it. On May 18, 1652, Rhode Island (in line with the traditions of Roger Williams) passed a law forbidding slavery, the first such law in North America. And, in April 1688, the Quakers of Germantown, Pennsylvania, issued a protest against slavery, the first antislavery document in North America.

The differences over slavery were as yet small, and no one

could foresee that the time would come when it would all but destroy a great nation. What men could foresee in those closing years of the 1600s was that trouble was brewing once again between England and France in Europe, and surely that would mean trouble in North America as well.

QUEEN ANNE'S WAR

Even as the Treaty of Ryswick was signed and King William's War came to an end, Europe was preparing for a new war. The different governments even knew what the cause of that war would be.

In Spain, the king, Charles II, was dying, and he had no heirs. In fact, he was such a sick man that all of Europe wondered what kept him alive so long; from month to month, the news of his death was expected.

Spain was no longer a great power, but it still had an enormous empire and the question was: Who would inherit Spain and its empire? If the inheritance fell to some minor princeling, to someone who would have as his realm Spain and its empire only, then well and good. Spain would be no stronger than before and no one would be threatened. If, on the other hand, Spain were to become the property of some vigorous monarch who was already king of a powerful nation, the combination might threaten all of Europe.

The most powerful nation in Europe was France, and, as it happened, the ambitious Louis XIV had a good claim on Spain for his wife was a half–sister of Charles II of Spain and his mother was an aunt of that monarch. There were some German princes with claims as good or better, however, and most of the adversaries of Louis XIV were anxious to have a certain Bavarian prince become the next king of Spain since he had the least power of any of the claimants.

Unfortunately, whereas Charles II lingered on alive, the Bavarian prince died, in 1699. That increased the chance that Louis XIV would manage to put Spain under the control of one of his family. The rest of Europe grew frenzied indeed.

As a matter of fact, Louis XIV had succeeded in maneuvering the dying Charles II into writing a will which left the succession to Louis's grandson, Philip. On November 1, 1700, Charles II finally died and Louis XIV promptly sent his grandson to Spain and recognized him as Philip V. Louis XIV promised that the governments of Spain and France would remain always separate, and that Spain would remain completely independent; but, of course, no one believed him.

William III was still king of England (his wife, Mary II, had died in 1694), and he certainly didn't believe his old enemy. He organized another alliance, including the Netherlands and the Empire, and war began again.

This "War of the Spanish Succession" began with a declaration of war by England and its allies, on May 4, 1702, but William did not live to see his preparations completed and the war actually begun. He had died two months before, on March 8. He had no children and was succeeded by his dead wife's younger sister, Anne; so in the colonies the new war with France was called "Queen Anne's War."

This new war had a new element of danger in itself as far as the colonies were concerned. Spain and France were both under the Bourbon family and were fighting in alliance. This meant that the English colonies had to face the enmity not only of the French in the north, but of the Spanish in the south. The southern colonies could not remain neutral in this war as they had in the previous one.

The first move came in the south, in fact, and it was the English colonials who took the offensive. James Moore, who was governor of Carolina, led an expedition of colonials and Indians against St. Augustine, the capital of Spanish Florida, in 1702. The town was reached and sacked in September, but the

Spanish garrison retreated into the fort where it held out stubbornly. The arrival of Spanish ships forced Moore to abandon his supplies and beat a hasty retreat back to Carolina. The accomplishments had been meager and the expense great. Carolina, like Massachusetts before her, had to issue paper money to cover her debts.

After that Carolina refused to do much as a colony; but Moore conducted additional raids, on his own, into the interior, making a profit by plundering Spanish missions and selling captured Indians as slaves. The Spaniards tried to retaliate by assaulting Charleston, in 1706, but that failed.

That is about all that happened in the south during Queen Anne's War.

In the north there was a repetition of the events of King William's War. The governor of New France, Marquis de Vaudreuil, labored to keep the Iroquois neutral and avoided raids into New York, which, thus, was spared the disasters of the previous decade. That merely shifted the pressure to New England, however.

On February 29, 1704, an Indian raiding party, led by Frenchmen, fell upon Deerfield in northwestern Massachusetts. The story of Schenectady, fourteen years before, was repeated. Fifty people were killed and a hundred carried away captive.

Again, the only way of striking back seemed to be by sea against French Acadia. The memory of the successful venture against Port Royal in the previous war lured Massachusetts on to try again.

In 1704, seven hundred men, mostly from that colony, sailed northward. This time Port Royal would not be bluffed into surrender and, after scavenging on the outskirts, the expedition returned with nothing of any value accomplished. A larger expedition, in 1707, accomplished just as little. In fact, the French took the offensive on their own and occupied some struggling English settlements that had finally been established in Newfoundland.

The colonials sank into frustration. Not only was England doing nothing to help, but there was considerable evidence that some of the well–to–do men in Massachusetts and the other colonies were making money out of trading with the French and were not anxious to prosecute the war vigorously.

And the Indian raids continued. On August 29, 1708, Haverhill, only 35 miles north of Boston, underwent an indiscriminate massacre in which 48 men, women, and children were killed.

Somehow, England had to be made to come to the rescue. She was winning great victories over France in Europe and surely she could spare a few ships and troops for her hard–pressed colonies.

It was Francis Nicholson who proved to be the man of the hour. He was the lieutenant–governor who had been driven out of New York at the time of Leisler's Rebellion twenty years before, but since then he had governed Virginia and Maryland. His last term in Virginia ended in 1705, and he was ready for some other action.

He burned to lead an overland attack on Canada, but for that he needed trained soldiers from England and though these had been promised, they did not arrive. He went to London in order to persuade the government to keep its promise. Along with him came a Major Peter Schuyler of Albany, New York, who brought along as part of his entourage five Iroquois warriors. The Iroquois took London by storm, and probably did more than anything else to shift English public opinion into a procolonial attitude. The English government, rather reluctantly, was forced to send troops.

Four thousand men arrived in New England, in July 1710, and, in September, Nicholson led them northward. On September 24, the flotilla lay off Port Royal and this time a serious siege was begun and the cannon began to fire into the port. Port Royal held out as long as it could, but it could not withstand a serious bombardment, and, on October 16, it surrendered.

This time the surrender was for good. The English renamed

the town "Annapolis Royal," in honor of Queen Anne, and it retains that name to this day.

As in the previous war, victory in Acadia produced visions of something greater still. Nicholson still wanted to lead a land expedition against Quebec but could only hope to succeed in this if a naval expedition was sent up the St. Lawrence River at the same time. The English government, pleased with the victory over Port Royal, was willing to provide the wherewithal.

In 1711, nearly seventy ships arrived in Boston with over five thousand fighting men aboard. Unfortunately, the officer in charge was General John ("Jolly Jack") Hill, whose only qualification for the post was that he was the brother of a woman who was a great friend of Queen Anne's. Admiral Sir Hovendon Walker, who was in charge of the ships, was equally incompetent.

They finally sailed off for the St. Lawrence and entered it, but got lost and managed to go aground during a fog. Ten ships were wrecked and seven hundred lives lost. After that, Hill and Walker gave up, decided they could never find Quebec, and blundered their way back to Boston. Nicholson, who had been waiting at Lake Champlain with his land force, was forced to turn back at the news of the fiasco.

The colonies did not have very long to brood over this failure. The war was rapidly coming to an end, and, on April 11, 1713, peace came with the Treaty of Utrecht (again signed in a Dutch town).

On the whole, France maintained itself pretty well in Europe although it had sustained some terrific defeats. Louis XIV's grandson remained king of Spain, but Louis had to give stiff guarantees to the effect that Spain would remain forever independent. He also had to agree to accept the Protestant monarchs of England and to recognize no longer the claim of James II's Catholic son to the English throne. From Spain, England took Gibraltar which it has kept ever since.

In North America, France lost less than it might if the Quebec expedition had not been so disastrously mishandled. Even so, it had to recognize the Hudson's Bay Company and agree to its right to handle the fur trade along the shores of the northern bay. It also had to recognize Newfoundland as English territory. Most important of all, France ceded Acadia to England and the peninsula became Nova Scotia once and for all, with Nicholson as its first governor.

8

THE STAKES ARE RAISED

FRANCE AND RUSSIA

The Treaty of Utrecht did not by any means settle the situation in North America or introduce a stable division of the spoils between England and France. For one thing, no clear boundaries were set anywhere. The continent simply wasn't known well enough to make such boundaries possible. There remained plenty of room for disputes and plenty of ground for new clashes.

Moreover, it was plain that France did not intend to accept her losses in Queen Anne's War permanently, but would make preparations for another struggle in which, perhaps, there might come a more fortunate result.

Immediately to the northeast of Nova Scotia, for instance, separated by so narrow a strait as to be virtually part of the mainland, is Cape Breton Island. That remained French when

Nova Scotia was lost to her. As soon as the Treaty of Utrecht was signed, France began to build a fortified post on the easternmost point of Cape Breton Island, naming it Louisbourg, after the aged Louis XIV (who was to die, in 1715, two and a half years after the end of the war, after having reigned for seventy–two years). Louisbourg was made steadily stronger, and it was clear that the French intended to have it dominate the mouth of the St. Lawrence in order to make impossible any further expeditions up the river to Quebec. Furthermore, it could serve as a base for raids southward against Nova Scotia and New England.

Nor was the fortified post at Louisbourg the only way in which the French were raising the stakes. All through Queen Anne's War they had been steadily extending their grip on the continental interior and turning La Salle's vision into reality.

The beginning of this task fell to Pierre le Moyne, Sieur d'Iberville, who had been active in King William's War. It was he, in fact, who had led the party that sacked Schenectady, in 1690. After the war was over, he and his brother, Jean Baptiste le Moyne, Sieur de Bienville, were placed in charge of the development of the lower Mississippi.

In 1698, they explored the delta of the Mississippi; and then, in 1699, they founded the first French settlement on the Gulf Coast, about 70 miles west of the river, near the present town of Biloxi. Iberville died in 1706 but his brother carried on.

In 1710, Mobile was founded, 50 miles farther west still; and then, in 1716, Natchez was established, 300 miles upstream on the Mississippi River. Finally, New Orleans was founded, in 1718, about 75 miles from the river's mouth. It flourished, and, by 1722, was made the capital of all of vast Louisiana.

The French hold on the upper Mississippi and in the Great Lakes region was also strengthened. At Detroit, between Lake Huron and Lake Erie, a settlement was established, in 1701, by Antoine de la Mothe Cadillac. In rapid succession Kaskaskia and Cahokia were established in what is now Illinois, and (in 1705) Vincennes, in what is now Indiana. Indeed, a whole chain of forts was established over the stretch from the Great Lakes to the Gulf.

All this the French did without serious European challenge. The Spaniards were distressed. In 1698, as soon as D'Iberville's expedition had begun nosing about the Delta, the Spaniards established a settlement at Pensacola on the Gulf Coast, in an attempt to block the French from expansion toward Florida. In 1718, they established San Antonio in Texas, to block them from expansion toward Mexico. The southeastern Indians prevented the French from moving too far east of the lower Mississippi.

However, Spanish strength in Florida was destroyed by the Carolinian raids during Queen Anne's War, and the Indians were weakened by their wars with the English colonists.

On the whole, the French expanded steadily so that, after Queen Anne's War, while England gained the frozen shores of Hudson Bay and the peninsula of Nova Scotia, France consolidated its grip on more than one million square miles of the interior, an area of incalculable potential strength and wealth. The stakes had been raised indeed.

And even as this was happening another nation was entering the race for land in North America, but in a totally different area.

In the two centuries following Columbus's voyages, the coast line of the Americas had been explored and mapped on the east all the way from Hudson Bay in the extreme north to the tip of South America in the extreme south. On the west, the exploration had traced out the shore line from the tip of South America northward to beyond the California coast.

Whatever large areas of uncertainty remained about the vast interior of the two continents, only in the northwest of North America was the coastline yet unknown. It was through that northwestern corner that the first human beings entered the Americas many thousands of years before, and, by the same route, a European nation was now coming.

The European nation was Russia.

The Russians lived on the large eastern plain of Europe, between the Baltic and the Black Sea. In the thirteenth century, they fell under the domination of the Mongols or Tatars, and it was not for a century and a half that portions of Russia began to break free.

In 1380, the ruler of the region about the city of Moscow (a region called Muscovy in the west) defeated the Tatar rulers in battle. Although that did not end the Tatar domination, it did make Muscovy the leader of Russian national feeling. Under a succession of strong rulers, Muscovy expanded. In 1478, Ivan III annexed the large, nearly empty sections of forested land to the north, and one could speak of Russia, rather than Muscovy. Then, in 1552, his grandson, Ivan IV inflicted a final defeat on the Tatars and annexed a large area in the east down to the Caspian Sea.

During the reign of Ivan IV, Russian fur traders, on their own and without governmental backing, had penetrated eastward beyond the area controlled by Russian forces. Farther and farther they went, with Russian governmental control laboring in their wake. In 1581, they crossed the Urals and plunged deep into the trackless forests of Siberia. By 1640, Russian adventurers stood on the shores of the Pacific Ocean well to the north of China.

With the ocean barring their way, they began to push south toward warmer lands, and that meant an inevitable clash with China. The Russians, 6000 miles from the center of their power, could not face up to the Chinese, and, in 1689, they had to sign the Treaty of Nerchinsk that set firm limits to their southern advance.

By then, though, Russia had met its destiny. In 1682, a ten-year-old boy came to the throne as Peter I. He grew into a remarkable seven–foot giant who was half–monster, half–prodigy. Under him, Russia was brought into the mainstream of European history. Peter did his best to introduce western techniques into a torpid, inert Russia by the sheer overwhelming force of his own drive. He managed, in 1709 (while Queen Anne's War was being fought out in North America), to defeat Charles XII, the half–mad, half–military–genius king of Sweden, and to fight the Turks to a standstill farther south.

Secure in the west, Peter's eyes turned toward the Far East. He was still not in any position to challenge Chinese strength and was blocked to the south in his vast Siberian dominion. But all the more reason, then, for Russia to move in other directions — eastward and still farther eastward.

In 1724, Peter I appointed Vitus Jonassen Bering, a Danish mariner in Russian service, as head of an expedition to the Siberian far east, intended to determine whether there was a land connection with North America.

Peter died the next year, but Bering carried on with the support of Peter's widow, who now ruled as Catherine I. In Kamchatka, a large peninsula jutting southward off far eastern Siberia, he built ships and began a sea exploration that ended with his discovery in 1728 that Siberia did indeed come to an end and that it was separated by water from North America.

That oceanic separation, now called Bering Strait in his honor, is not wide, however, and did not represent much of a barrier to an advance into the neighboring continent.

Bering went on to explore the arm of the sea south of the strait (Bering Sea it is now called) and, in 1741, discovered the chain of islands bounding it on the south — an arc of islands running from Siberia to North America which are now called the Aleutian Islands. In this final expedition of 1741, he also sighted the southern coast of what is now known as Alaska.

Soon after, Bering died of exposure; but his discoveries laid the foundation for a Russian claim to the northwestern corner of North America.

GREAT BRITAIN

The dawn of the new century saw important changes in the English colonies as well. Indeed, they ceased being English colonies because England ceased to be England.

For a century, since James I had ascended the English throne in 1603, England and Scotland had been ruled by the same king, but had maintained their separate legislatures, laws, and governments. They were independent nations united by a king alone.

After the overthrow of James II, however, England became increasingly worried over the possibility that Scotland would seek the return, for itself, of James II, or, after his death, his son, who called himself "James III" and who would be "James VIII" of Scotland.

To diminish the chance of a truly independent Scotland on the island, Queen Anne's government put through the Act of Union, on March 6, 1707. Scotland gave up its separate parliament and the two nations were to be ruled as one henceforward. The united island was to be known thenceforward as the "United Kingdom of Great Britain" (usually referred to, more briefly, as either "the United Kingdom" or "Great Britain"). The subjects of the queen, while they might think of themselves as Englishmen or Scotsmen were henceforth officially "British."

And so, from 1707 on, we must speak of the coastal colonies which had been founded by Englishmen or taken by them, as the "British colonies."

The British colonies were growing in population and strength and they spread steadily westward — not by establishing isolated forts as the French did but by extending the farmlands and multiplying the towns. They covered more and more

ground more and more solidly, and that, too, represented a
steady raising of the stakes.

Nor did the increase in population mean a purely British expansion. No bars were placed on immigration, and, during the
years of Queen Anne's War, for instance, over 30,000 Germans
flooded into the colonies. Most of them went to Pennsylvania,
and the areas west of Philadelphia are to this day inhabited by
the "Pennsylvania Dutch," who are the descendants, to a large
extent, of these early immigrants.

As though the westward push had given Pennsylvania less
reason to worry about the easternmost extension of her area, she
granted the three southeastern counties (which had once been
New Sweden) the right to have an independent legislature.
This legislature met for the first time on November 22, 1704,
and the counties became the colony of Delaware. Delaware,
however, continued to accept the governor of Pennsylvania as
its own also, for another three–quarters of a century.

A reverse change took place east of Pennsylvania, where two
colonies became one. On April 17, 1702, East Jersey and West
Jersey gave up their separate charters and were combined once
more into the single colony of New Jersey.

Beyond Pennsylvania, the two southernmost colonies, Virginia and Carolina were also pushing westward. Of the two,
Carolina's position was the shakier. It was large in area, and its
population was small and, worse, continued to be concentrated
in the Albemarle area in the north, near Virginia, and in the
south near Charleston; a deputy governor in the north was responsible to the governor in the south; and there was a wide
stretch of unsettled country between.

In 1710, New Bern was established at the mouth of the
Neuse River, eighty miles southwest of the northern settlements in Albemarle, and the movement to fill in the space between north and south began.

The Tuscarora tribe of Indians, which lived along the coast

south of Albemarle, watched its territories being encroached on and its children kidnapped to serve the White settlers as slaves. Goaded beyond endurance, they went to war in the usual Indian fashion of surprise attack. They struck, on September 22, 1711, massacring all the settlers they could find in New Bern and surrounding territory. There were 200 dead, including eighty children.

The Albemarle section was so hard–hit, it was unable to mount the counterattack that almost always followed the initial Indian massacre — and returned ten for one. It therefore appealed for help. The response showed how disunified the colonies were and how indifferent one might be to its neighbor.

Virginia had long disputed the boundary between itself and Carolina, and, when the appeal for help came, the older colony demanded territorial concessions as the price. Carolina refused, so Virginia remained aloof.

Men arrived, however, from the southern section of the colony and, during 1712 and 1713, the Tuscaroras were defeated in three battles and their strength smashed. The tribe, fortunately for itself, had links to the Iroquois confederation, so the survivors trekked northward to New York and took up new hunting grounds there.

The Tuscarora War, however, showed the impracticality of trying to rule the Albemarle section from Charleston. On May 9, 1712, the Albemarle section was given the right to have a governor of its own, and the colony of Carolina became the two colonies, "North Carolina" and "South Carolina" (with the former the larger and the latter the richer), a separation that has existed ever since.

In 1715, another and even more desperate Indian war struck South Carolina. The Indian tribe known as the Yamasees had moved from Spanish territory northward into South Carolina and attacked. Again no help was received from populous Virginia. It was only when the Cherokee joined the White men and attacked the Yamasees that the uprising was put down, in 1717.

The southern colonies were also plagued by piracy, which is the hijacking of vessels, the theft of their cargoes, and often the murder of their crews and passengers, on the high seas. It can be a profitable occupation when sea lanes are improperly patrolled.

For pirates to ply their profession, however, some safe haven on land is needed, some place where they can rest between voyages, repair their ships, pick up supplies, recruit new crewmen, and so on. There were innumerable such places in the lesser islands of the West Indies. There were also places on the virtually unpopulated Carolina shore where pirates could be quite secure.

During Queen Anne's War, the colonials had been glad for the presence of pirates since they confined themselves to the rich pickings available in French and Spanish vessels. Afterward, when they turned on British and colonial vessels, too, their popularity waned sharply.

Some individual pirates became famous (and, like picturesque bandits of all kinds, were idealized after they were safely dead). Captain Kidd is the most famous, perhaps, even though he was actually a small–time practitioner in the field. He was born William Kidd, the son of a Presbyterian minister, in Scotland. In 1695, he was commissioned to capture pirates who were preying on British shipping in the Indian Ocean. Instead he took a few ships, becoming a pirate himself.

He then sailed to the West Indies, where he found he was being sought as a pirate. He tried to prove his innocence, maintaining that he was forced into piratical acts by a mutinous crew resentful over the fact that they weren't being paid. His story was not convincing. On July 6, 1699, he was taken into custody in Boston. He was sent to England for trial and was convicted. On May 23, 1701, he was hanged.

His real fame does not arise out of his penny–ante exploits

as a pirate, but from the report that he had buried some of his loot in eastern Long Island. Rumors concerning caches of his treasure all up and down the coast continued for many years afterward and kept his memory green.

A much more effective pirate was Bartholomew Roberts, who was born in Wales and who reportedly took more than 400 ships before he died in action, in 1722, at the age of forty. He was supposed to have conducted his affairs in strictly business-like fashion, keeping his crew sternly up to the mark. He was a teetotaler himself, and, while he allowed his men to drink in moderation, he permitted no gambling and would have no women aboard.

Then there was Edward Teach, who was a privateer (a kind of government–supported pirate) during Queen Anne's War, when he confined his depredations to the French and Spanish. Afterward he continued his activities, less discriminatingly. Because of his luxuriant facial hair, which he wore in long curls, he was widely known as "Blackbeard."

In 1717, he captured a French merchant vessel, fitted her out with forty guns, and made a formidable warship out of her. He wintered in the islands off the coast of North Carolina and may have gained immunity there by seeing to it that some of the colonial officials got a cut of his gains.

It was Virginia that brought Blackbeard to his end. His coziness with officials of the Carolinas made him the less popular with Virginia's administration, which were apt to consider the Carolinas enemy regions rather than sister colonies. In 1718, Virginia sent out ships under Lieutenant Robert Maynard. Blackbeard was cornered off one of the long islands that rim North Carolina's shore. In a fierce fight, with many casualties on both sides, Maynard himself managed to kill Blackbeard in hand–to–hand combat.

The pirate menace simmered down after that, but the memory of those days has been immortalized in Robert Louis Stevenson's classic *Treasure Island*.

GEORGIA MAKES THIRTEEN

The growing strength of the Carolinas and the continuing decline of Spain faced the South Carolinians with the temptation
to push southward, partly for new land and partly to force the
Indians back. This they did, over Spanish protests, and, in
1727, there was virtual war between South Carolina and Florida. A South Carolinian expedition raided nearly to St. Augustine and it was clear that Spain could no longer hold all the territory between St. Augustine and Charleston.

This meant there was room for another British colony south
of South Carolina, and this seemed a godsend to James Edward
Oglethorpe, a British soldier and an outstanding humanitarian.

In his youth, Oglethorpe had fought with the Austrians
against the Turks and, then, turning to the pursuits of peace,
entered Parliament, in 1722. There he served on a committee
which looked into the prison situation in Great Britain.

The prisons in those days were horrible beyond conception.
To make it worse, imprisonment for debt was common. Since
the imprisonment itself made it impossible for the prisoner to
pay off his debt, it often meant a life sentence for "crimes" that
were very often the result of nothing more vicious than poverty
and helplessness.

Oglethorpe's heart bled, and it seemed to him that if colonies
could be established in America as a refuge for people of a particular religious belief, one could be established as a refuge for
the poor and unfortunate of any sect.

On June 9, 1732, he procured a charter for such a colony to
be settled in the space which now seemed available south of
South Carolina. The British government was perfectly happy
to grant such a charter since it felt no loss in sending shiploads of debtors and paupers out of the country to a place where

they might serve to blunt Spanish and Indian thrusts against the Carolinas.

At that time, a new dynasty ruled Great Britain. Queen Anne had died in 1714, soon after the Treaty of Utrecht, and had left no heirs. Parliament scorned the Catholic son of James II and turned instead to George of Hanover. He was a great–grandson of James I and a second cousin of Queen Anne.

He ruled as George I. Speaking only German and utterly uninterested in British affairs, he was content to reign as a do-nothing, leaving the entire conduct of the government in the hands of the Prime Minister — thus initiating the modern form of government of Great Britain in which the monarch, however beloved, is a figurehead.

George I died, in 1727, and was succeeded by his son, George II, also primarily German in background and also content to let the Prime Minister rule. It was George II who granted the charter to Oglethorpe, and in his honor, the new colony was named "Georgia."

In January 1733, Oglethorpe and a party of 120 colonists landed in Charleston, then moved south to the mouth of the Savannah River, which formed the southern boundary of South Carolina. There, on the southern bank, he founded Savannah, on February 12.

Oglethorpe did his best to establish the new colony on humanitarian principles. He tried to prevent the formation of large estates, prohibited the sale of hard liquor, and forbade the importation of Black slaves. As time went on, however, the rules were relaxed and Georgia came to take on the sort of culture found in the other southern colonies. By 1755, when the number of White settlers in Georgia was still only 2000, there were already present 1000 Black slaves as well.

In 1733, then, the list of colonies, as usually given, reached the number of thirteen. From north to south, these were: New Hampshire, Massachusetts, Rhode Island, Connecticut, New

York, New Jersey, Pennsylvania, Delaware, Maryland, Virginia, North Carolina, South Carolina, and Georgia.

Of these, six had the boundaries we now associate with them: Massachusetts (excluding its Maine settlements), Connecticut, Rhode Island, New Jersey, Delaware, and Maryland. The remaining seven (plus the Maine section of Massachusetts) were still expanding.

The thirteen colonies were advancing in many ways. The attitude toward religion was liberalizing steadily. In 1696, for instance, South Carolina had formally established liberty of worship for all Protestants. In 1709, Quakers were able to establish a meeting house in Boston, where, half a century before, Quakers had been hanged just for being Quakers.

As yet, however, toleration did not extend, officially at least, to Catholics. Even Maryland, which had begun as a Catholic–sponsored colony had not been Catholic since Cromwell's time. In 1704, in fact, public worship was forbidden to Catholics. After the fall of James II, in 1688, the control of the colony had been taken from the Catholic Baltimores and was not given back to them till 1715, when one of them had turned Protestant.

Nevertheless, active persecution of Catholics (or Jews, for that matter), did not take place.

There continued to be halting steps toward ending slavery, at least in the north. In New York City, on April 12, 1712, there was a slave revolt which was quickly crushed; twenty Blacks were killed or executed. However ineffective, the revolt showed that being a slave master was not all fun. On June 7, 1712, therefore, Pennsylvania (with its Quaker heritage) passed a law forbidding the further importation of Black slaves. The difference in attitude toward slavery between north and south widened a bit further.

The liberalization of social affairs and the increase in civil liberties continued in another direction. The colonists, with the tradition of English self–government behind them, were deeply concerned to retain in their new land all the rights of free–born Englishmen (even those among them whose origins were not English). This meant the privilege of speaking one's mind freely, either in speech or in print.

On April 24, 1704, the *Boston Newsletter* began publication. This was the first regularly issued newspaper in America. Others soon followed, and it was not long before these began to publish material critical of the colonial government.

It was in New York that the matter came to a head and involved a German–born journalist, John Peter Zenger, who had come to New York in 1710.

In the early decades of the 1700s, the *New York Gazette* was the chief newspaper of the colony, and it was controlled by the governor, William Cosby, and his officials.

On November 5, 1733, Zenger began to publish the *New York Weekly Journal,* which took issue with the official version of the news, exposed hypocrisy and corruption (as it saw them), and did not hesitate to attack Cosby himself in virulent terms. In 1734, an election for aldermen produced an anti-Cosby majority.

Cosby, furious, was sure that Zenger's editorials were responsible and had him arrested for libel, on November 17, 1734.

There had to be a jury trial, of course, but Cosby hounded the lawyers who attempted to defend Zenger and insisted, furthermore, that only the judges could decide whether a libel was committed and that a libel was anything uncomplimentary, whether true or not. The task of the jury was merely to decide whether the libel was actually published. (All that meant that Zenger could not possibly be considered innocent.)

The trial took place, in August 1735, and Zenger would certainly have been convicted but for the sudden appearance of the aged Andrew Hamilton, a lawyer from Philadelphia who was the most respected legal mind in America.

In a moving and spirited address, Hamilton maintained that the truth, however uncomplimentary, is no libel; that the jury should decide whether something was libellous or truthful; and that the freedom to publish the truth, however uncomplimentary, was part of the rights of Englishmen. The jury, and public opinion, too, upheld Hamilton vigorously.

The decision, which was to acquit Zenger, did not end the attempts of the colonial governors to control the press, but it made it much more difficult for them to do so. Newspapers multiplied in the colonies, and even Virginia, where Berkeley had once gloated that no printing press existed, saw the establishment of its first newspaper, the *Virginia Gazette*, on August 6, 1736.

Criticism of the governing officials continued vigorous (and at times even vicious), and there was a steady drift of power away from the executive, whether a proprietor or a royal governor, and toward the popularly elected legislatures. (To be sure, though, the legislatures were chosen by a limited electorate, since in all the colonies, only men of a certain amount of property could vote.)

The advances of the colonies presented Great Britain with certain economic problems, too. As roads improved and as the colonists could travel more freely, intercolonial trade became a factor. It became possible for men in one colony to buy goods in another colony rather than from England. This the home country did not approve of.

In 1699, for instance, she passed the "Woolens Act" which forbade one colony to ship wool or woollen products to another. Those colonies which had wool to sell could sell neither to another colony nor to England, but had to use it themselves. Those colonies which needed wool, on the other hand, had to buy it from England. This was another example of England's attempt to turn a profit for its own manufacturers at the expense of the colonists.

What seemed even more unfair, Great Britain, a generation following, tried to mulct the thirteen colonies for the sake of still other colonies.

You see, thirteen colonies weren't all there were. We speak of thirteen because it was those thirteen that eventually gained their independence from Great Britain. Actually, though, anyone counting the British colonies in North America in 1733 (after the founding of Georgia) would count more than thirteen.

Nova Scotia was a fourteenth colony, and Newfoundland a fifteenth. To be sure, Nova Scotia's inhabitants were still largely French and Newfoundland's were largely nonexistent, so they were no real threat to the thirteen, and Great Britain had no reason to favor them.

In the south, though, there were two more colonies. These were the West Indian islands of Jamaica (taken from Spain, in 1655) and Barbados Island which had been settled even earlier. They were far more profitable and far less troublesome than the mainland colonies and were regarded with considerably more favor by the British crown.

Jamaica was almost as large as Connecticut in area and, in 1733, had a population of more than 50,000, nearly twice that of Connecticut. Barbados, only half the area of the present New York City, had a population of 75,000. (To be sure, most of the population of these island possessions were Black slaves; not more than 15,000 on both islands were Whites.)

These British islands were sugar producers and their great money-making exports were molasses and rum. For these the mainland colonists, the New Englanders particularly, could trade their own produce. With the rum thus obtained, the New Englanders could go on to Africa and trade it for Black slaves. The slaves they could then sell in America. At every step of this so-called triangular trade, which had begun as early as 1698, the enterprising traders could turn a handsome profit.

When French and Dutch islands in the West Indies increased their own sugar production and offered prices that undercut those in the British islands, the mainland colonists cheerfully went where the greater profits lay. The British islands suffered a serious depression and began to put pressure on the home government, which responded. On May 17, 1733, Great Britain passed the "Molasses Act" which placed huge tariffs on non–British sugar and rum. In effect, this meant the colonists would be forced to trade with the British islands at higher prices so that their profits would syphon into the pockets of the island plantation owners.

The colonists countered this by continuing and extending their smuggling practices. The whole policy of economic control brought very little good to Great Britain and, by sowing ill feeling among the colonists, finally brought the British great harm.

KING GEORGE'S WAR

From 1700 on, France and Spain were under the rule of the same family, but their interests remained distinct. The first Bourbon king of Spain, Philip V, thought he could return his country to its expansionist role of a century and a half before. In 1717, therefore, he sent armies to Italy and intrigued for the succession to the French throne, then occupied by his nephew, the eight–year–old Louis XV.

The result was that Great Britain, the Empire, the Netherlands, and France as well, combined in a Quadruple Alliance to put Spain back in her place. This was quickly and easily done.

This "War of the Quadruple Alliance" did not affect the British colonies in North America at all. Instead, there was involved some fighting between France and Spain across the stretch of Gulf Coast from Florida to Texas. The French attacked Pensacola in northwestern Florida, while the Spaniards sent expeditions far northward, reaching what is now Nebraska.

Both offensives failed, and when the war was over in Europe in 1720, the fighting stopped in North America also, with no territory changing hands. Spain's weakness had, however, become so patent that the other nations were ready to take offense with her over trifles.

Spain, for instance, like all the colonizing nations of the time, was desperately trying to control colonial commerce for her own profit. That meant that she punished smugglers severely whenever she could catch them. One such smuggler was the English sea captain, Robert Jenkins. His story was that when he was caught smuggling (he called it trading), in 1731, his ear was cut off by the Spaniards.

Jenkins kept the ear and, in 1738, when he was questioned by a committee of the House of Commons, he displayed the dried–up ear. His tale caught the imagination of the British public, which was already fired up by stories of Spanish atrocities, and the demand for war became overpowering. On October 19, 1739, Great Britain declared war on Spain and there began one of the more curiously named conflicts in history — "The War of Jenkins's Ear."

In part, the war was fought at sea. One of the leading hawks of the time, Edward Vernon, had clamored for war and had offered to take Portobello on the northern coast of Panama with no more than six ships under his command. On November 22, 1739, he accomplished the task easily. He could hold Portobello only briefly, however, for Spain would be sure to counterattack; so he destroyed its fortifications, abandoned the city, and returned home.

This temporary capture of Portobello, though it served little purpose, was treated as a great victory. Vernon was therefore placed in charge of a much greater force intended for a much greater feat, the capture of the large city of Cartagena, in what is now Colombia.

The result was a fiasco. In 1741, Cartagena was placed under siege, but bombardment accomplished nothing and more than half the men in Vernon's fleet died of yellow fever. Vernon had to raise the siege and return.

Yet in two respects, Vernon (who might otherwise be easily forgotten) lives in our language and memory. He wore a grogram cloak in bad weather (that is, one woven of coarse silk) and was consequently called "Old Grog." He was the first to issue rations of rum, diluted one to five, to the crew (to avoid getting them helplessly drunk with undiluted drink), and this came to be called "grog" in nautical slang.

More important to Americans, however, is the fact that a contingent of Virginians served with Vernon at Cartagena. Among these was a man named Lawrence Washington, who admired Vernon greatly. In 1743, after he returned to Virginia, Lawrence Washington built a house near the Potomac River and called his holdings "Mount Vernon" in honor of the admiral. It is this same Mount Vernon that is now an American shrine through its associations with Lawrence's young half-brother, George, memorializing forever (though few realize it) the name of Old Grog.

The War of Jenkins's Ear was also fought on land, with Georgia bearing the brunt of the struggle, for Spain saw the war as an opportunity to wipe out the colony that had been founded on what it viewed as territory usurped from itself.

Oglethorpe of Georgia, however, was not caught napping. In good time, he had constructed a fort at the mouth of the St. Mary's River, a hundred miles south of Savannah, and only sixty miles north of St. Augustine. (St. Mary's River is now the boundary between Georgia and Florida.)

As soon as war was declared, Oglethorpe moved southward and, in May 1740, with a combined force of Georgians and South Carolinians, laid siege to St. Augustine. There was poor cooperation between the two sets of colonials, however, and the Spanish struck to his rear, so Oglethorpe was forced to retreat to Georgia once more.

Vernon's failure at Cartagena then followed, and it was Spain's turn to plan a large naval expedition. A fleet of thirty ships left Cuba, took on reinforcements at St. Augustine, then, in 1742, landed on the Georgian coast, fifty miles south of Savannah.

Oglethorpe retreated northward but, on July 7, 1742, managed to maneuver a contingent of Spaniards into a trap and killed many of them at what was called "The Battle of Bloody Marsh." The repulse disheartened the Spaniards, who abandoned their attempt against Georgia.

In 1743, Oglethorpe again tried to invade Florida and take St. Augustine and again failed. By then the War of Jenkins's Ear had been reduced to a stalemate and would probably have come to an end but that it merged into another and larger war.

This new war again revolved about a disputed succession in Europe. In 1740, the Holy Roman Emperor, Charles VI (also Archduke of Austria), had died, leaving no sons. He did, however, have a daughter, Maria Theresa; and he had spent many years trying to negotiate agreements with other powers to the effect that they would recognize his daughter as his successor.

Once he died, however, the vultures moved in despite any promises. Prussia, a north German nation, was growing in strength at that time; and, in 1740, it, too, had a new monarch, Frederick II. Frederick acted at once by seizing Silesia, an Austrian province adjoining Prussia. Other nations quickly joined Prussia against Austria in order to share in the loot, and among these were France and Spain.

There was no real need for Great Britain to get involved, but the British king, George II, was also ruler of Hanover, a state in western Germany. In his Hanoverian role, George found his interests causing him to side with Austria. The British did not mind this since it put them at war with France again, with whom they had been fighting almost continuously for half a century anyway.

In North America, the war was, naturally enough, known as "King George's War," and it swallowed up the War of Jenkins's Ear.

Once King George's War flared up, the French attempted to

use their new fort at Louisbourg as a base for offensive opera-
tions. They were hampered in this by the fact that the French
navy was weak and the British controlled the sea. Nevertheless, they raided Annapolis Royal in Nova Scotia and harassed
the Massachusetts fishermen.

As in previous wars, Massachusetts had attempted to take
Port Royal to neutralize the direct French danger; they now
found they would have to do something about the much
stronger Louisbourg.

The governor of Massachusetts at this time was William
Shirley, a capable man who kept the colony's economy on an
even keel. He saw the necessity of removing the Louisbourg
menace and felt it would take an effort more than Massachusetts alone could apply. So forceful and eloquent was he that
he collected volunteers for the task not only in Massachusetts,
but in New Hampshire and Connecticut as well. Supplies came
from all New England and from New York as well. It was the
most elaborate example of colonial cooperation seen up to that
time.

The expedition was placed under William Pepperrell, a
Maine–born merchant, who had had some military experience.
On March 24, 1745, the transports sailed north, with 4000 men
on board. Three British warships joined them, and, on April 30,
the colonials landed near the Louisbourg fortress.

For six weeks, the undisciplined colonials attempted assaults
on the fortress whenever enough of them felt like doing so and
whenever they were sober enough to do so. The French held
them off, but they were few in number and dispirited, and they
knew they could not be relieved as long as the British warships
hovered offshore. The colonials created a kind of exuberant and
drunken chaos that further depressed the French, and, on June
17, 1745, the fort surrendered even though it had not been
seriously and methodically assaulted.

It was the greatest military victory yet achieved by the
colonials. Pepperrell was made a baronet by George II, the first

time such an honor had been given a colonial. (It is an odd coincidence that Phips, the first colonial knight, and Pepperrell, the first colonial baronet, were both born in Maine.)

The French organized a fleet to recapture Louisbourg, and all of Nova Scotia if it could, but the project failed. The fleet encountered storms and sickness and was forced to turn back with nearly half its men gone and not a shot fired.

The war then petered on with Indian raids and frontier scuffles, until October 18, 1748, when the war ended in Europe with the Treaty of Aix–la–Chapelle.

Great Britain and France did some horse–trading at the treaty table. France had taken the British–held city of Madras in India in the course of the war, and Great Britain wanted it back so she offered to return Louisbourg in exchange. The deal went through, and the New England colonists had to face the bitter realization that Great Britain valued the profits of the Far East trade more than she did the security of her North American colonies.

The New Englanders knew that war with France would come again, probably soon, and then they would face the Louisbourg menace all over again. There was nothing they could do about it, of course, but they did not forget.

9

MANEUVERING FOR POSITION

THE GROWING COLONIES

By the end of King George's War, the British colonies had a population of about 1,250,000 Whites and 250,000 Black slaves; the mark of the wilderness was beginning to disappear from the older coastal areas. It had been a century and a quarter now since the first settlements were begun, and it was no longer a matter of isolated groups of men, huddling behind palisades.

Virginia, the most populous of the colonies, numbered 231,000 (though 100,000 of these were slaves). The four New England colonies together had a population of 360,000, and included very few slaves. The largest city in the colonies was Boston which, in 1750, had a population of about 15,000. Philadelphia and New York followed, with 13,000 apiece. All were growing rapidly and new towns were being established — Baltimore, Maryland, in 1730; Augusta, Georgia, in 1735; and so on.

From New Hampshire to the North Carolina border, the land was continuously occupied. Roads had been improved, and, in 1732, the first commercial stagecoach was established. By mid-century, stagecoaches were carrying people from New York to Philadelphia in three days. Men began to travel from one colony to another routinely. That, together with a common language and the common danger associated with the French and the Indians, helped break down the feeling of separation and produced at least the beginnings of a sense of union.

The sophistications of culture continued to increase, with Philadelphia usually showing the way. In 1731, the first circulating library in the colonies was established in Philadelphia; in 1744, the first novel (Richardson's *Pamela*) to see a colonial edition was printed in Philadelphia; in 1752, the first permanent hospital in the colonies was established in Philadelphia.

It was during this period, too, that the colonies went through an experience that was to become typical of the nation into which they were to develop — a religious revival.

This revival began, in a way, in Great Britain, where John Wesley organized a group of men at Oxford University who dedicated themselves to a stricter observance of a religious way of life. The group was called "methodists" in derision, because Wesley drove them all to go about their readings, their prayers, their good works in a methodical by-the-clock manner. The joking name became the real one, as in the case of the Quakers and Puritans.

In 1735, shortly after the founding of Georgia, John and his brother Charles Wesley crossed the sea to the infant colony to serve as ministers to the colonists and missionaries to the Indians. The venture was a humiliating failure, for the brothers did not take well to frontier life.

After they returned to England, however, a follower, George Whitefield, volunteered to take up the task; and, on February 2, 1738, he arrived in Georgia. He proved the man for the job, for he was the first of the great evangelists in North America; he preached to thousands. In 1740, after a short return to Great Britain to raise funds, he made a tour that carried him through all the colonies from Savannah to Boston and wherever he went he roused great enthusiasm and made many converts.

In Boston, he met Jonathan Edwards, a hell–fire preacher who, since 1734, had been delivering extremely effective sermons that dealt in great detail with the dangers, and even certainty, of going to hell if one did not follow a path so narrow as to be almost invisible.

Between Whitefield and Edwards, and other lesser lights, the colonies went through a few years of what was called "the Great Awakening." It didn't last long, of course (revivals never do), and the more conservative elements among the religious leadership were hostile. Still, it succeeded in shaking up the churches and breaking their holds on the colonial government, thus encouraging the continuing movement toward religious tolerance. It also stimulated the founding of colleges, which in those days were all connected with religious bodies. Columbia, Princeton, Brown, and Dartmouth were all founded after the Great Awakening and, to some extent, as a result of it. In addition, since the revivalism affected all the colonies, a common experience served to add to the growth of the feeling of unity among them.

But always, as the British colonies grew and prospered, there remained the shadow of France. King George's War had settled nothing, any more than the earlier wars had; and both sides, the French and the British, continued to prepare for another, and possibly more decisive, round.

Both maneuvered for position, and each tried to fill in such areas of no–man's–land as still existed between the two colonial powers. The largest gap, and potentially the most important, was that south of the Great Lakes and north of the Ohio River, from the Mississippi River on the west to the Allegheny Mountains on the east, a vast stretch of land usually referred to in those days as the "Ohio Territory."

If the French could make their hold on Ohio firm, then the British colonies would be penned east of the Alleghenies and might well be choked to death.

To prevent this, the colonials (who were, in any case, perpetually land–hungry) pushed westward. To be sure, they had been pushing westward for a century and a half and had already reached the line of the Alleghenies; but, after the Treaty of Aix–la–Chapelle, with the feeling growing that the final showdown with France would soon be at hand, the push went into high gear. The effort was particularly made to establish settlements beyond the Alleghenies.

In 1748, Virginia frontiersmen established a settlement at Draper's Meadow in the Appalachian country, two hundred miles from the Atlantic Ocean. Leading men in Virginia established the "Ohio Company," organized expressly to colonize the upper reaches of the Ohio River. In 1750, Christopher Gist was sent out to explore the area and moved up the Ohio to a point not far short of the site of the modern city of Cincinnati. Another explorer, Thomas Walker, penetrated due westward into what is now Kentucky; he was the first white man to explore the area in detail.

Nor was it only Virginia. In 1750, Pennsylvania traders had established a base on the Miami River, well past the Alleghenies and, indeed, farther west than the present boundary of Pennsylvania.

As for Great Britain, she played no part in this. As always, she was content to leave the colonies to themselves. Where she did interest herself in their development, it was to remember to hamper that development in the interest of British manufacturers. In 1732, she forbade one colony to manufacture hats for sale to other colonies, for the benefit of British hatters. In 1750, she forbade any further construction of mills for the smelting of iron and steel, for the benefit of British mills. In 1751, she forbade any of the New England colonies to issue paper money (which made it easier for colonial debtors to pay off their British creditors with cheap money).

Great Britain felt greater concern for Nova Scotia which, of all the colonies, was the weakest and the nearest to center of French power. She could not count on hard–bitten colonials fighting her battles in Nova Scotia, for, after forty years of British rule, the colony still had no British settlers. In fact, the colony was worse than empty, for it still held the French settlers who had ruled the peninsula in the days when it had been Acadia. The Acadians had not forgotten, and during King George's war they had maintained a grim silence or a muttering hostility to the British.

In 1749, George Montague Dunk, Second Earl of Halifax, who had lately become president of the British Board of Trade (the department which had the duty of dealing with colonial problems) took vigorous action. He sent out 1400 colonists, drawn from the debtors' prisons, under the leadership of a governor named Edward Cornwallis. In June 1749, they settled on the east central coast of the peninsula and the town so founded was named Halifax. Other settlers followed and it was soon a flourishing town of 4000. It became the center of the British government and has remained the capital of Nova Scotia ever since.

GEORGE WASHINGTON

While the British and the colonials were strengthening their positions, the French were not idle. They were still far fewer in numbers than were the British colonials. In all their vast dominions they numbered only 80,000 men or so, yet they restlessly extended their exploratory tentacles ever farther westward. In the 1730s and 1740s, Pierre Gaultiers de Varennes, Sieur de la Verendrye, pushed out from Lake Superior and established forts as far west as Lake Winnipeg. In 1742 and 1743, he reached the Black Hills in what is now South Dakota. And, in 1739, two other French explorers, Pierre and Paul Mallet, caught a glimpse of the Rocky Mountains in what is now Colorado.

Closer to home, they continued to tighten their grip on the Great Lakes. They established posts at Niagara Falls between Lake Erie and Lake Ontario; at the site now occupied by Toronto on the northern shore of Lake Ontario; and at the site now occupied by Ogdensburg, New York, on the St. Lawrence River.

The crucial area, however, lay south of the Great Lakes. They already had forts in the Ohio Territory, and perhaps as many as a thousand French occupied it. These, however, were concentrated in the western half of the territory and, in view of the steady infiltration of the British colonials across the Allegheny, the French felt they had to move eastward.

The governor of New France, Marquis Duquesne, organized the necessary expedition, in 1753. They were to travel through the Ohio Territory and establish French claims there. They were to put up markers, officially proclaiming the territory to be French, and were to warn any British colonials they were to encounter that they must leave.

What's more, the French began to construct forts as far eastward as they could, notably in several places in what is now northwestern Pennsylvania.

It was Virginia that was particularly disturbed by news of the French penetration. Virginia, of all the colonies, had been most active in westward exploration and settlement and had no hesitation in claiming for herself all the territory in her latitudes, stretching westward indefinitely.

Furthermore, the leaders of the colony were deeply engaged in land speculation, in buying up large blocs of western land very cheaply and then selling it at considerably higher prices to settlers. French occupation of the territory would obviously ruin this.

The governor of Virginia at this time was Robert Dinwiddie. He was himself a land speculator, but even if that were not true, he could not help but see the French advance as a danger to the colonies. He tried to rouse the British homeland to the dangers of the situation and failed. His next step was to try to do something himself, by sending someone westward to warn the French to pull out. It would be a bluff, since he was in no position to use force; but it might work.

His choice for the difficult job of carrying out the bluff was a young Virginian planter, then only twenty–one years of age. The name of the planter was George Washington.

Washington was born on February 22, 1732, by the Gregorian calendar then in use in most of Europe (and now in use just about everywhere). The birth date was February 11, by the Julian calendar which was then in use in Great Britain and in the British colonies. On January 1, 1752, however, Great Britain and the colonies adopted the Gregorian calendar, and young Washington changed the date to suit.

Washington came of an upperclass family; his great–grandfather, John Washington, being a supporter of Charles I, fled Cromwell's England, in 1657, and settled in Virginia.

Washington's father, Augustine Washington, had children by two wives, four by the first, six by the second. Among the children by the first wife was Lawrence Washington, who fought with Vernon at Cartagena and then built the house at Mount Vernon. The eldest of the children by the second wife, was George. Augustine Washington died in 1743, when George was eleven, and the elder half–brother, Lawrence, whom George idolized, brought up the boy.

(The best–known tale of George Washington as a boy — that business about the cherry tree and "I cannot tell a lie" — is itself a lie. The story, however edifying, was an outright fabrica-

tion by a bookseller named Mason Locke Weems. He wrote a
life of Washington in 1800 — the year after Washington's death
— which he eventually fleshed out with admitted fiction in order to enhance its appeal.)

In 1748, at the age of sixteen, Washington turned to survey-
ing as a profession, and, for several years, he familiarized himself with the wilderness and with frontier life as he tramped
through the forests mapping the territory.

In 1751, Lawrence Washington, suffering from tuberculosis,
went to Barbados Island, taking George with him (the only
venture the latter was ever to make outside the thirteen colonies). Washington had a mild attack of small pox there and his
face was permanently scarred as a result. In 1752, Lawrence
and his only daughter both died, and, in 1754, George bought
Mount Vernon from his brother's widow. He thus became one
of the most important land owners in Virginia. Eighteen Black
slaves came with the estate, and, although Washington disapproved of slavery, he kept slaves all his life.

Inspired, perhaps, by memories of Lawrence's fight at Cartagena, George longed for a military career, and he accepted a
post as a military aide under Dinwiddie, when the latter became governor in 1752. Naturally, then, it was to George Washington that Dinwiddie turned. Washington was a large man,
six feet two inches tall, an excellent horseman, and had a strong
constitution. He had extensive experience of the wilderness,
was courageous and eager.

On October 31, 1753, Washington left Williamsburg with a
small party that included Christopher Gist, the explorer. It was
a difficult 400–mile journey through the gathering winter, but,
on December 4, Washington reached a body of French soldiers
at Fort Le Boeuf on the site of what is now Waterford, Pennsylvania, about 20 miles south of Lake Erie.

The French captain commanding on the site was pleasant
enough. He saw to it that Washington and his party were fed
and warmed, and agreed to send the message, warning the

French out of the Ohio, on to Quebec. He made no secret, however, of the fact that the French had no intention of moving,
that they were going to take the Ohio country and keep it,
too.

Washington had to leave, carrying that message with him;
and, after a return journey even more fraught with danger than
the one outward (including a fall into an icy river and being
shot at by hostile Indians at point–blank range — and being
missed), he made his way back to Virginia. All that had been
gained were such observations as Washington's shrewd survey-
or's eyes could make of the territory he had passed over, and of
French preparations and fortifications.

Dinwiddie had failed in his bluff, and it was clear there could
be no peaceful solution. The French would not move out of the
Ohio territory without being pushed. He tried to get other colonies to cooperate in preparing the necessary push and got nowhere. Only North Carolina seemed ready to venture a little
support, and Virginia's own legislature could be persuaded to
vote funds for some warlike move only with the greatest difficulty. As for Great Britain, it was at peace with France and
was reluctant to start another war over some North American
backwoods.

Washington had told Dinwiddie of a spot on the upper Ohio,
where the Allegheny River and the Monongahela River join,
and assured him the site would be an ideal place for a fort.
Some settlers were already present but what was needed was
something strong that would dominate all the country round
about.

Dinwiddie was impressed and sent a party of 160 men to establish such a fort, putting Washington at its head with the rank
of lieutenant–colonel.

Off they went, in April 1754; but, by the time they had made
their way to Fort Cumberland in what is now western Maryland, two hundred miles northwest of Williamsburg and still
eighty miles short of the spot for which they were aiming,

Washington received the depressing news that he had been anticipated. The French, too, had noted the usefulness of the site. On April 17, 1754, after expelling the few Virginians there, they had established Fort Duquesne, the name honoring the governor of New France.

Washington might have turned back, but he was burning for military action; and the surrounding Indians, who were friendly, offered to help against the French. Washington thought he would try to see what a surprise attack might do.

He therefore continued his forward march till he came to a point some 45 miles short of Fort Duquesne, and there set up a base of his own which he called "Fort Necessity." (It is near the modern city of Uniontown, Pennsylvania.)

It was located on a poor choice of ground, too low and marshy for use in wet weather, but Washington hoped to use it only as a base for marshalling his offensive. Men flocked to him and before long, he found himself commanding four hundred men.

On May 28, Washington led a sizable party out of Fort Necessity and encountered a small body of thirty Frenchmen. The Frenchmen were unaware of the presence of Washington's men and since there was peace between the nations, there was no legal right for either side to fire.

Washington (only 22 years old, remember) could not hold back. Eager for action, he persuaded himself that the French were spies who would, unless stopped, carry back the message of Washington's weakness to Fort Duquesne and ruin the effect of surprise. Feeling that the safety of his party was at stake, Washington ordered a surprise attack on the outnumbered and thoroughly unsuspecting Frenchmen. In almost no time, ten of them were killed, including the commander, Sieur de Jumonville, and the rest were taken prisoner.

This colonial version of a Pearl Harbor carried out against the French was the start of one more war between France and Great Britain in North America.

Quebec

Montreal

LAKE
CHAMPLAIN

Fort Frontenac

Crown Point
Fort Ticonderoga
Fort
William
Henry
LAKE GEORGE
x Battle of Lake
George
Fort Edward

ONTARIO

Fort Oswego

N.H.

Fort Niagara

Albany

MASSA-
CHUSETTS

ERIE

NEW YORK

CONNEC-
TICUT

Allegheny R.

Delaware R.

Hudson R.

Ohio R.

PENNSYLVANIA

New York

LONG ISLAND

Monongahela R.

Fort Duquesne
✕ Braddock's Defeat
Fort Necessity
Cumberland

Philadelphia

NEW
JERSEY

MARYLAND

DELAWARE

DELAWARE BAY

VIRGINIA

CHESAPEAKE BAY

MAP V

The French and Indian War

It could not be named for the British monarch, for George II, who gave his name to King George's War, was still on the throne. The new war has come to be called "The French and Indian War" (a poor name, since all the colonial wars could be described in that fashion).

Washington's preliminary success brought him a promotion to full colonel and further reinforcements. However, the French, infuriated at what they considered (and with some justification) an act of base treachery, were issuing angrily out of Fort Duquesne.

Washington found himself facing five hundred Frenchmen and four hundred Indians. Far outnumbered, he prudently retreated to Fort Necessity, but now the inadequacy of the fort ruined everything. It was raining, and its defenders found themselves wallowing in mud. The French made no attempt to storm it, but, screened by the woods, patiently shot down every animal they could see inside the walls, making sure that Washington's forces would be deprived of their food supply.

On July 3, three days after entering the fort, Washington, with food and ammunition nearly gone, was forced to surrender.

Since France and Great Britain were still not formally at war, the French troops (who would have found that many prisoners an embarrassing load to care for) were willing to free them and allow them to return to Virginia. First, however, they had to do something about the man who had treacherously killed good French soldiers. They therefore set the condition that Washington sign an admission that he was responsible for the murder ("l'assassinat") of Sieur de Jumonville. In order that his men might be freed, Washington signed.

His admission to murder led to his being criticized rather strenuously, even at the British court. Young George Washington was terribly embarrassed and humiliated and offered the rather lame excuse that, being unfamiliar with the French language, he did not realize that "l'assassinat" meant "the murder."

BENJAMIN FRANKLIN

The determined French advance into the Ohio Territory alarmed the colonies to the north of Virginia as well. Among those who saw the dangers of colonial disunity in the face of the menace from without was Benjamin Franklin of Philadelphia. He was the most remarkable man to be produced by the British colonies prior to their independence (even including George Washington) and certainly the first colonial to achieve renown in Europe.

Benjamin Franklin was born in Boston, Massachusetts, on January 17, 1706, so he was a quarter century older than Washington. His father, Josiah Franklin, was an Englishman who had come to Massachusetts in 1682, bringing his wife and three children with him. He had four more children after he arrived in America, and, when his wife died, in 1689, Josiah married a second time and went on to have ten more children by his second wife. Of the seventeen children, Benjamin was the fifteenth — the tenth and last of his father's sons.

The family was not well–to–do and Benjamin Franklin had little opportunity for schooling. When he was ten, he left school and went to work in a candle maker's shop. This was no fun for Benjamin, who threatened to run off to sea, so his father persuaded James Franklin, a son by his first wife, to employ his young half–brother. James had a printing establishment and was putting out a successful paper. At the age of twelve, therefore, Benjamin Franklin became a printer and had the opportunity both to read and write — and to profit hugely by his surroundings.

Benjamin didn't take kindly to being ordered about by anyone, however, even by an older brother, and the two quarreled bitterly. Eventually, Benjamin decided to leave James and find a job with some other printer. The angry James had him black-listed in Boston, and there was nothing for Benjamin to do but leave town.

In October 1723, Benjamin Franklin, now seventeen years old, left for Philadelphia, and that city remained his home for the rest of his long life. He arrived in Philadelphia with only one dollar in his pocket, but got a job as a printer and, thanks to ability and industry, was soon doing quite well. He did well enough to find the funds to go to London and spend two years learning about the great European world across the ocean.

He returned to Philadelphia, in October 1726, and within a year was able to set up a printing shop of his own. In 1729, he bought a newspaper called *The Pennsylvania Gazette*. It had been losing money, but under Franklin's lively guidance it began to show a tidy profit.

Franklin turned his hand to everything. He bought and sold books; he published books; he established branch printing offices in other cities.

In 1727, he started the "Junto," a debating club where intelligent young men could gather and discuss the issues of the day, and, by 1743, it had become the "American Philosophical Society," which encouraged scientific studies throughout the colonies. He started the first circulating library in America, in 1731, and the first fire–fighting company in Philadelphia, in 1736. In 1749, he became president of the Board of Trustees of the newly founded Philadelphia Academy, an establishment which eventually became the University of Pennsylvania.

His most successful business effort was an almanac, which he began to publish in 1732, and of which he put out an edition each year for twenty–five years. This included the ordinary contents of almanacs: calendars; the days of the phases of the moon; the times of sunrise, sunset, moonrise, moonset, high and low tides for each day; days of eclipses; and so on.

In addition, however, Franklin filled it with interesting and clever articles on matters of interest to the colonials. He also

included many short and pithy sayings, many of which he made
up himself, and which, for the most part, praised thrift and hard
work. Many of his sayings entered the common language; and
the one which turned out to be the most famous, and which is
still repeated today (though not always seriously), is: "Early to
bed, and early to rise, makes a man healthy, wealthy, and
wise."

The almanac was published by Franklin under the pen name
of Richard Saunders, and he called it *Poor Richard's Almanac*.
The pithy sayings were usually preceded with "Poor Richard
says. . . ."

The almanac sold very well indeed — up to 10,000 a year, a
figure enormous for the times. It made him wealthy, and, by
1748, Franklin had enough money to retire. He let others
handle his business interests with a minimum of supervision
from himself and moved to the outskirts of the city where he
could devote himself to scientific research. Nor was he a failure
in that direction, either; he turned out to be the first great
American scientist; he had already proven himself the first great
American inventor.

For instance, in those days, houses were heated by fires in
fireplaces. This was very wasteful of fuel, for most of the heat
went straight up the chimney. In fact, it was even worse than
that, for the rising hot air stirred up a draft that actually
brought in the cold air from outside, and, on the whole, cooled
the house rather than warmed it. To get any heat at all, one
had to crowd around the fire.

It occurred to Franklin that what was needed was an iron
stove, standing on bricks, and set out in the room. Inside that,
a fire could be built. The metal would heat up and that would
heat the air; the warm air would stay inside the room instead
of vanishing up a chimney, but the smoke would be carried off
by a stovepipe into the chimney.

The first "Franklin stove" was built in 1742, and it worked
very well. It has been in use ever since. The furnaces in the

basements of modern houses are, in essence, Franklin stoves.

People suggested to Franklin that he patent the Franklin stove so that he could charge a fee to any manufacturer who wanted to build and sell them. This might have made Franklin a millionaire, but it would also have raised the price of the stoves, so Franklin refused. He said that he enjoyed the inventions that other men had made before his time, and therefore he should be willing to have others enjoy his inventions freely.

He also invented bifocal glasses and a musical instrument constructed out of hemispheres of glass which were kept moist and rubbed with the fingers. Toward the close of his life, he devised a long–handled pincer for getting books down from high shelves, something still used in grocery stores and other such establishments for reaching top shelves without a step ladder.

Franklin also was the first to notice the "Gulf Stream," a band of warm water moving up the North American coast, and made sensible suggestions (in which he was far ahead of his time) concerning weather prediction and the use of daylight saving time.

What really made Franklin famous, however, were his experiments with electricity.

The 1700s were the so–called Age of Reason. It was a time when gentlemen of leisure interested themselves in scientific experiments and when experiments with the newly explored phenomenon of electricity were all the rage. Something called the "Leyden jar" (because it was developed in Leyden, a city in the Netherlands) could be used to store a large electric charge, and every man of science was experimenting with it.

Franklin showed, in 1747, that while a Leyden jar ordinarily discharged with a spark and crackle, it could discharge much more quickly, and without either spark or crackle, if the metal rod through which it discharged ended in a point instead of a rounded structure.

The spark and crackle with which a Leyden jar discharged

itself reminded Franklin (and others) of lightning and thunder. Was it possible that, during a thunderstorm, the earth and the clouds acted like an enormous Leyden jar which discharged itself with a spark of lightning and a crackle of thunder?

In June 1752, Franklin flew a kite in a gathering thunderstorm (taking precautions against being electrocuted, for he was experienced in the behavior of Leyden jars, which sometimes store enough electricity to knock a person down on discharge and jar him to his eye teeth). He was able to draw electricity down from the clouds along the kite string and use it to charge an uncharged Leyden jar. In this way, he showed that thunderstorms did indeed involve electrical effects in the heavens, the same electrical effects (but much more enormous in size) as those produced by men in the laboratory.

Franklin decided that what worked for the Leyden jar would also work for the clouds. If a Leyden jar was easily discharged without spark or crackle through a pointed metal end, why not set up pointed metal rods on rooftops and link them to the ground. In that case, electric charges built up in the earth during a thunderstorm could easily and quietly be discharged through the pointed metal rod. No charge would accumulate to a degree so high as to discharge all at once as a bolt of lightning. A structure with such a "lightning rod" on it ought to be protected from being struck by lightning.

In the 1753 edition of *Poor Richard's Almanac*, Franklin announced this and suggested ways for outfitting structures with lightning rods. The device was so simple, and lightning so dreaded, that everyone was tempted to try it. After all, what was there to lose?

Lightning rods began to rise over buildings in Philadelphia by the hundreds, then in Boston and New York. And they worked!

Franklin had already gained a reputation in Great Britain as a scientist; but now his name and deeds spread over all Europe as the lightning rod came into use in region after region. For the first time in history, one of the great dangers to mankind had been beaten — and through science.

Franklin's world fame made him appreciated even in his homeland. In July 1753, he was given an honorary degree by Harvard University, and, in September of that year, another by Yale. Then in November, Franklin was awarded the Copley gold medal, its greatest honor, by the Royal Society of London. These were enormous accomplishments for someone whose formal schooling had stopped at the age of ten.

Even Louis XV of France sent Franklin a complimentary letter.

Louis's letter did not prevent Franklin from seeing, quite clear-sightedly, the gathering menace of France. In fact, he saw it all the more clearly because his own colony of Pennsylvania saw it so dimly. Pennsylvania was still a proprietary colony, and was still owned, so to speak, by the Penn family. That family, and many of the influential settlers, were Quakers, and they consistently refused to vote money for military preparedness.

Franklin had, amidst all his many and varied activities, involved himself in politics. In 1748, he had been elected to the Philadelphia city council; and, in 1750, he was elected to the Pennsylvania legislative assembly. In 1753, he was appointed postmaster-general for all the colonies, and he promptly turned the financially unsuccessful institution of the post office into a money-maker.

As a member of the Pennsylvania assembly, Franklin was a ringleader of those colonists who opposed the do-nothing attitude of the Penns toward the gathering war clouds. He fought hard to persuade Pennsylvania to establish a kind of volunteer army that would support itself and would not be dependent for money on the Penns. In this, he failed.

So he and others like him in the north viewed the situation with growing apprehension and with a disturbing feeling of helplessness.

It wasn't only the French advance that darkened the clouds over the colonial future. The Indian situation was equally disturbing.

In all the previous wars with France, most of the actual damage done the colonies had been at the hands of France's Indian allies. That the situation was not even worse than it was rested entirely on the fact that the intrepid Iroquois tribes could be counted on to remain anti–French. But would they always do so?

In the years since King George's War, they had remained loyally pro–British, to be sure; but that was the result of the work of a remarkable man named William Johnson.

Johnson was born in Ireland, in 1715, and had emigrated to America, in 1737, in answer to his uncle's call. That uncle, Sir Peter Warren, had an estate in upstate New York on the southern bank of the Mohawk River, about 25 miles west of Schenectady. Johnson settled there and, at his uncle's request, undertook its management.

Johnson bought land on the north side of the river, too, and became a great landholder. This was Iroquois country but Johnson tried the rather novel experiment of treating the "savages" with sincere friendship. He mediated in disputes between Indians and colonials and did so with scrupulous fairness. He encouraged education among the Indians, traded with them honestly, wore Indian clothes, spoke in their language, perfected himself in the knowledge and use of their ways and customs. Then, when his European wife died, he married an Indian girl.

As always seemed to happen, when Indians were treated with friendship and respect, they responded in the same way. Johnson was adopted into the Mohawk tribe and even made an official among them. He remained the man through whom the British and the colonials treated with Indians for all his life.

Nevertheless, Johnson was but one man, and the Iroquois could not remain blind to the facts of life. One fact was that the French were far more enlightened in their treatment of the Indians than the British were (despite the single example of Johnson). The steady outward thrust of dense colonial settlements was a greater danger to the Indian way of life, to his very existence, than the thin expansion of French traders and soldiers.

Finally, in the early 1750s, the French were pursuing an aggressive and successful policy in the Ohio territory, and were wooing the Iroquois with great ardor. The Iroquois could not help but listen, particularly since they had the very natural desire to be on the winning side.

For the first time since the British–French wars had begun there seemed a real danger that the Iroquois might actually defect to the French. And if this happened, nothing in the world would prevent New York and, possibly, New England from being crushed. After that, the other colonies might follow.

The result was that a very worried British Board of Trade suggested, in 1753, that the various colonies negotiate with the Iroquois and try to settle any grievances the Indians might have.

New York, at least, was perfectly willing, since it was upon her that the brunt of Iroquois hostility would certainly fall with the most deadly force. Governor James DeLancey of New York sent out an invitation to the other colonies to meet in general congress with the Indians at Albany.

Those colonies who felt directly endangered by the Iroquois responded. These included Pennsylvania, Maryland, and the four New England colonies. These, with New York itself, meant that seven colonies were represented at the congress. Proceedings began officially, on June 19, 1754.

Present, along with the twenty–five colonial delegates, were one hundred and fifty Iroquois. These were feverishly buttered up with promises and presents and were then sent off with much in the way of smiles and inflated oratory. In that respect the "Albany Congress," as it was called, was a complete success, for the Iroquois did not defect to the French side.

The congress then made recommendation for the appointment of regular officials to deal with the Indians and with westward settlement. William Johnson, who was at the Albany Congress, was appointed "Indian superintendent," a kind of official ambassador to the Iroquois and their Indian allies. He held the post till his death, and while he lived Indian troubles were held to a minimum.

But even with Indian matters settled as far as possible, some delegates remained concerned. What about the French? Washington's expedition, going on at the time, had recorded an initial victory of very small proportions, but did not seem now likely to accomplish much.

Benjamin Franklin was a delegate to the Albany Congress, and it was his view that the colonies could not defend themselves efficiently if they remained separate and, indeed, often hostile among themselves. He had actually dreamed up a scheme of colonial unification the previous March, and now he proposed it to the congress, on June 24. He actually persuaded the congress to adopt it; a motion carried, on July 10 (a week after Washington's surrender at Fort Necessity); and the plan was then submitted to the colonies generally and to Great Britain.

Franklin's proposal was that all the colonies be governed by a governor–general, appointed and paid by the British crown. He was to have extensive powers but he was to be no autocrat either. Partner with him was to be a 48–member "grand council," to which each colony was to send delegates. The number of delegates was to vary from two for some colonies, to as many as seven for others, the number being apportioned roughly in accordance with population. (As time went on, Franklin planned to have the delegate number become proportionate to the financial contribution made by each colony.

This would, in theory, encourage each colony to compete with the others in generosity of financial support to the confederation.)

The grand council would meet annually and would deal essentially with those problems which the colonies held in common, leaving the internal affairs of each colony under its own control. Thus, the grand council would deal with Indian treaties; with expansion into territories not clearly within any colony; and with military matters such as fortifications, armies, navies, and war taxes.

The proposal, actually signed on July 4 (of all days), makes great sense in hindsight, but was met with frozen disapproval from all sides. The British government felt it gave too much power to the colonies and would have nothing to do with it. The colonies felt it gave too much power to the Crown and those who did not express their disapproval openly, simply ignored the plan. Not one colony was willing to abandon any of its rights to the common good, even though another war with France had started in North America.

BRADDOCK'S DEFEAT

The British government, though not sufficiently impressed by the crisis to be stampeded into supporting Franklin's plan of colonial union, did recognize the need of doing something in the wake of Washington's defeat. They decided to send regular soldiers to North America even though they were still officially at peace with France.

Two regiments, therefore, adequately supplied and financed, were sent to Virginia to take the situation in hand there. Over them was placed General Edward Braddock, who had fought in the Netherlands during the War of the Austrian Succession.

On February 20, 1755, Braddock and his men arrived in Virginia.

No doubt the British felt that with such a force in Virginia, there would be no problem whatever in whipping the colonists into shape, using them as auxiliary forces, then beating down the few French and their barbarian allies.

That might have been possible, but militating against it was the character of Braddock himself. His experience was entirely in European warfare which, in that time, was fought with parade-ground maneuvering in what were called "linear tactics." A line of soldiers marched to the battlefield where they formed into a line three ranks deep. Standing shoulder to shoulder, they raised their muskets in unison and fired, together, on command. It was a military chorus line with no room for individual initiative.

This sort of fighting was enforced by the nature of the weapon. The musket was an inaccurate weapon, so inaccurate that soldiers were not trained in precision firing since such a thing was not possible. For the musket fire to have effect, it must be delivered in quantity and in unison so that, by sheer statistical chance, a number of hits might be made.

This worked well enough if the enemy also formed a line and went through similar military motions: the side which was better trained in following commands and better able to stand up against enemy fire would win. But what if the enemy chose to fight otherwise?

Braddock was not the man to recognize that tactics must be altered to suit the occasion. He was a narrow and limited man, sixty years old, opinionated, tactless, and with strong prejudices. He did not think much of the colonials, and, unfortunately, the latter did little to convince him he was wrong. Where Braddock counted on colonials to supply his armies with food and other necessities, he met with delays, inefficiency, and, all too often, outright dishonesty from men intent on profiteering and on reaping special benefits out of general disaster. Only Benjamin Franklin supplied what he promised in full and on time, and Braddock loudly proclaimed him the only honest colonial on the continent.

Braddock also took a liking to Washington. Washington had resigned from the army the previous fall out of pique at a British order that placed any colonial officer, of however high a rank, under the command of any British officer, of however low a rank.

Now, however, Braddock rather graciously offered to accept Washington into his own official family as his aide–de–camp, with the rank of colonel; and Washington quickly and gratefully accepted — eager, as always, for military action.

On April 14, 1755, Braddock began conferences with the governors of six of the colonies, and elaborate schemes for intermeshing offensives against the enemy were drawn up. These were simply too complicated to carry through over the distances and through the type of country characteristic of the colonies. (Braddock was somehow convinced he was still fighting on the narrow, flat, and tame countryside of Europe.) In the end, Braddock's own advance was the only military effort of consequence.

Franklin warned Braddock that the Indian allies of the French had their own way of fighting and that he must be wary of ambushes, so it cannot be said that the general had no advance knowledge of what might lie ahead. Braddock, however, with an air of irritating superiority, stated that the Indians might be able to fight effectively against mere colonials, but that it was not possible that they could oppose British regulars.

Washington suggested that Braddock avail himself of the offers of friendly tribes and make use of Indians as scouts and guides. Braddock had no trick of dealing with the Indians, however, nor could he really make himself believe they had any usefulness. In the end, virtually no Indians marched with him. A famous colonial Indian hunter, Captain Jack, offered to serve as scout; but Braddock refused to accept him unless he conformed to military discipline, which the old hunter refused to do.

Braddock's army formed at Cumberland, the outskirts of civilization at the time, and prepared to march blindly into the wilderness. Early in June 1755, 1500 British soldiers and seven hundred Virginia militia set off on the 80–mile march north-westward to Fort Duquesne, which was Braddock's first objective. It was a horrible march through wild forest and bogs, made all the worse by the fact that Braddock insisted on traveling heavy, carrying with him all the supplies and equipment an army would need if it were marching in Europe.

So slow was the progress, that, on June 18, Washington suggested in desperation that 1200 of the men move on ahead with light baggage, leaving the rest of the army to struggle on afterward with the main supplies. This served only to weaken the army, for it cut Braddock's manpower nearly in half, since the rear guard would not be likely to arrive in time to support the advance party in case of sudden battle. Braddock accepted the suggestion.

On July 8, the advance party, led by Braddock and including four hundred and fifty Virginians under Washington, reached the Monongahela River, 8 miles south of Fort Duquesne. Here they paused to consider the next move.

Washington now urged that he and his Virginians lead the initial attack, having in mind, undoubtedly, that they would fight frontier style. Then, if they successfully achieved surprise and won an initial advantage, the heavy weight of the British regulars could be added.

This Braddock refused. The battle would be fought his way, that is, the European way that he considered the only proper way.

Meanwhile, though, the French, unlike the British, were not fighting blind. Their efficient Indian scouts had brought back all the news needed concerning the British advance. The French at Fort Duquesne knew exactly how many British troops faced them, and their first impulse was to beat a prudent retreat from an outnumbering enemy force. A certain Captain de Beaujeu, however, had a different idea. It seemed to him from the reports that Braddock didn't really have a grasp of the situation, so he asked permission to be allowed to lead a harassing attack before the French retreated in order to see what would happen.

De Beaujeu was given permission. He had only two hundred Frenchmen at his disposal, but he delivered a stirringly effective speech that brought several hundred Indians to his side.

On July 9, De Beaujeu's force, still less than half the total of the enemy it faced, moved noiselessly through the forest toward Braddock's men. As soon as they saw the French force, the British started firing; but the French and Indians sank out of sight behind the trees and began to pick off the British regulars, bright in their red uniforms.

The British soldiers, with the natural instinct of sane men, tried to do the same; but Braddock was on the field, cursing and using the flat of his sword to beat his regulars back into line, to make them advance and fire in the Pennsylvania forests as though they were on a Dutch battlefield.

The British did manage to inflict some casualties, killing de Beaujeu among others, but by and large they were simply mowed down by an enemy they could not see and could not effectively retaliate against. In three hours of fighting, nearly two–thirds of the British soldiers were killed or wounded — 877 of them, including sixty–three of the eighty–six officers. The casualties on the other side were a mere sixty, and of these only sixteen were Frenchmen.

Braddock himself was faultlessly brave and faultlessly stupid. He was everywhere, exposing himself recklessly. Four horses were shot under him; shortly after he realized that the British soldiers had broken completely and were no longer an effective fighting force, he was himself badly wounded. He had just ordered the retreat at last, and the British soldiers were fleeing.

None would move to help him off the field. It was a British officer and two Virginians who took him in charge.

Washington was the only one of Braddock's aides–de–camp left alive. He had exposed himself with as great a courage as Braddock's. Two horses were killed under him, and four bullets ripped through his clothes without touching him. Unbelievably, he fought through the entire holocaust without receiving a scratch.

And now he took over. Most of his Virginians were dead, but the few who remained took to the trees. It was thanks to their fire that what was left of the British could leave the field. Once they had left, they were safe; for the French were too few to risk a pursuit, and the Indians wanted only to loot the camp and to collect the scalps of the dead and dying.

The wounded Braddock was carried onward by the retreating troops. He was silent, except for an occasional mutter of "Who would have thought it?" He died, with Washington at his bedside, on July 13, and was buried on the spot. The retreating army marched over the grave to conceal its location, reached Fort Cumberland at last, and finally found refuge in Philadelphia.

"Braddock's Defeat" is what the disastrous battle is almost invariably called, although "the Battle of the Monongahela" or "the Battle of the Wilderness" are its more formal names. The popular instinct is correct in this case, for the defeat was Braddock's, entirely his.

And its immediate result was to open the entire frontier to French and Indian attacks and to plunge the colonials into a new slough of insecurity. From the standpoint of military history, it represents the low point of the colonial situation.

For Washington, however, the battle was no defeat. He was the hero of the occasion. The month after the battle he was made commander of all Virginia forces, even though he was still but 23. It did him little good, however. The remnant of the British forces would not allow him any authority over them.

Indeed, with only a colonial commission, he found he was still exactly nothing in British eyes.

Washington sickened with frustration. He was ordered home by his physicians and played no further part in the war. When he could not get a royal commission, he finally resigned from the army a second time (bearing the worthless rank of brigadier–general).

In 1758, he was elected to the House of Burgesses and switched from a military to a political career, though in politics he was muted, and for the most part he spent his time as a wellto–do Virginia planter. From then on, though, he maintained a strong and steady dislike of the British, something that was to prove a matter of supreme importance in years to come.

10

THE FINAL DECISION

LAKE CHAMPLAIN

In the months after Braddock's defeat, Governor Shirley of Massachusetts, the organizer of the Louisbourg campaign a decade before, took over as commander–in–chief of the British forces in North America. His son had died in the horrible fight on the Monongahela River, and he was anxious to strike back.

The colonials had a foothold on Lake Ontario, at least, in the form of Fort Oswego; and it was Shirley's plan to move westward along the shore of that lake and northward along the shores of Lake Champlain.

He himself attempted to lead an attack on Fort Niagara, between Lakes Ontario and Erie, but bad weather and reports of of the arrival of French reinforcements forced him to turn back. He dared not risk another defeat on the scale of Braddock's.

Another attack was planned against Crown Point, which was

near the southern end of Lake Champlain (a lake that was firmly in French hands in those days) and which was only 90 miles north of Albany. This part of the plan was entrusted to William Johnson, the Indian supervisor, who was made a general for the occasion. Johnson had about 3400 colonials and Iroquois under him, representing New York; and six thousand New Englanders (chiefly from Governor Shirley's colony of Massachusetts) came to join him.

Toward the end of August 1755, Johnson's men advanced to the southern tip of what the French called Lac St. Sacrament, 40 miles south of the Crown Point objective. Lac St. Sacrament was a southwestern offshoot of Lake Champlain, and Johnson, in order to symbolize British dominion over it, renamed it Lake George after King George II. It has retained this name ever since.

The French did not choose to wait passively. Under General Ludwig August Dieskau, a German soldier fighting in the French service, they pushed southward. News of the French advance reached Johnson, and he sent out a party of a thousand men, under Colonel Ephraim Williams, to intercept them. It wasn't enough. They fought well, but the colonials were driven back and Williams was killed. (He had made out a will leaving money to found a school in western Massachusetts, and it exists today as Williams College.)

When the fleeing detachment reached Johnson's camp, he hastily ordered the throwing up of a barrier of felled trees. The French attacked overconfidently, but it was the reverse of the situation on the Monongahela. Now it was the colonials who were behind cover, shooting from security, and the French who were in the open. They were driven off, and Dieskau was wounded and taken prisoner. The Battle of Lake George was considered a great victory by the British and colonials, who badly needed one. Johnson was made a baronet and was awarded 5000 pounds by a grateful Parliament.

The victory was not followed up, however, and came to

nothing. Unfortunately, Johnson, who had been the soul of honor and decency in treating with the Indians, now showed a meanness of spirit. He had been wounded in the course of the Battle of Lake George, and General Phineas Lyman of Connecticut took over the leadership. It was Lyman who carried the battle to victory and who was hailed by the soldiers, with whom he was very popular.

Johnson, in a fit of jealousy, neglected to mention Lyman at all in his report on the battle. When Lyman supervised the building of a fort on the upper Hudson, Johnson had its name changed from Fort Lyman (as it was originally called) to Fort Edward, after Prince Edward, a grandson of George II. A fort which Johnson had built at the site of the battle, he called "Fort William Henry," after another grandson of the King's.

Even worse than the friction between Johnson and Lyman was the fact that New York and Massachusetts, whose men had fought and won the battle together, were virtually at war among themselves. There was a boundary dispute between them, and New York was not as eager as Massachusetts to make a too-aggressive strike against the French (with whom many important New York businessmen carried on a lucrative trade).

So Johnson resigned his commission, and no further advance was made in the direction of Lake Champlain.

To this list of defeats and empty victories, there was added that year a further blot on the British reputation — farther north, and a blot of another sort.

Despite the foundation of Halifax, the British position in Nova Scotia was not secure. The French settlers (the Acadians) were by no means reconciled to British rule; rather the contrary, in fact. As French fortunes rose in the 1750s, the Acadians became more openly and more aggressively pro-French.

Gentler means having failed, the British finally placed a harsh alternative before the Acadians. Colonel Charles Lawrence, then governor of Nova Scotia, announced that all must either

swear allegiance to the British crown (and therefore lay themselves open to the charge of treason for any anti–British action)
or suffer deportation.

By and large, the Acadians refused, and Great Britain then
did to the French of Nova Scotia what they had not done to the
Dutch of New York. They shipped them out. Deportations began, on October 8, 1755, and from six to eight thousand Acadians were taken out of Acadia and distributed among the other
British colonies.

It was an act of cruelty that was not forgotten. Ninety years
later, the American poet, Henry Wadsworth Longfellow was to
tell the story in his long narrative poem, "Evangeline." The tale
of how two lovers were separated on their wedding day by the
British and of how Evangeline finally found her Gabriel only on
his deathbed, has wrung the hearts of generations of school
children and has placed the British in the role of villain.

Actually, things were not quite as bad as that. A number of
the Acadians returned to Nova Scotia, swore allegiance to Great
Britain, and were given new lands. Some made their way to
southern Louisiana, still French then, and persist there even
today. Their descendants live along the Gulf shores of the states
of Louisiana and Alabama and still call themselves "Cajuns" (a
corruption of "Acadians").

One short–term result of the eviction of the Acadians was the
angry stiffening of French determination both in Europe and in
North America. Louisbourg remained in French hands, and
France labored to strengthen it further. By now, if not before,
Great Britain had cause to regret the carelessness that had
allowed them to return the place to France after King George's
War.

And, in 1756, there was a further intensification of the situation when war broke out in Europe.

As a result of the War of the Austrian Succession (the European end of King George's War), Prussia under its remarkable
king, Frederick II, had become a great power. Austria, how-

ever, could not forgive Prussia the defeats Frederick had inflicted on her in the previous war and finally organized a formidable coalition. With France, Russia, Sweden, and some German states on her side, she launched an attack on Prussia.

Only Great Britain supported Prussia, and this largely because she dared not allow France to grow stronger through victory in Europe. This only made official the unofficial warfare that was going on with France, not only in North America, but in India, too. As a result, this war, called "The Seven Years' War" in Europe, is the first conflict in history that can truly qualify as a world war, since it involved fighting on three continents and on the high seas.

LOUISBOURG

The coming of war in Europe did not, however, magically transform colonial fortunes in North America. In fact, the situation for the colonies grew worse, if anything.

On May 13, 1756, five days before Great Britain's declaration of war on France, a new general arrived in Quebec. He was the Marquis Louis Joseph de Montcalm, a capable soldier who had fought gallantly in the War of the Austrian Succession. Unfortunately for France, he was given authority only over the French regular troops; while Marquis de Vaudreuil, the governor of New France, retained control over everything else. This divided authority weakened the French forces, all the more so since Vaudreuil, a not very competent man, disliked and envied Montcalm and was not usually disposed to cooperate with him.

On the British side, John Campbell, fourth Earl of Loudon, was appointed commander–in–chief of the British troops in North America, replacing Shirley. He arrived in New York, on July 22, 1756, and quickly proved himself incapable of getting along with the colonials.

Montcalm began vigorous actions on the New York frontier, taking and destroying the fortifications at Oswego on the southern shore of Lake Ontario, on August 14, 1756, and depriving the British of their only hold on the Great Lakes.

A year later, on August 9, 1757, he laid siege to Fort William Henry and forced its surrender, making himself master of a great store of supplies and war materiel, and wiping out the effect of Johnson's victory at Lake George. He guaranteed the safety of the garrison and agreed to allow them to retire with all honors of war, but was unable to prevent his Indian allies from attacking and killing many of them. (These events are central to the action in James Fenimore Cooper's famous novel, *The Last of the Mohicans*.)

As for Loudon, he intended to strike against Louisbourg. He had six thousand British regulars, and, on July 13, 1757, he reached Halifax where he was reinforced with 6000 more troops and eleven ships. Then, with all that in hand, he found he had to face French reinforcements, the damaging effect of adverse weather on his own ships, and the failure of the various colonial legislatures to support him vigorously. He decided that he wasn't strong enough for the task. He returned to New York with nothing accomplished. It was one more fiasco.

Three years had now passed since George Washington had started the French and Indian War during his expedition against Fort Duquesne, and the record had been one of almost unrelieved British defeat.

But now changes were taking place in Great Britain, where discontent over reverses in North America, and elsewhere, too, were rising. George II, like his father, was far more interested in the vest–pocket electorate of Hanover in Germany, than he was in Great Britain. He concentrated on Europe, therefore, and the vast British sea empire, which even then was growing in North America and in India, was neglected.

Opposed to his course were a group of politicians who called themselves "patriots" and who wanted British overseas interests to take precedence. They were intent on building an empire and not on fighting over a few hamlets in Europe.

Chief among the politicians in opposition to the Hanoverian policy was William Pitt. He entered Parliament, in 1735, while still only twenty–three, and at once joined the party of Frederick Louis, the Prince of Wales. (Among the Hanoverian kings of Great Britain, it was traditional for the King and the Prince of Wales to hate each other and to fight bitterly.)

Through his years in Parliament, Pitt showed himself (despite constant illness, gout in particular) an extremely formidable person, thanks to his great powers of oratory and to the way in which he could swing public opinion behind him. George II, however, could not endure Pitt, because of his bitter attacks on the Hanoverian policy. The King therefore kept Pitt out of the government as long as possible, even though he grew more and more popular with the country at large (not only for his point of view but for the honesty that kept him a poor man when all about him accepted graft as a matter of course).

The disasters of 1755 and 1756, however, brought Pitt to the fore. Popular demand could no longer be denied, and Pitt's self–confidence was such that he said, "I know that I can save the country and that no one else can." (Pitt was, in fact, a kind of eighteenth–century Winston Churchill.)

By November 1756, he was in the ministry, and, although the King managed to force him out, he was soon in again. In June 1757, a new ministry was formed under the Duke of Newcastle, and Pitt, as Minister of War, was its heart and soul. He was in entire control of the war; and he infused new vigor into British policy, concentrated with all his might on the overseas ventures, and sifted the armed forces for capable leaders. As for Europe, he took no direct action there, nor did he need to. He merely gave Frederick II plenty of money and let him do the fighting, something he did remarkably well.

On December 30, 1757, Pitt recalled Loudon and got him out of North America. He sent large contingents of British regulars to America and began to make proper use of colonials. He paid them out of the British treasury and recognized the ranks of their officers. A new, fresh wind was blowing over the continent.

In 1758, a triple–pronged offensive against the French was planned. The British and colonials began to prepare expeditions against Louisbourg, against Fort Ticonderoga on Lake Champlain, and against Fort Duquesne, where Braddock's forces had been smashed. Pitt supplied plenty of men and supplies for all three and would brook no delay.

In some ways, the land offensive against Fort Ticonderoga was most important since a success there would open the way right into the heart of New France. Here, however, Pitt was working with a holdover, Major–General James Abercrombie, who had been second in command to Loudon and who had automatically succeeded to the post of commander–in–chief when the latter had been relieved of command.

Abercrombie was a heavy, slow-witted man, subject to the pains of indigestion, and he did not move fast. Partly, it was not his fault; for he depended on colonial militia to a considerable extent, and they were slow in gathering. Once they had come, however, they proved valuable. This was particularly so in the case of a company of hard–fighting scouts (Rogers's Rangers) who had been organized, in 1756, by Robert Rogers of New Hampshire. Abercrombie promoted Rogers to the rank of major.

With Abercrombie also was Brigadier General Lord Augustus Howe, who knew how to work with colonials, had fought with Rogers's Rangers, and was the real brains of the expedition.

Abercrombie finally got under way at the beginning of July 1758, and almost at once disaster struck. A contingent, scouting forward, skirmished with the enemy, on July 6, and Lord Howe was killed. Abercrombie was left with nothing but his indigestion to guide him.

By July 8, Abercrombie was at Ticonderoga with 16,000 men. Opposing him was Montcalm with only 4000. (Montcalm could be there at all only because he had somehow managed to argue and cajole the Iroquois into remaining neutral.) Abercrombie could easily have surrounded Ticonderoga and starved it out, but his scouts told him that the French were expecting reinforcements. Abercrombie therefore hastened to attack before those reinforcements could come.

So far, so good. That wasn't in itself a bad idea, but the attack ought to have been carried through intelligently. Without Howe to guide him, Abercrombie could think of nothing better to do than to order his men blindly forward. He did not wait to bring up his artillery, nor did he pay sufficient attention to the fact that the French were entrenched behind fallen trees, as the British had been at Crown Point.

Abercrombie pressed a useless and bloody frontal attack through seven separate assaults before his dim mind could recognize disaster. He reeled back with nearly two thousand casualties as against less than four hundred on the part of the French. It was worse than Braddock's defeat.

That broke Abercrombie's spirit, and he attempted nothing more. Nor would a furious William Pitt have allowed him to do anything more after the news reached him. Abercrombie was relieved of his command, on September 18.

As it happened, though, the Battle of Ticonderoga was the last French victory. Even as it took place, Louisbourg was under close siege.

On June 8, 1758, nine thousand British regulars and five hundred colonials, carried on 157 warships and transports, were at Louisbourg. The expedition was under the command of Colonel Jeffery Amherst who had distinguished himself at the Battle of Dettingen in western Germany, in 1743, when British troops, under the personal leadership of King George II, defeated the French. (It was the last battle in which a British

monarch commanded troops on the field.) Pitt promoted Amherst to major–general before sending him off.

Second in command was a 31–year–old brigadier–general,
James Wolfe, who had also fought at Dettingen. Wolfe was
an eccentric who, despite constant ill health and premonitions
of early death, had been in the army since he was thirteen and
had given ample proof of the possession of a rather erratic bril-
liance. Pitt had an eye on him as a result of the excellent way
in which he had organized attacks on French seaports the previous year.

Wolfe was an eccentric. For one thing, he was a teetotaler in
an age when army officers were hard drinkers as a matter of
course. He had effeminate mannerisms and a rather unpredict-
able way about him. He would have none of the staid wigs
worn by officers of the time, but insisted on exposing his own
flaming–red hair, which he wore long and bound in a queue.

His manner was strange enough so that when, later in the
war, he was entrusted with great responsibilities, the Duke of
Newcastle nervously expostulated, "But he's mad, sir." To which
George II growled in answer, "Mad, is he? Then I wish he'd
bite some of my other generals."

Wolfe, carrying only a cane and with his long red hair making
him an unmistakable target, personally led the landing force
that disembarked southwest of the fort. For seven weeks, even
while Abercrombie's offensive gathered and then came to disaster, the British bombarded the fort. Its strong walls, designed
to withstand bombardment, remained; but the French guns
were silenced one by one, and a thousand of the French defenders, isolated by the British fleet, died one by one. On July
26, there seemed no reasonable hope for further defense, and
Louisbourg surrendered. The British loss was only half that of
the French. Louisbourg was promptly destroyed, and only its
ruins survive to this day.

The fall of Louisbourg was the turning point of the war and, indeed, the turning point of the entire colonial struggle between France and Great Britain. It more than made up for the disaster at Ticonderoga, and French morale plummeted. With the British in command of the sea and with the British navy in firm control of the mouth of the St. Lawrence, the French in North America were virtually isolated. It had to be, now, a matter of time only before they were defeated — unless the British somehow managed to defeat themselves.

But the British were not going to. With Pitt driving them on and morale zooming, they did nothing wrong. Even before Abercrombie was relieved, one of his subordinates, Lieutenant Colonel John Bradstreet took three thousand men, made his way to Lake Ontario, crossed it in a flotilla of small boats, and attacked Fort Frontenac (where Kingston, Ontario now stands). Bradstreet, unlike Abercrombie, made proper use of his artillery, and, after two days of bombardment, the fort surrendered, on August 27.

Farther south still, Brigadier–General John Forbes, with seven thousand men, labored to repeat Braddock's march and bring it to a more successful conclusion. The march began, in July 1758, with George Washington one of the officers serving under Forbes in one last and useless attempt to achieve some real status, despite the fact that he was a mere colonial.

As the British approached, the French, finding themselves deserted by their Indian allies (who scented the turn of the tide without difficulty), destroyed Fort Duquesne, on November 24, 1758, and retreated northward. The next day the British were on the site and erected Fort Pitt instead (named for the war minister, of course). About that nucleus, the city of Pittsburgh, Pennsylvania, grew up.

As 1758 drew to its close, then, Pitt could see that all was going well. He made Amherst, the victor at Louisbourg, commander–in–chief of the British forces in North America and prepared for the kill.

QUEBEC

For 1759, Pitt ordered Amherst to carry the fight into the heart of New France and to take Quebec itself. Amherst therefore planned a triple–pronged offensive. The first was against Fort Niagara, the closest strong point still held by the French in the Great Lakes area. The second was against Fort Ticonderoga, where the British had had their one failure the year before. And the third was against Quebec itself.

In June 1759, Brigadier–General John Prideaux, with two thousand men, did as Bradstreet had done the year before. He marched to Lake Ontario, sailed over the lake to Fort Niagara, and took it, on July 25, after a steady nineteen–day artillery barrage (although Prideaux himself died in the course of the bombardment, being hit accidentally by a British shot). Sir William Johnson and one hundred Iroquois were present at this action.

Meanwhile, Amherst himself was leading 11,000 British regulars to the attack on Fort Ticonderoga. Since the French, whose Indian allies continued steadily to fade away, were extremely short of manpower, it was necessary for them to hoard every man for the supreme battle which would be, of course, at Quebec. They therefore abandoned Ticonderoga (Fort Carillon to the French), on July 26, and Crown Point (Fort St. Frederic), on July 31. Both points were quickly refortified by the British, and, by August, all of Lake Champlain was in British hands.

As for Quebec, what was planned was a sea–borne assault from captured Louisbourg. James Wolfe was quite ill, but he was pressured to take command. (It was on this occasion that George II said he hoped Wolfe would bite some of his other generals.)

Wolfe, with nine thousand men and a number of colonials (including contingents of Rogers's Rangers) moved up the St. Lawrence River with a fleet of 22 warships and many transports and, on June 26, disembarked on Orleans Island, 4 miles down river from Quebec.

The task that Wolfe found himself assigned to undertake was not an easy one. Quebec was situated on a prominence high above the St. Lawrence and it was impregnable if it were resolutely defended. Concerning the resolution of the defense there seemed no question since Montcalm himself was in command; and he had a total of 16,000 men under him, nearly twice that of Wolfe's command.

Montcalm had his difficulties of course. Many of his soldiers were French colonials who might not be steady under fire. Furthermore, since he was on the defensive, he had to spread his men out to cover every possible weak point while the British were free to concentrate at any one point as they chose. Last, and worst of all, Vaudreuil, the governor of New France chose to hamper Montcalm at every point in a manner that went beyond incompetence and approached malice.

Montcalm's difficulties were of no immediate help to Wolfe. Lacking forces large enough to surround the city and try to starve it out, he could do nothing but bombard the city from the river, hoping it would force Montcalm out into the open to give battle.

Montcalm knew better than that. He would not be lured into a fight. He intended to endure the shelling and was counting on the fact that winter would eventually come and that the fleet, on which Wolfe depended, would have to leave.

Through July, the tug of war continued. Both sides attempted offensive actions that failed. On July 31, Wolfe attempted a quick frontal assault in the hope that the French would be surprised enough and disheartened enough to give way. They weren't, and they didn't; the British fell back with over 400 casualties, while the French remained virtually untouched.

A few days before that, on July 27, Montcalm had tried a fire–ship tactic. Ships loaded with inflammables were set floating downstream toward the British fleet. At the last minute they were to be set on fire and the hope was that the wooden warships of the British would catch fire, too, and be disabled or, at the very least, have to retire for repairs. Unfortunately for Montcalm, the ships were fired too soon, and British sailors had time and space to row out to the burning ships and tow them to shore where they could quietly reduce themselves to ash without doing harm.

But the days passed, and each one was a day of summer gone to French advantage. The news arrived of the defeats suffered by the French on Lake Ontario and Lake Champlain, but that did not halt the passing of summer. Although the steady bombardment was damaging the French, the British troops were melting away with disease and desertion also. On August 20, Wolfe himself was too ill with fever to rise from his bed.

Then September came, and the fleet was growing anxious. By September 10, Admiral Saunders, who was responsible for the safety of the ships, argued strenuously that unless something happened quickly, the attack must be broken off. Once the river began to ice up, the fleet might be lost and with it the entire expeditionary force.

Wolfe had to do something soon. At this low point he became aware of a path that led from the river to the heights, one that seemed to lead to a place that was but thinly defended. According to one tale, he spied it himself through his field glass, a thin, nearly invisible track going up the cliff. According to another tale, it was pointed out to him by a British officer who had once been prisoner in Quebec and knew the terrain.

It was necessary for Wolfe to keep the French from guessing the place where the British would make their attempt, for if they sent men to cover that path, all was lost. Wolfe therefore kept British ships scouring the river as though looking for a place for a landing. He set up bombardments in the wrong places, where he knew the French were well defended, in order to force Montcalm to keep those places well defended with men who were, in that way, kept far from the real objective.

In the early hours of the morning, on September 13, Rogers's Rangers, together with a detachment of British soldiers under Colonel William Howe, began to scramble up the path. Simon Frazer, a young Scottish officer answered sentries' challenges in French with a self-confident calm that carried conviction. By the time the French outposts at the point realized it was the British army coming up, enough British troops had reached the top to overpower them. The rest followed.

When morning came, a British army of nearly five thousand men, sprung as though from nowhere, stood outside Quebec. They were on the Plains of Abraham, named after its one-time owner, a river pilot named Abraham Martin. (The city of Quebec has now expanded to include the site as a park within the city limits.)

Montcalm, caught in utter surprise, hastened to do what he could. The men he could lay his hands on at a moment's notice were only 4500 in number and most of them were colonials, not regulars. He could not wait to bring up more men; nor could he bring up artillery, for Vaudreuil withheld that from him.

It was a battle in the traditional style of linear tactics. The French moved forward while the British regulars waited. Wolfe judged the exact moment, then gave the signal. The British raised their muskets, fired in unison, and the French line withered and turned in flight. Now it was the British turn to charge with wild abandon and drive the foe into the city. In that charge, both Montcalm and Wolfe were mortally wounded.

Wolfe, upheld by men who came to his support, heard the cry, "See how they run!"

"Who run?" murmured Wolfe.

"The enemy," came the answer.

And Wolfe said, "Then I die in peace."

As for Montcalm, he was helped into the city. He was told he would die, and quickly. "So much the better," he said, "I will not live to see Quebec surrender." He died the next day.

Vaudreuil, bottled up in the city, still had available an army which was larger than the British forces. He might yet have made a fight for it, but he dared not. With Montcalm gone, he could think only of escape and abandoned the city, on September 17, making his way to Montreal. The British marched into Quebec, on September 18.

But the French still had an army in Montreal, and they were not yet done. When the winter closed in, the British fleet had to leave the St. Lawrence, and the British soldiers occupying Quebec were isolated. In the spring, a French army marched downstream to Quebec, and a British force came out of the city to meet them. On April 27, 1760, the French won the second battle of Quebec and promptly placed the city under siege.

Sea power made all the difference, however. The British held out for nearly three weeks, and then, on May 15, the river ice broke and the British ships came sailing upstream. The French had to return hurriedly to Montreal.

In September 1760, the British were advancing on Montreal from three directions. They were moving toward Montreal upstream from Quebec, downstream from Lake Ontario, and cross stream from Lake Champlain and the Richelieu River. On September 8, 1760, Vaudreuil bowed to the inevitable and gave up Montreal. Meanwhile Rogers's Rangers were sweeping up French forts on the farther Great Lakes, taking Detroit on November 29, 1760. New France came to an end after a century and a half of existence.

Simultaneously with her victories in North America, Great Britain was winning victories in India, too, and it was in 1759 that the British Empire may be truly said to have been founded. It was then that Great Britain began its two–century career as the world's dominating power.

It seemed to be of little moment that in Europe itself, Great

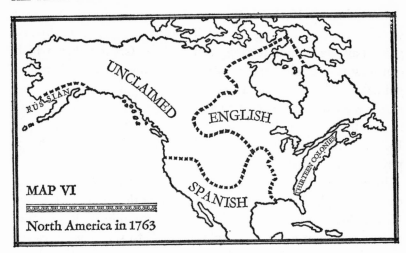

MAP VI

North America in 1763

Britain's ally, Frederick II of Prussia, seemed sure to be crushed by an overwhelming array of enemies. Even there, though, British fortune held. Desperately, Frederick II hung on till, on January 5, 1762, his most bitter enemy, the Empress Elizabeth of Russia, died. That shattered the alliance against him and enabled him to survive.

Meanwhile, however, Spain, fearing an overwhelming British victory and the consequent loss of her own overseas possessions, prepared to join the French side. Great Britain did not wait. On January 2, 1762, she declared war on Spain and in quick succession took some of the smaller West Indian islands, together with Cuba and, on the other side of the world, the Philippine Islands.

Great Britain could not be halted, and France found only one way of staving off utter loss. In the secret Treaty of Fontainebleu, signed on November 3, 1762, France ceded all her claims west of the Mississippi to Spain. That would at least keep that area out of the hands of Great Britain, and someday, when the pendulum swung back, it would not be difficult to force Spain to disgorge again.

On February 10, 1763, the war came to an end all over the world with the signing of the Treaty of Paris. The British gained all the French territory north of the Great Lakes, which can now be called Canada, rather than New France. She also gained all of Louisiana east of the Mississippi, leaving the territory west of the river to Spain in accordance with France's earlier treaty with that country. From Spain, however, Great Britain took Florida in return for handing Cuba and the Philippines back.

France was thus completely evicted from the North American mainland. All she retained of her vast dominions were two islands, St. Pierre and Miquelon (93 square miles in total area) off the southern coast of Newfoundland, to serve as bases for her fishing fleet. (Those islands remain French to this day.) France also retained her holdings in the West Indies.

In 1763, then, North America was divided between Great Britain and Spain. The Mississippi River separated the holdings of the two nations. Only the northwestern quadrant of the continent remained a no man's land, to whose shores British, Spanish, and French ships all occasionally ventured, but where the Russians were most active.

A NEW BEGINNING

Great Britain, in 1763, had reached a peak in its history. Its triumph in the world outside Europe was nearly absolute. It controlled the seas; it held the northeastern portion of North America; it had a strong foothold in India. Those other nations who had overseas dominions held them only by grace of the British navy.

In particular, North America had finally received its shape. Two and a half centuries after Columbus's great voyage, one

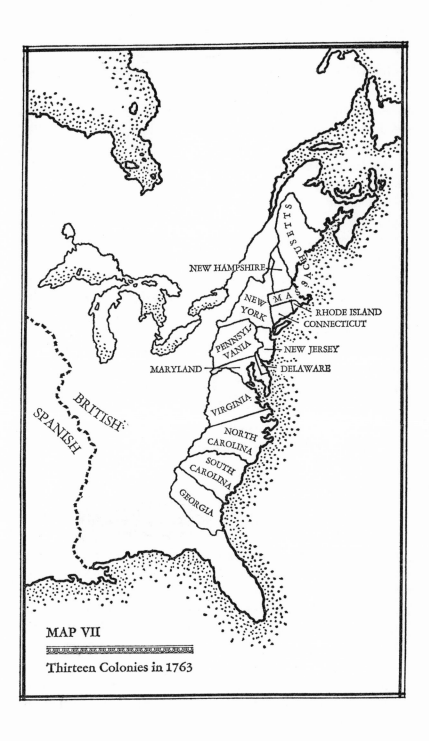

NEW HAMPSHIRE

MASSACHUSETTS

NEW
YORK

M A

RHODE ISLAND
CONNECTICUT

PENNSYL
VANIA

NEW JERSEY

MARYLAND

DELAWARE

VIRGINIA

NORTH
CAROLINA

SOUTH
CAROLINA

GEORGIA

BRITISH

SPANISH

MAP VII

Thirteen Colonies in 1763

and a half centuries after England had planted its first colony on the continent, the decision had come.

North America was to be British in heritage. Those who lived there, whatever their origins, would speak the English language and be heir to English traditions. How much of North America would be Anglicized in this way could not be foretold just then, but with only feeble Spain standing in the way, it would surely be most of the continent and possibly all of it.

That much seemed certain, and that much has indeed come to pass.

Yet not all was decided. Even if North America spoke English, would it therefore necessarily be subject to the British crown? In 1763, there must have been few if any British subjects, either in Great Britain or in North America who doubted that it would, and yet. . . .

On what terms would the British colonials of North America remain subject to the British crown?

To the British themselves this must have seemed a foolish question if anyone had raised it. The answer to them would have been, quite obviously, on those terms which the British government would set.

To the colonials that answer was not quite so obvious. They had always been difficult to govern, even when the French and the Indians were a constant menace and the British soldiers and ships were needed for defense. Now that the French were gone and the Indians were but a minor problem, the colonials would surely be far harder to govern. They could afford to feel offended and to complain loudly where previously they had dared only grumble beneath their breaths.

There were a million and a quarter White men in the colonies, in 1763, with the population going up rapidly. To these might be added the unpaid labor of over a quarter of a million Black slaves, mostly in the southern colonies. This was nearly 20 percent of the population of Great Britain and what's more, the colonials were spread over an area far greater and potentially far richer than the home country.

The colonials could not be expected to remain quiet while Great Britain continued to act under the calm assumption that she could treat North America as her own to do with as she wished. They would not be content to endure Great Britain's laws that restricted the territories they could settle, or constricted their economy for the profit of British manufacturers, or settled taxes on them at will.

The British, on the other hand, were utterly blind to the powder keg in the colonies. A new king, George III, had succeeded to the throne, in 1760. He was a kindly and decent man who was, however, not very intelligent and who was enormously stubborn to boot.

There was going to be a quarrel, a new beginning of a new kind of trouble. Great Britain had beaten France and shaped North America, but there are no final decisions in history and much of what had been won was now to be lost after all.

What was to come was the birth of the United States, a story which we must leave for another book.

THE END

A TABLE OF DATES

1420 Henry the Navigator establishes exploration center at Sagres, Portugal

1431 Azores discovered by G. V. Cabral (Portuguese)

1445 Cape Verde reached by Dinis Dias (Portuguese)

1455 Cape Verde Islands discovered by Cadamosto (Portuguese)

1460 13 November Henry the Navigator dies

1474 12 December Isabella I becomes queen of Castile

1479 Ferdinand II becomes king of Aragon; with Isabella rules over a united Spain

1481 John II becomes king of Portugal

1482 Cão (Portuguese) reaches mouth of Congo River

1483 Christopher Columbus appeals to John II of Portugal for support for western voyage

1485 22 August Henry VII becomes king of England

1486 Columbus's first appeal to Ferdinand and Isabella for backing

1488 Bartholomeu Dias (Portuguese) reaches southern tip of Africa

1492 2 January Ferdinand and Isabella take Granada

3 August Columbus leaves on first voyage westward

12 October Columbus reaches San Salvador; "discovers America"

28 October Columbus discovers Cuba

6 December Columbus discovers Hispaniola

1493 13 March Columbus returns to Spain

4 May Pope Alexander VI establishes Line of Demarcation

25 September Columbus leaves on second voyage

19 November Columbus discovers Puerto Rico

1494 7 June Treaty of Tordesillas, moves Line of Demarcation westward

1497 19 May Vasco da Gama (Portuguese) rounds Africa and reaches India

24 June Cabot discovers Newfoundland

1498 30 May Columbus leaves on third voyage

1500 22 April Cabral discovers Brazil

1501 Corterreal sails past Labrador and names it

1502 9 May Columbus leaves on fourth voyage

1504 Vespucius maintains western lands to be part of separate continent

1506 20 May Death of Columbus

1507 Waldseemüller uses name "America" for first time

1508 Ponce de León founds permanent colony in Puerto Rico

1509 21 April Henry VII dies; Henry VIII becomes king of England

1510 San Juan, Puerto Rico, founded

1513   11. April   Ponce de León
       discovers Florida
       25 September   Balboa
       sights the Ocean (Pacific)
       west of Americas
1515   Havana, Cuba, founded
       1 January   Francis I be-
       comes king of France
1516   23 January   Charles I
       becomes king of Spain
1519   20 September   Magellan
       leaves Spain on voyage of
       circumnavigation
       21 October   Magellan
       discovers Strait of Magel-
       lan
       18 November   Cortez en-
       ters Tenochtitlán (Mexico
       City)
       28 November   Magellan
       enters   Pacific   Ocean;
       names it
1521   27 April   Magellan dies
       in Philippine Islands
1522   7 September   Del Cano,
       with one ship of Magel-
       lan's   fleet,   returns   to
       Spain; first circumnaviga-
       tion of Earth
1524   17 April   Verrazano   en-
       ters New York Bay
1528   Narváez   explores   Gulf
       Coast west of Florida
1534   10 August   Cartier enters
       Gulf of St. Lawrence
1536   De Vaca returns to Mexico
       City after exploring Texas
       and northern Mexico
1540   Coronado explores Ameri-
       can southwest
1541   18 June   De Soto discov-
       ers Mississippi River
1542   21 May   Death   of   De
       Soto

1547   28 January   Henry VIII
       dies; Edward VI becomes
       king of England
1553   6 July   Edward VI dies;
       Mary I becomes queen of
       England
1556   16 January   Charles I ab-
       dicates; Philip II becomes
       king of Spain
1558   17 November   Mary I
       dies; Elizabeth I becomes
       queen of England
1560   5 December   Charles IX
       becomes king of France
1564   Huguenots establish col-
       ony in northern Florida
1565   Menendez de Avila de-
       stroys Huguenot colony
       8 September   St. Augus-
       tine, Florida, founded
1567   Hawkins and Drake at-
       tacked by Spaniards in
       Vera Cruz
1573   3 February   Drake in
       Panama; sights Pacific
       Ocean
1576   June   Frobisher   discov-
       ers Baffin Island
1577   13 December   Drake sets
       sail on circumnavigation
       of Earth
1578   20 June   Frobisher redis-
       covers Greenland
       6 September   Drake en-
       ters Pacific Ocean
1579   Drake explores west coast
       of North America
1580   Philip II of Spain be-
       comes king of Portugal as
       well
       26 September   Drake re-
       turns to England; com-
       pletes   circumnavigation
       of Earth

1581 Black slaves brought to Florida for first time

1583 Gilbert attempts to establish English colony in Newfoundland

1584 Raleigh names east coast of North America "Virginia"

1587 Davis explores west coast of Greenland

English settlement at Roanoke Island by White

18 August   Birth of Virginia Dare, first child of English parentage born in territory of United States

1588 England defeats Spanish Armada

1589 2 August   Henry IV becomes king of France

1591 15 August   White returns to Roanoke, finds colony gone

1598 De Onate explores New Mexico

13 September   Philip II of Spain dies

1602 15 May   Gosnold explores Cape Cod

1603 3 April   Elizabeth I dies; James I becomes king of England

1604 Champlain explores New England coast

1606 10 April   London Company and Plymouth Company founded

1607 13 May   Jamestown founded; beginning of colony of Virginia

December   John Smith saved by Pocahontas

1608 3 July   Quebec founded by French

1609 30 July   Champlain fires at Iroquois; beginning of French–Iroquois feud

3 September   Hudson enters New York Bay

12 September   Hudson begins sail up Hudson River

5 October   John Smith recalled from Virginia

1610 Santa Fe, New Mexico, founded by Spaniards

14 May   Louis XIII becomes king of France

8 June   Lord De La Warr's ships prevent abandonment of Jamestown

3 August   Hudson enters Hudson Bay

1612 Rolfe develops Virginian tobacco

1614 John Smith explores New England shore

Block explores Connecticut shore

Fort Nassau (Albany, New York) founded by Dutch

1615 Champlain discovers Great Lakes

1619 30 July   House of Burgesses established in Virginia; first representative assembly in colonies

August   First Black slaves brought to Virginia

1620 16 September   Pilgrims leave England

9 November   Pilgrims reach Cape Cod

21 November   Pilgrims sign Mayflower Compact

16 December   Pilgrims anchor off Plymouth

1621   3 June   Dutch found Dutch West India Company

1622   22 March   Opechancano's Indians attack Virginia colonists

10 August   Gorges and Mason receive charter to colonize New England shores; beginning of colony of New Hampshires

1624   Manhattan Island settled by Dutch

1625   27 March   James I dies; Charles I becomes king of England

1626   4 May   Minuit buys Manhattan Island from Indians for $24

1629   English take Quebec

7 June   Dutch found patroon system in New Netherland

1630   7 September   Boston founded; beginning of colony of Massachusetts

1632   English return Quebec to French

16 November   Christina becomes queen of Sweden

1634   27 March   St. Mary's founded; beginning of colony of Maryland

1635   9 October   Roger Williams banished from Massachusetts

October   Hartford founded; beginning of colony of Connecticut

1636   June   Providence founded; beginning of

colony of Rhode Island

28 October   Harvard College founded

1637   26 May   Pequot Indians defeated along Mystic Bay; Indian power broken in Connecticut and Rhode Island

8 November   Anne Hutchinson exiled from Massachusetts

1638   29 March   New Sweden founded along shores of Delaware Bay

15 April   New Haven founded

1640   Portugal regains independence from Spain

1642   French defeat Spaniards at Battle of Rocroi; Spanish military preeminence destroyed

1643   New England Confederation formed

14 May   Louis XIII dies; Louis XIV becomes king of France

1644   18 April   Opechancano leads second attack on Virginia colonists; Indian power in Virginia broken before end of year

1647   Peter Stuyvesant becomes governor of New Netherland

First woman hanged as witch in colonies (in Conneticut)

1648   24 October   Treaty of Westphalia; Netherlands officially independent

1649   30 January   Charles I of England beheaded

21 April Toleration Act passed in Maryland

1651 Stuyvesant establishes Fort Casimir in Delaware Bay

9 October England passes first Navigation Act

1652 18 May Rhode Island forbids slavery; becomes first free colony

1654 Swedes take Fort Casimir

1655 26 September New Netherland absorbs New Sweden

1658 3 September Oliver Cromwell dies

1659 Virginia recognizes Charles II as king of England

1660 8 May Charles II formally accepted as king of England

1661 Virginia recognizes slavery as legal institution

1662 23 April Charles II grants Connecticut a charter

1663 24 March Charles II grants charter to eight courtiers to colonize land south of Virginia; beginning of colony of Carolina

8 July Charles II grants Rhode Island a charter

1664 24 June Cartaret and Berkeley granted charter for southern New Netherland; beginning of colony of New Jersey

7 September New Amsterdam surrenders to English; beginning of colony of New York

1665 5 January New Haven merges with Connecticut

1666 Allouer founds missions along Great Lakes

1667 21 July Treaty of Breda; Netherlands formally recognizes English possession of New York; French possession of Acadia recognized

23 September Virginia law keeps Black a slave even after he is converted to Christianity

1670 First settlements at Albemarle south; beginning of colony of North Carolina

April Charleston founded; beginning of colony of South Carolina

2 May English establish Hudson's Bay Company

1672 Count Frontenac governor of New France

1673 17 June Joliet and Marquette reach upper Mississippi River; give it its name

30 July Dutch fleet retakes New York

1674 10 November Dutch return New York to English

1675 24 June King Philip's War begins in New England

19 December King Philip defeated at Battle of Great Swamp

1676 20 April Bacon leads Virginians against Indians

1 July New Jersey divided into East Jersey and West Jersey

12 August King Philip

killed; Indian power broken in Massachusetts
19 September   Bacon burns Jamestown
26 October   Bacon dies

1679   24 July   Charles II grants New Hampshire a charter

1680   Pueblo Indians revolt; take Santa Fe from Spaniards

1681   14 March   Charles II grants William Penn right to settle west of Delaware River; beginning of colony of Pennsylvania

1682   9 April   La Salle reaches mouth of Mississippi; claims the entire river basin ("Louisiana") for France
27 April   Peter I becomes Czar of Russia
27 October   Philadelphia founded

1683   Carolina colonists settle Port Royal

1684   5 September   Last meeting of New England Confederation
23 October   Massachusetts charter annulled

1685   6 February   Charles II dies; James II becomes king of England
18 October   Louis XIV revokes Edict of Nantes; Protestantism no longer tolerated in France

1686   3 June   Dominion of New England established; Andros governor
17 August   Spaniards drive Carolinians out of Port Royal

1687   15 March   Anglican church established in Boston
19 May   La Salle dies

1688   April   Quakers of Germantown, Pennsylvania, issue protest against slavery
November   James II driven from throne of England

1689   King William's War begins
13 February   William III and Mary II rule England
18 April   Andros arrested; Dominion of New England breaks up
1 June   Leisler rebellion in New York begins
4 August   Iroquois massacre at Lachine in New France
1 December   Leisler proclaims himself governor of New York

1690   8 February   French and Indian massacre at Schenectady, New York
1 May   Leisler calls for united colonial action against French and Indians
11 May   Colonials under Phips take Port Royal, Acadia
31 July   French and Indian massacre at settlement at site of Portland, Maine
7 October   Phips reaches Quebec, but fails to take it

1691   16 May   Leisler executed
7 October   Massachusetts
gets new charter; absorbs
Plymouth
1692   Witchcraft mania in Salem
Spaniards retake Santa Fe
1693   8 February   College of
William and Mary
founded
1694   28 December   Mary II of
England dies
1696   South Carolina establishes
freedom of religion for all
Protestants
1697   10 September   Treaty of
Ryswick ends King Wil-
liam's War; no change in
North America
1698   Pensacola, Florida,
founded by Spaniards
1699   Capital of Virginia transferred from Jamestown to
Williamsburg
Biloxi established on Gulf
Coast by French
1700   1 November   Charles II
of Spain dies; grandson of
Louis XIV becomes king
of Spain as Philip V
1701   23 May   Captain Kidd
hanged
24 July   Detroit founded
by French
1702   Carolinians sack St. Augustine, Florida
8 March   William III
dies; Anne becomes queen
of England
17 April   East Jersey and
West Jersey reunited to
New Jersey
4 May   Queen Anne's
War begins

1704   29 February   French and
Indian massacre at Deer-
field, Massachusetts
24 April   *Boston
Newsletter* begins publi-
cation; first regularly issued newspaper in the
colonies
1705   Vincennes (Indiana)
founded by French
1706   17 January   Benjamin
Franklin born
1707   6 March   Act of Union;
England, Wales and Scot-
land   became   "United
Kingdom of Great Britain"
22 November   Counties
on Delaware Bay get own
legislature; beginning of
colony of Delaware
1708   29 August   French and
Indian massacre at Haver-
hill, Massachusetts
1709   Quakers establish meeting house in Boston
1710   Mobile (Alabama)
founded by French
16 October   Colonials
take Port Royal, Acadia;
rename it Annapolis Royal
1711   British attack against Quebec fails
22 September   Tuscarora
War begins with massa-
cre at New Bern, Carolina
1712   12 April   Revolt of Black
slaves in New York
9 May   Carolina divided
into North Carolina and
South Carolina
7 June   Importation of
Black slaves forbidden in
Pennsylvania

1713 11 April   Treaty of
Utrecht ends Queen
Anne's War; Acadia be-
comes British as Nova
Scotia; France recognizes
shores of Hudson Bay as
British
Fortress   of   Louisbourg
built

1714 1 August   Queen Anne
dies; George I becomes
king of Great Britain

1715 Yamasee Indian war in
South Carolina
1 September   Louis XIV
dies; Louis XV becomes
king of France

1716 Natchez (Mississippi)
founded by French

1718 New Orleans founded by
French
San Antonio (Texas)
founded by Spaniards

1724 Peter I of Russia appoints
Bering to explore Siberian
Far East

1725 8 February   Peter I dies;
Catherine I becomes cza-
rina of Russia

1727 12 June   George I dies;
George II becomes king
of Great Britain

1728 Bering discovers Bering
Strait; shows North Amer-
ica not connected with
Asia

1729 8 August   Baltimore,
Maryland, founded

1731 Franklin starts first circulating library in colonies

1732 Franklin starts *Poor Richard's Almanac*
First commercial stage-

coach established in colonies in New Jersey
22 February   George
Washington born

1733 12 February   Savannah
founded; beginning of colony of Georgia
17 May   Great Britain
passes Molasses Act

1734 Great Awakening starts

1735 Augusta, Georgia, founded
August Zenger tried for
libel in New York and ac-
quitted

1736 Franklin establishes first
fire-fighting company in
colonies

1739 Pierre and Paul Mallet
sight Rocky Mountains in
what is now Colorado
19 October   Great Britain
declares war on Spain;
"War of Jenkins's Ear"
22 November   Vernon
takes Portobello, Panama

1740 King George's War begins
May   Georgians lay seige
to St. Augustine, Florida
31 May   Frederick II be-
comes king of Prussia
20 October   Maria The-
resa becomes archduchess
of Austria

1741 Bering discovers Aleutian
Islands; sights Alaska
Vernon lays siege to Carta-
gena and fails; Lawrence
Washington serves under
Vernon

1742 Verendrye reaches Black
Hills (South Dakota)
Franklin invents "Frank-
lin stove"
7 July   Georgians defeat

Spaniards at Battle of
Bloody Marsh

1743 Lawrence Washington
builds Mount Vernon

1744 First novel published in
colonies

1745 17 June Colonials under
Pepperrell take Louis-
bourg

1748 18 October Treaty of
Aix-la-Chapelle ends King
George's War; Louisbourg
returned to France

1749 Halifax, Nova Scotia,
founded

1750 Gist explores upper Ohio
River

1752 First hospital established
in colonies in Philadelphia
1 January Colonies adopt
Gregorian calendar
June Franklin flies kite
in storm; proves lightning
is an electric discharge

1753 Franklin invents lightning
rod
Franklin appointed post-
master-general of colonies
French explore and lay
claim to Ohio territory
4 December Washington
delivers message to French
ordering them out of Ohio

1754 17 April French build
Fort Duquesne
28 May Washington at-
tacks French detachment
and starts the French and
Indian War
19 June Albany Con-
gress opens meetings
3 July Washington sur-
renders at Fort Necessity
10 July Albany Congress

adopts Franklin's plan of
Union

1755 20 February Braddock
arrives in Virginia
9 July Battle of Monon-
gahela, "Braddock's De-
feat"
August Johnson defeats
French at Battle of Lake
George
8 October British begin
deportations of Acadians

1756 13 May Montcalm ar-
rives in New France as
commander-in-chief
18 May Great Britain
declares war on France
22 July Loudon becomes
commander-in-chief of
British forces in North
America
14 August Montcalm
takes Fort Oswego
November Pitt enters
ministry

1757 June Pitt becomes Minister of War
July Loudon fails at
Louisbourg
9 August Montcalm
takes Fort William Henry
30 December Abercrom-
bie replaces Loudon as
commander-in-chief

1758 8 July Montcalm de-
feats Abercrombie at Bat-
tle of Ticonderoga
26 July Louisbourg
taken by British under
Amherst
27 August Bradstreet
takes Fort Frontenac
18 September Amherst
replaces Abercrombie as

commander-in-chief
24 November Forbes occupies Fort Duquesne; builds Fort Pitt

1759 26 June British under Wolfe land near Quebec
25 July British take Fort Niagara
26 July French abandon Fort Ticonderoga
27 July Montcalm's fire ships fail against British
31 July French abandon Crown Point; Wolfe's assault against Quebec fails
13 September British defeat French at Plains of Abraham; Wolfe killed; Montcalm mortally wounded
18 September Quebec surrenders to British

1760 27 April French defeat British at Quebec; place city under siege
15 May British break siege of Quebec
8 September British take Montreal
25 October George II dies; George III becomes king of Great Britain
29 November British take Detroit

1762 2 January Great Britain declares war on Spain
3 November Treaty of Fontainebleu; France cedes Louisiana, west of Mississippi to Spain

1763 10 February Treaty of Paris ends French and Indian War; France loses Canada and all land east of Mississippi to Great Britain; Spain loses Florida to Great Britain

INDEX